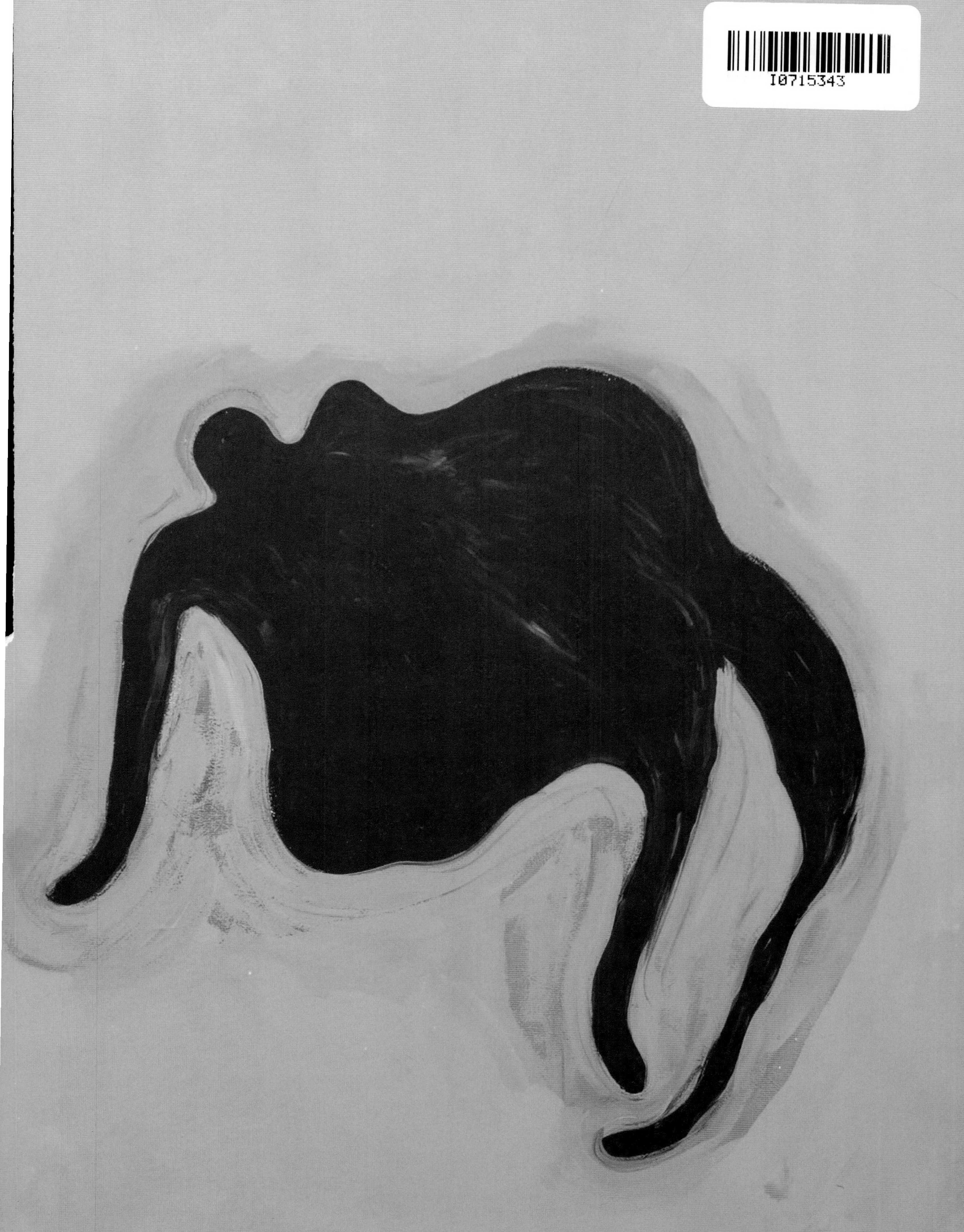

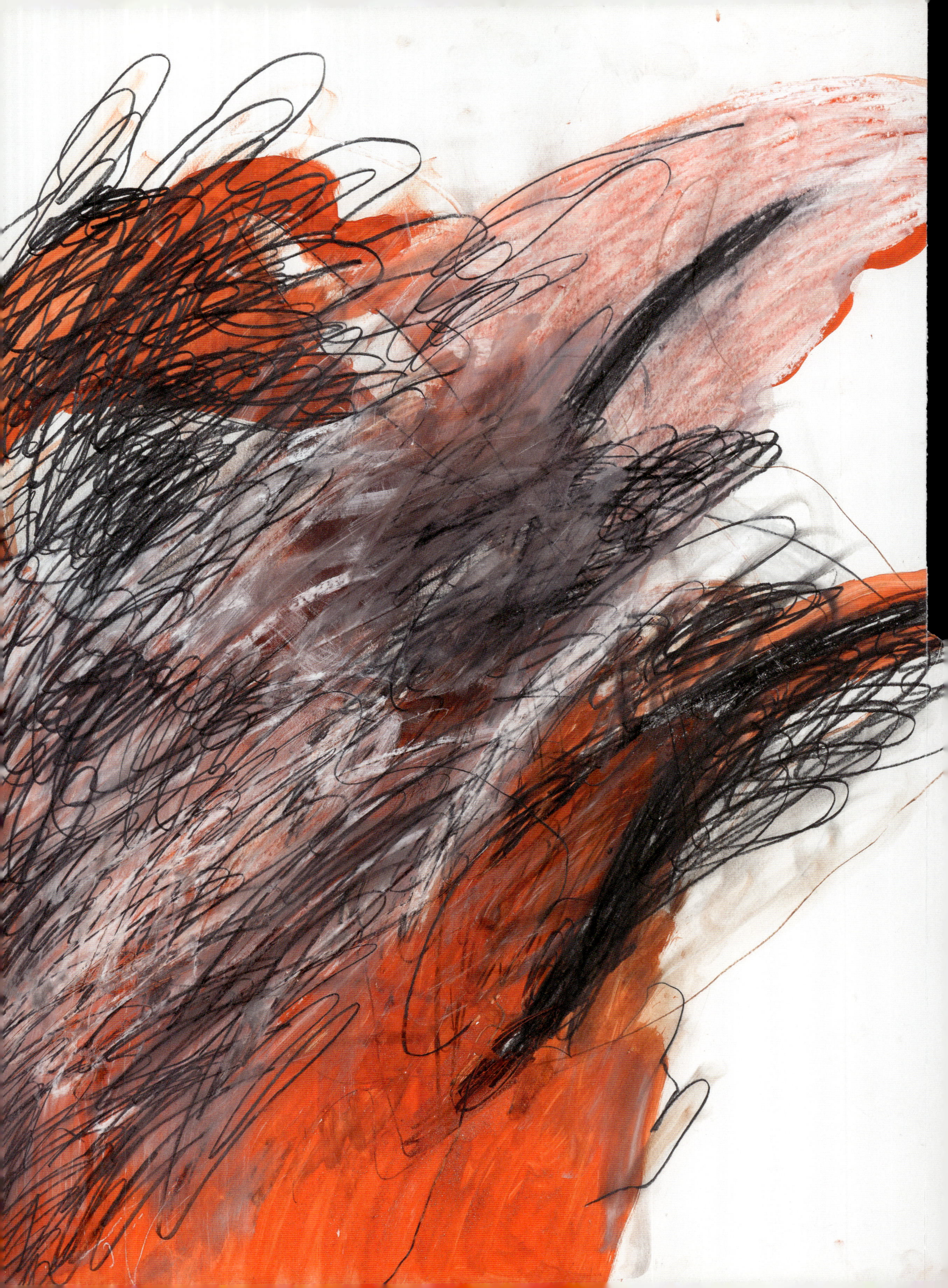

MARIANNE EIGENHEER

A Lifelong Search Along the Lines

VON BARTHA

THE ESTATE OF MARIANNE EIGENHEER

black dog press

Contents

Untitled, c. 2012
multipart wall–work, dimensions variable

The formal language of the work is based on the series *Peterchens Mondfahrt* and *Les guédés dansent toujours.*

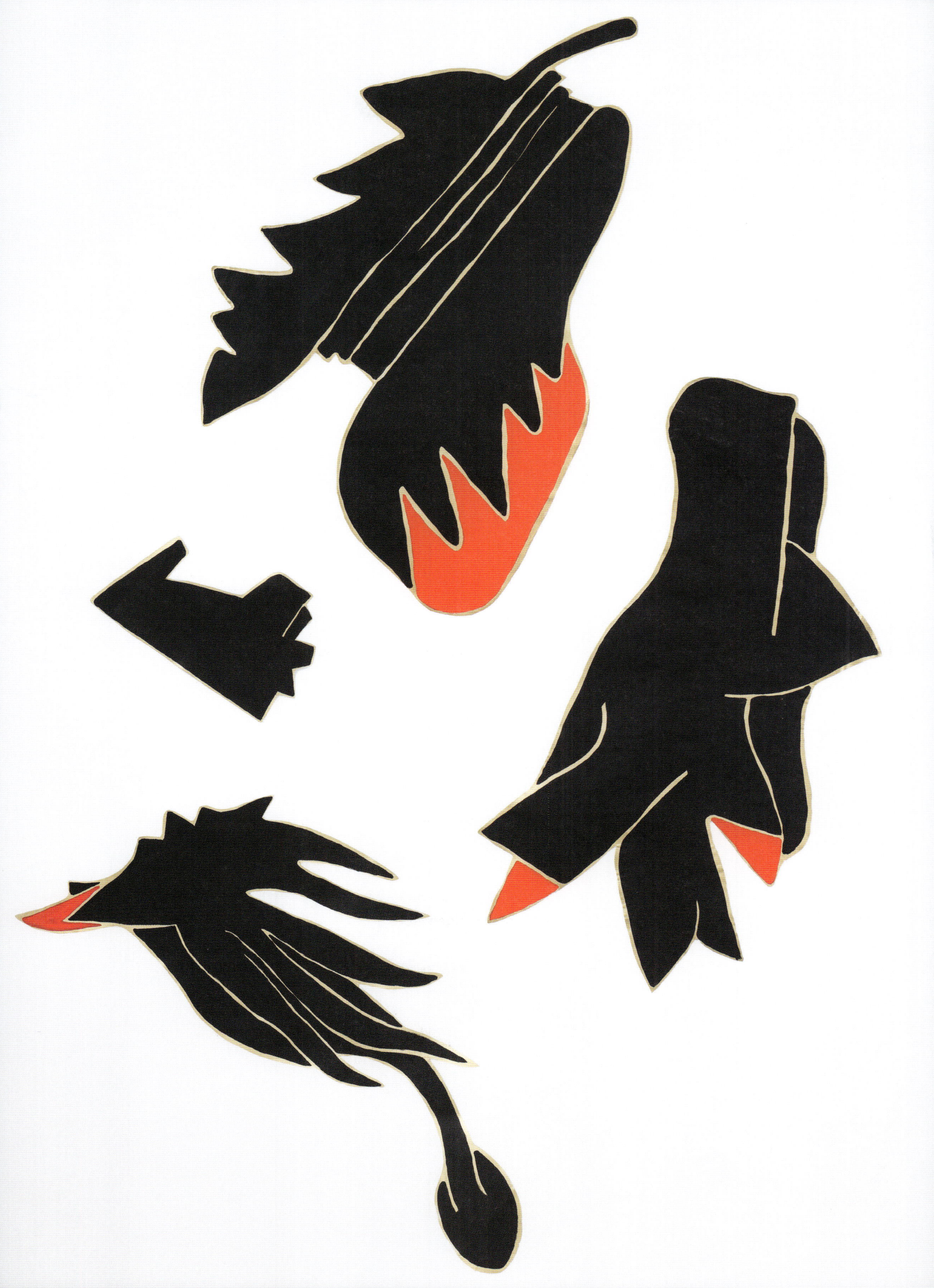

Foreword

By Stefan von Bartha, Owner and Director, von Bartha, Basel & Copenhagen

Years ago, I recall, our exhibition openings were almost invariably attended by one particular person. She was small, very kind and very enthusiastic; I knew peripherally that she was an artist and was based in Basel, but we had never officially met. Not until one day, that is, when this particular person addressed me directly and invited me to visit her at her studio. This person was, of course, the subject of this book: the incomparable Marianne Eigenheer.

As much as I like to visit artists' studios, it can be tricky as a commercial gallerist to not raise hopes or make promises you can't fulfil. So I tried to postpone the visit – but she insisted. One day, I finally gave in – I called and asked if she would be available that afternoon. To my surprise, she was, and it turned out that her studio was conveniently close to our gallery. I arrived in front of a wonderful house in a rather nice area of Basel and Marianne buzzed me in. The staircase had certainly seen better days, but there, I first encountered her work. On the third floor, she greeted me and accompanied me up to the next floor, where her studio was located. The door opened and I entered a world of many forgotten treasures that had been forged along the path of a unique and incredible journey.

Marianne did not hold back in giving me a thorough overview of her practice – which by this time already spanned 40 years – and what was supposed to be a short visit turned into a long and fascinating afternoon. I tried my very best to understand why she had not exhibited more in recent years, and I failed. Her story was more than unique. She had lived, taught, worked and exhibited at so many places all over the world. She had contacts in all realms of the art world. But Marianne was an artist fighting against a current; throughout her life, the male-dominated art scene had made it very difficult for her to get the recognition she deserved. But it was clear to me even then: Marianne was a revelation.

So, even if she was not, let's say, a "logical fit" for our programme, I felt the urge to get to know her better. We started a very close and extremely amusing conversation, mostly accompanied by studio visits or very long coffees at the gallery. She always had a story to tell about the countless encounters that didn't turn out the way she imagined. Looking back, I think it is fair to say she did have some bad luck along the way. But her stories revealed that old-school misogynist attitude that plagued the commercial art world back then (and now, too). I became acutely aware that her journey was more complex and difficult than it should have been.

Through our regular conversations, our friendship grew and I became only more fascinated by her life story. Over time, my team and I felt the urge to represent her. I clearly remember calling her and asking her, in the same straightforward manner she always had, "Marianne, can you trust another man in your life? If yes, I would love to represent you. Let's start planning the future together." She obliged, and we announced the representation in 2017. Her time with von Bartha started with a smaller project in our showroom, as we wanted to have more time to prepare her inventory and to start planning her comeback show at the gallery in 2019. It was wonderful to realise how many people knew and respected her and her practice. It was clear to us that ours would be a very long and wonderful story together. But unfortunately, her health began to falter. We spoke plainly about how she was not yet allowed to leave us. She always promised me that she would live another 20 years – at minimum.

When the Gegenwartsmuseum invited her to create a wall work for a group show in 2017, we all believed this was the point of inflection that would bring the attention she deserved. She felt better and was again full of energy; she was excited to start planning her upcoming solo exhibition at the gallery. But sadly, and very unexpectedly, her body decided against her and after a very short illness, she passed away in January 2018. It all happened too fast, and the story we wanted to share together remained untold.

Even though Marianne is no longer with us, I am determined to keep the promises I made to her – to give her the stage, the recognition and the renown that she so deserved. This book is just the beginning of our attempt to honour Marianne's life and work.

This book is a collage of powerful artworks and strong voices; it is an attempt to take hold of and grapple with the myriad variations in Marianne's œuvre. Expressive and delicate at the same time, her strong compositions are the manifestation of a driven soul and directly linked to her personality and her life's journey. While she was skilled in many media – she was well versed in photography, sculpture and on canvas – she always returned to paper. It proved a lifelong companion and an abundant venue for her bursting lines and sign-like symbolic figures, all attributes of an artistic creation rooted in music, poetry and history.

The most outstanding quality of Marianne's work is her ability to express herself in a powerful but also nuanced, delicate manner. It didn't matter if she was successful in her career; the inner urge to express herself through her art had always been present, and this was reflected in her work. Marianne's expressions are even more relevant today, ringing out as the clear voice of a woman who had something to say and claimed her right to be seen.

Her work is emotional – sometimes even overwhelming – yet never reproachful; her gestures were often light and joyful. In her works, we can recognise winks and nods to moments in history, art, music and the natural world; we can also catch a glimpse of the vast interior life of the woman who wielded the brush. Her art is sensually charged, demonstrating Marianne's unending development as an artist. I will never forget her incredible passion and energy.

This book is dedicated to Marianne as some small token of thanks for her years of friendship, inspiration, and her tireless spirit that made us aware of all the things that must change in our society. Marianne, thank you.

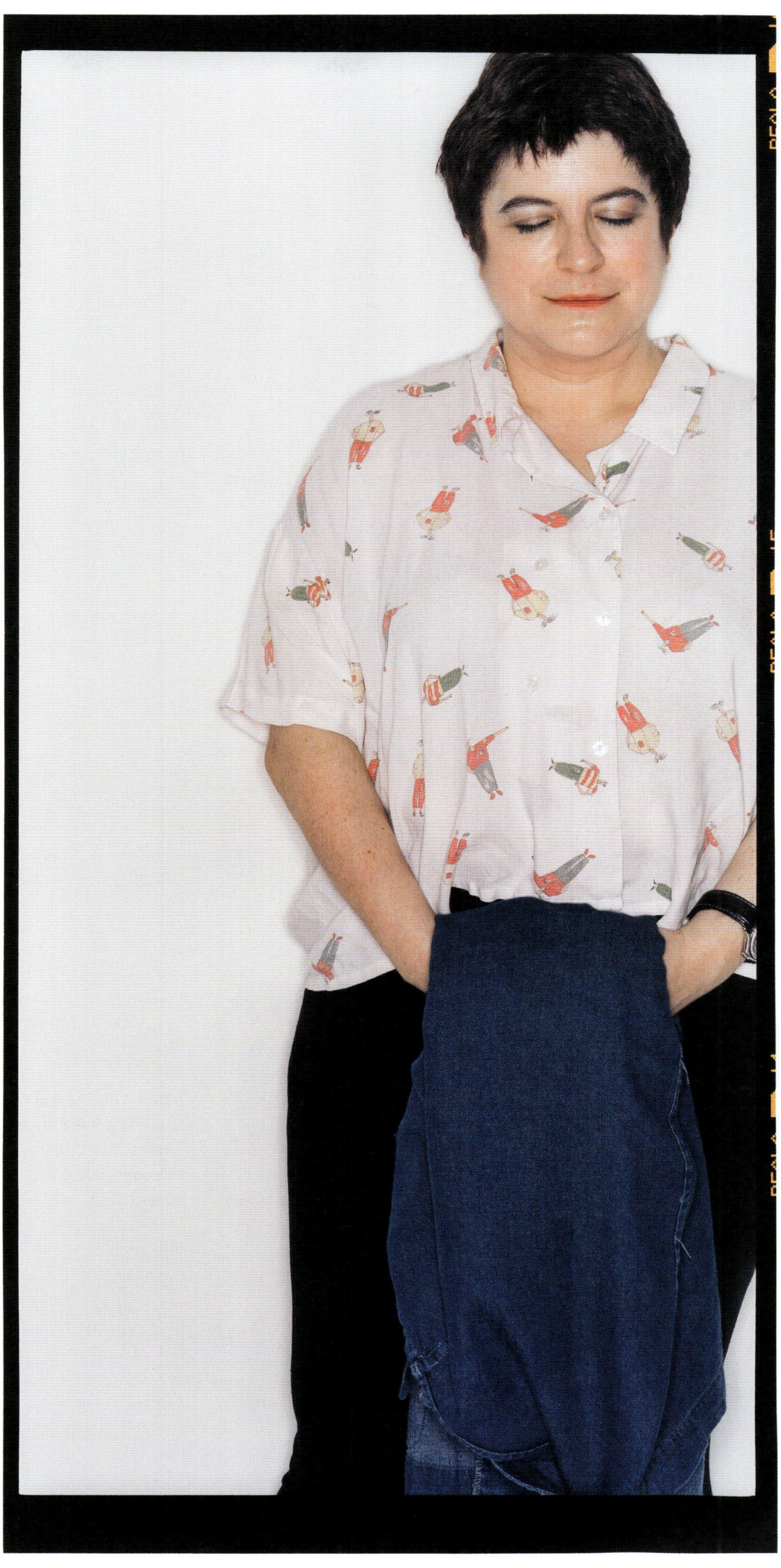

Portrait of Marianne Eigenheer
Unknown photographer

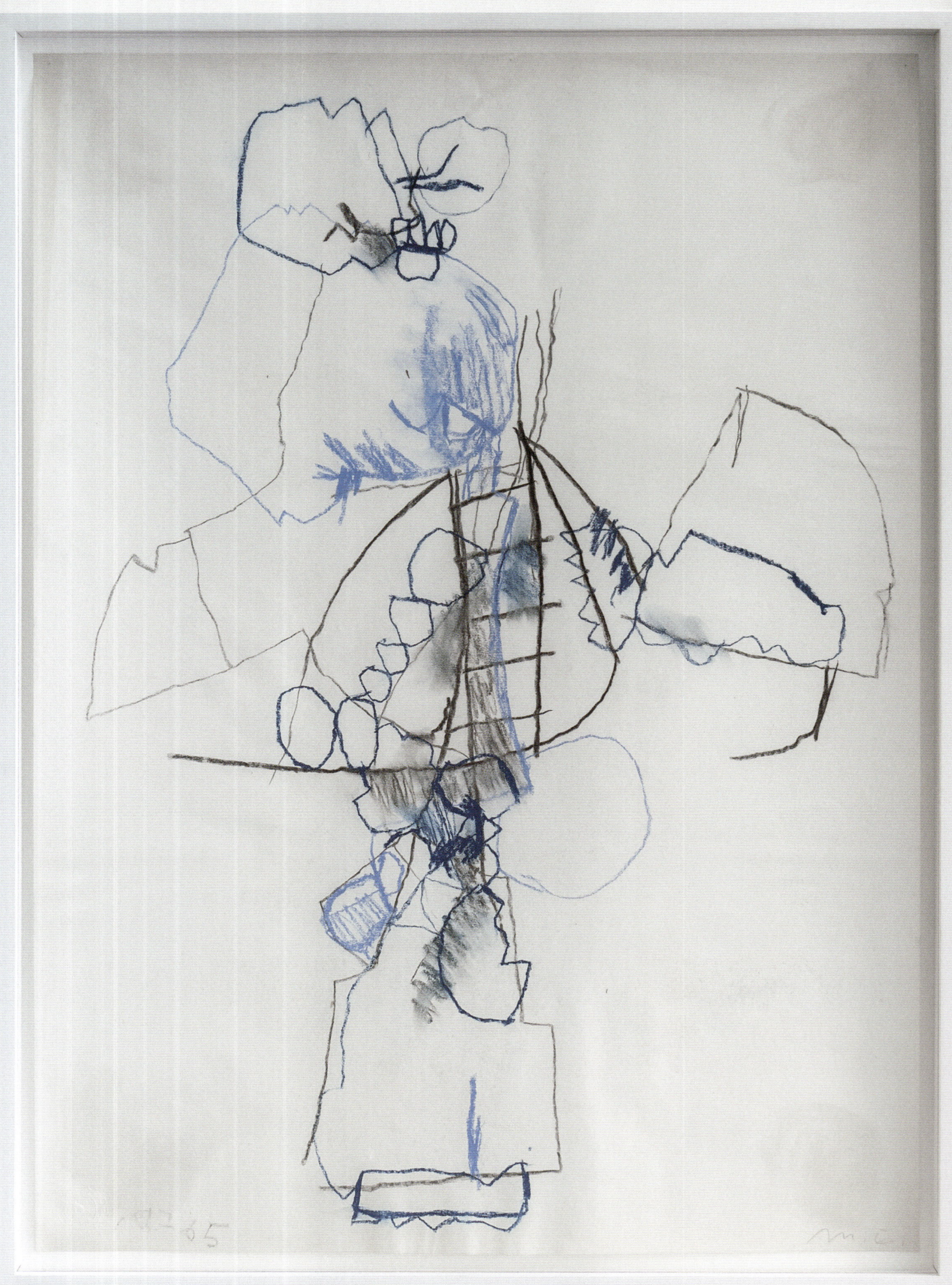

Untitled, 1965
coloured pencil on paper, 61.5 x 44cm

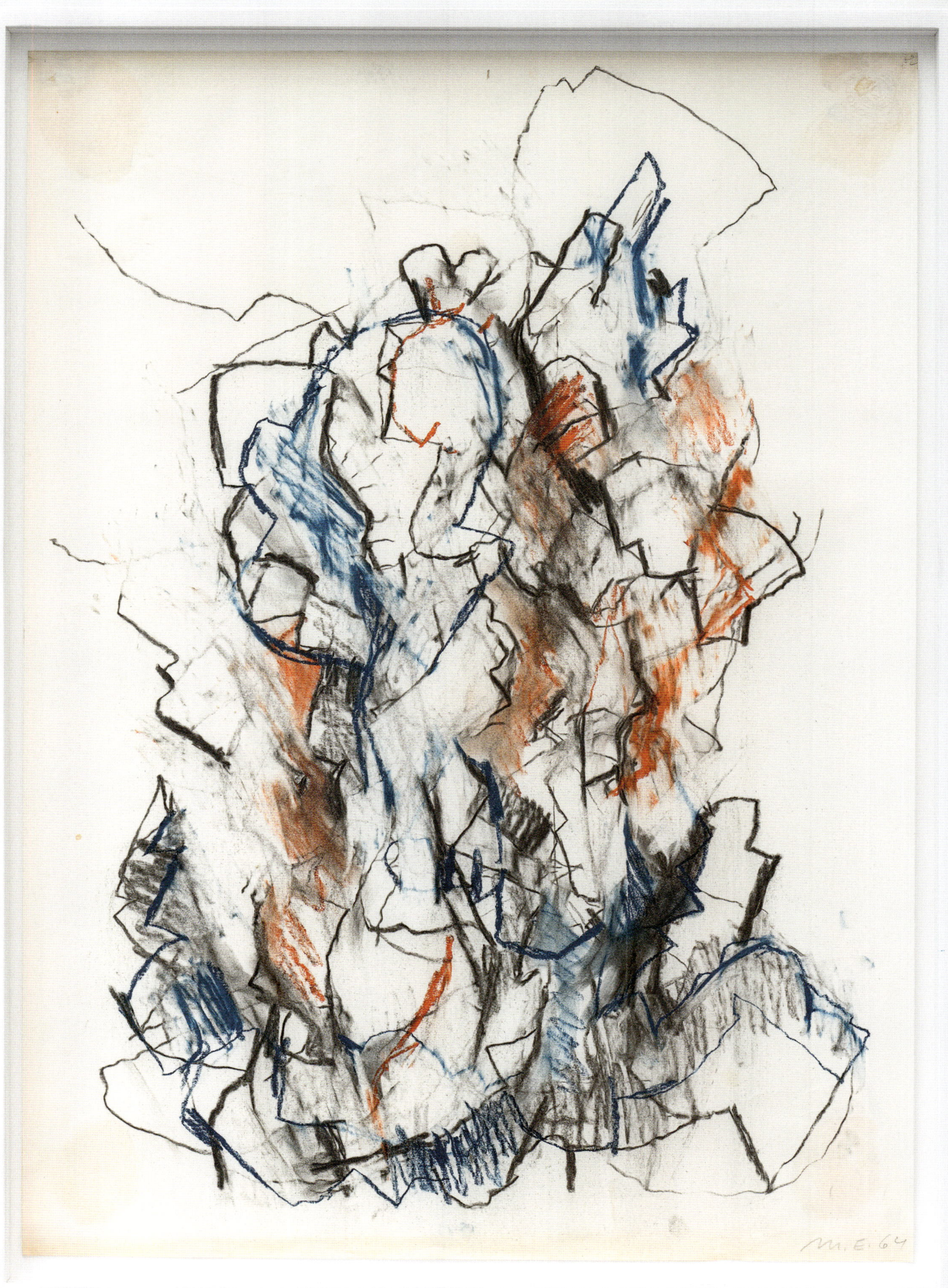

Untitled, 1964
coloured pencil on paper, 62 x 45.5cm

Legacy I, 2014
photograph, 112 x 91cm

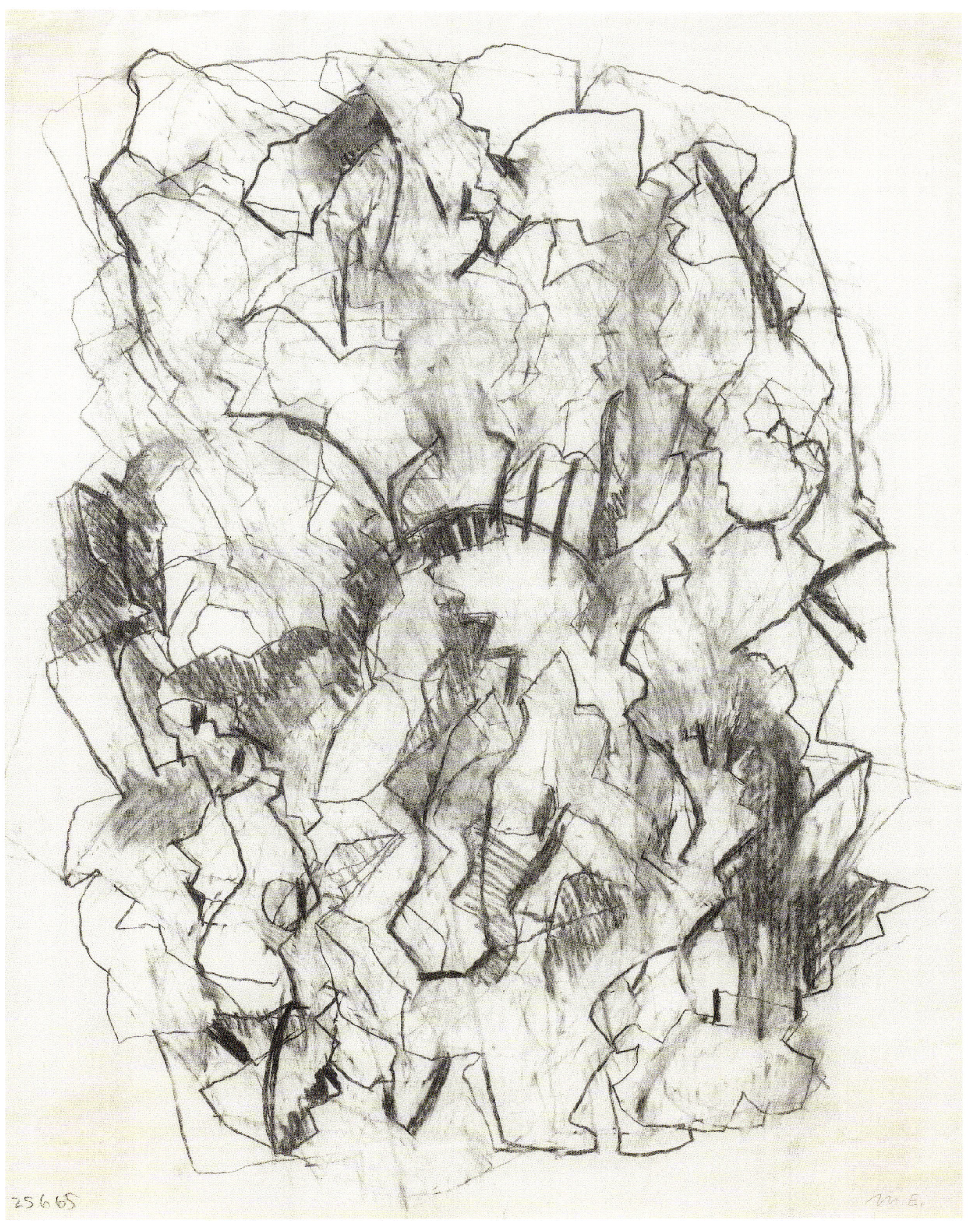

Untitled, 1965
pencil on paper, 65 x 50cm

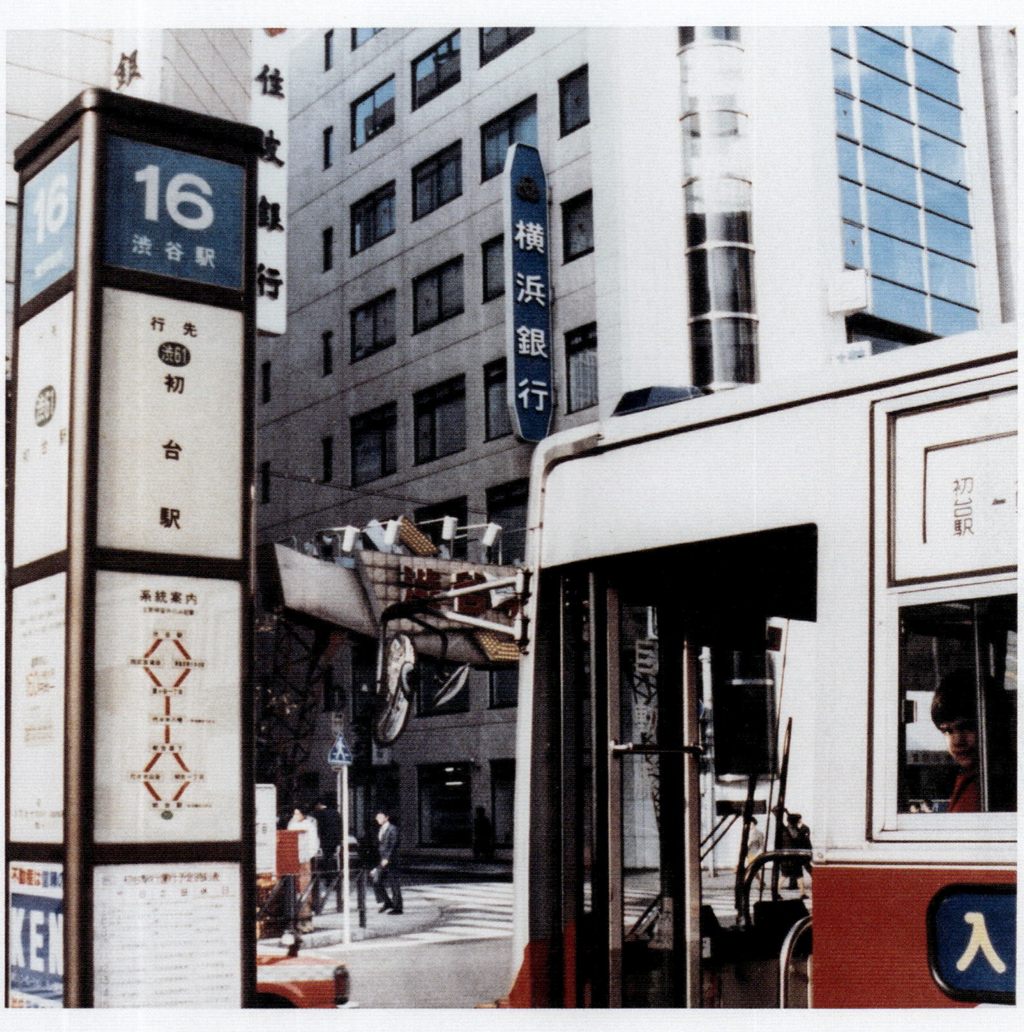

Untitled, n.d.
photograph on aluminium,
Two parts, each 73 x 73cm

This work forms part of Marianne Eigenheer's publication
The Oxford Bar published in Basel in 1999
(A little book about
"A PLACE FOR ART
A PLACE AS ART
A PLACE LIKE ART
ART AS A PLACE
ART LIKE A PLACE".)

Most of Marianne's photographic work has
been titled *Your time, my world* and was
made around 1998.

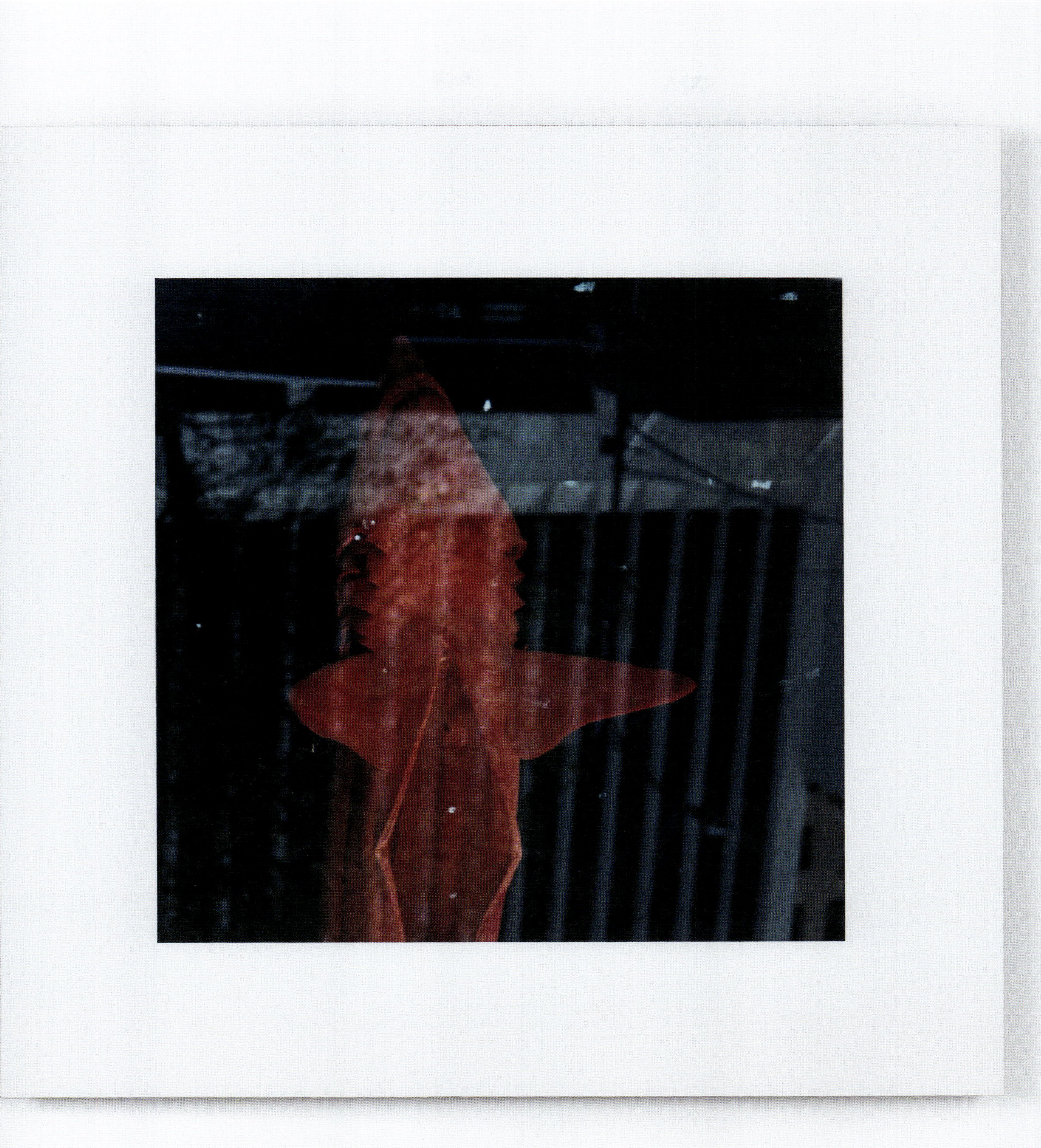

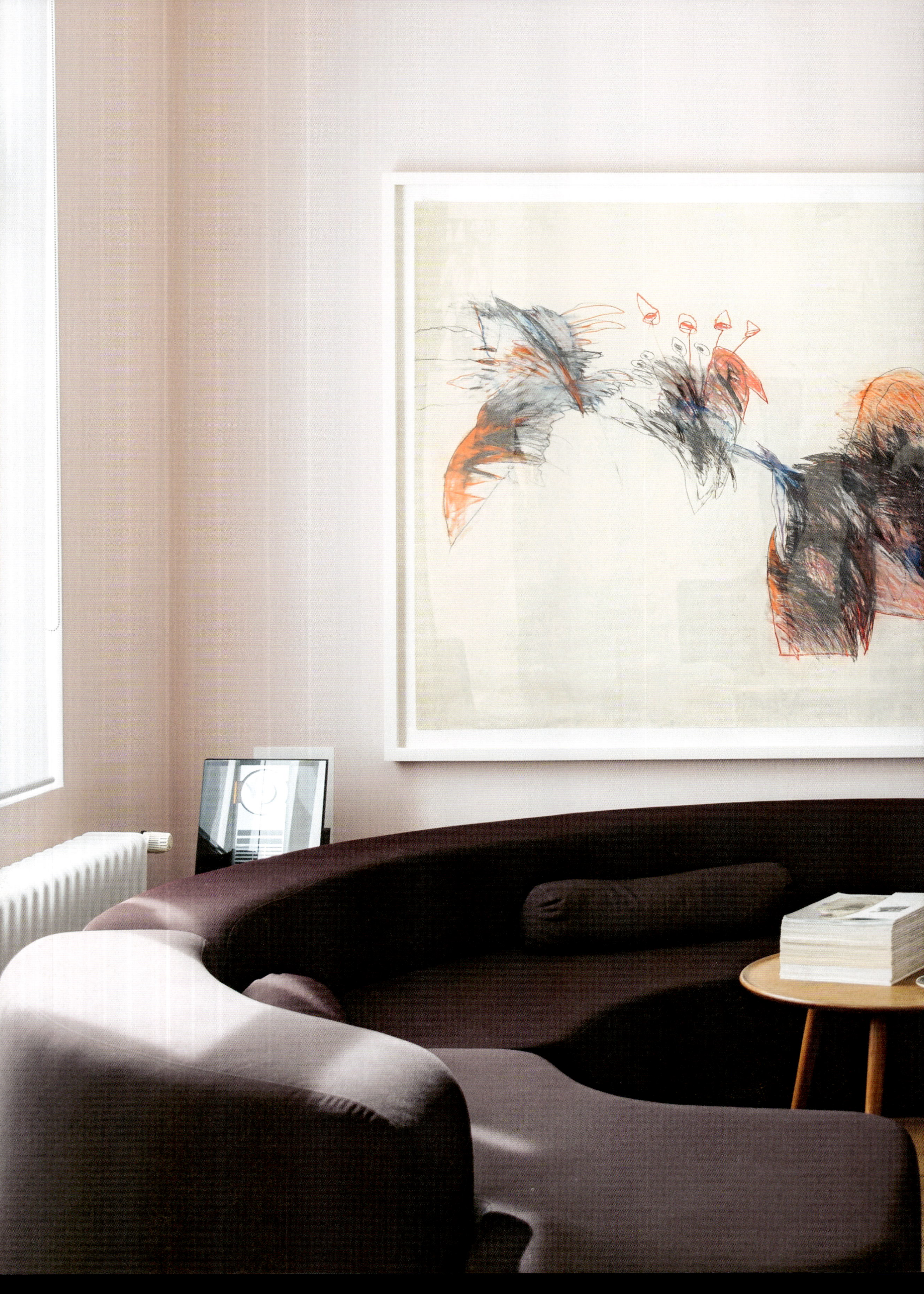

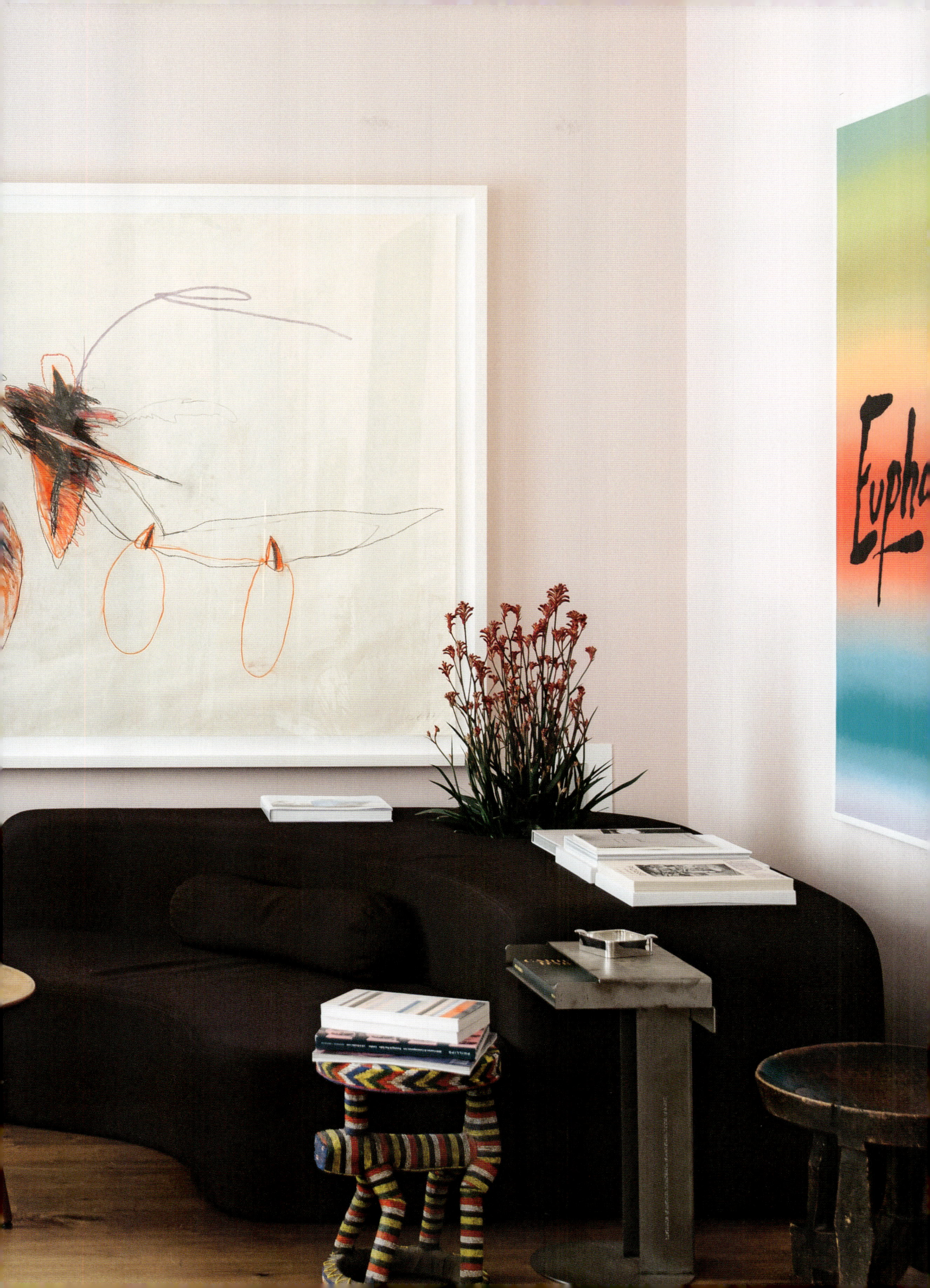
Eupha

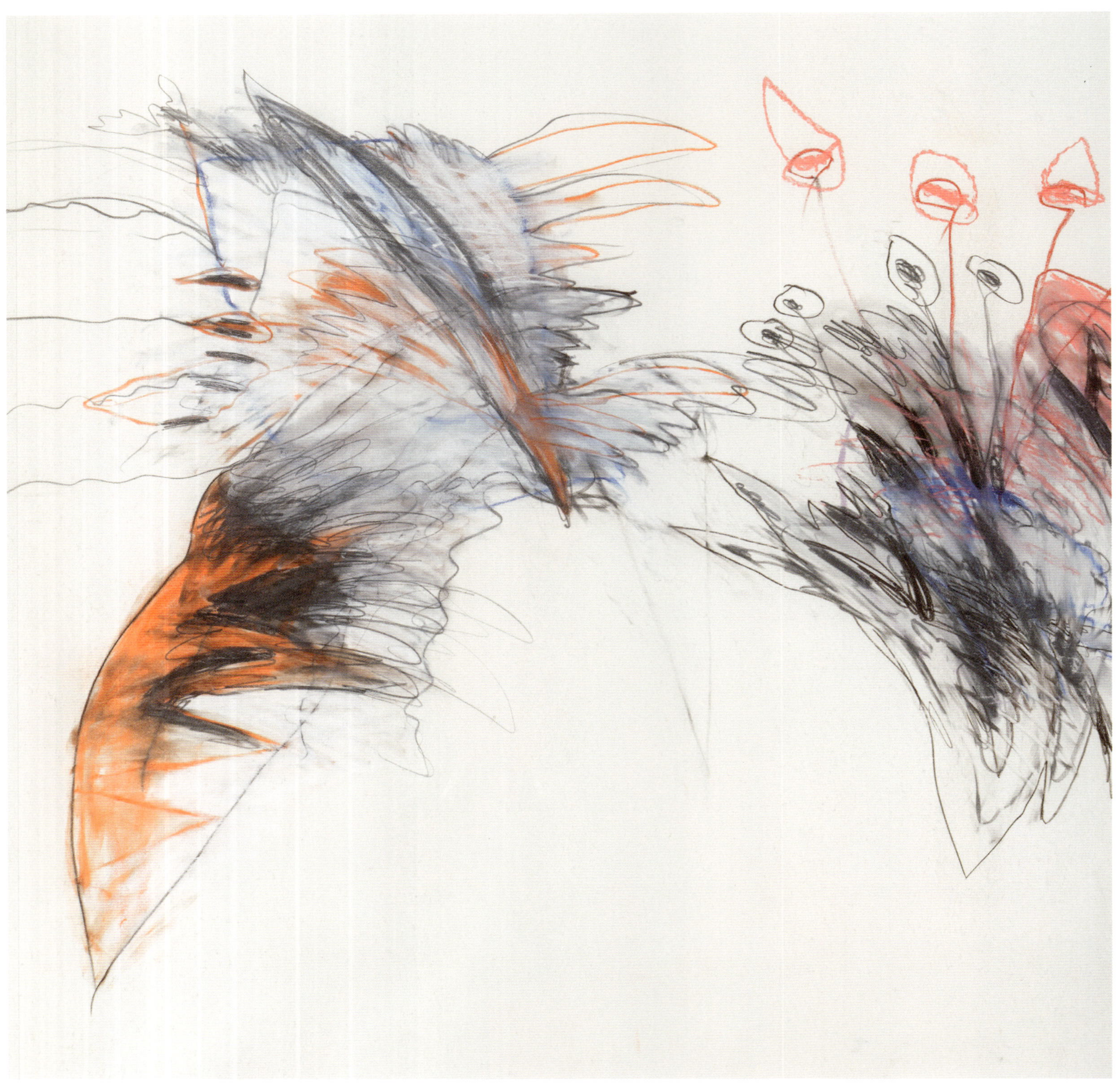

Der Traum von Panama, 1977
pencil and pastel chalk on paper
300 x 150cm

Previous page: The Imaginary Collection,
von Bartha x Mike Meiré, 2018,
Cologne, Germany

This page: details

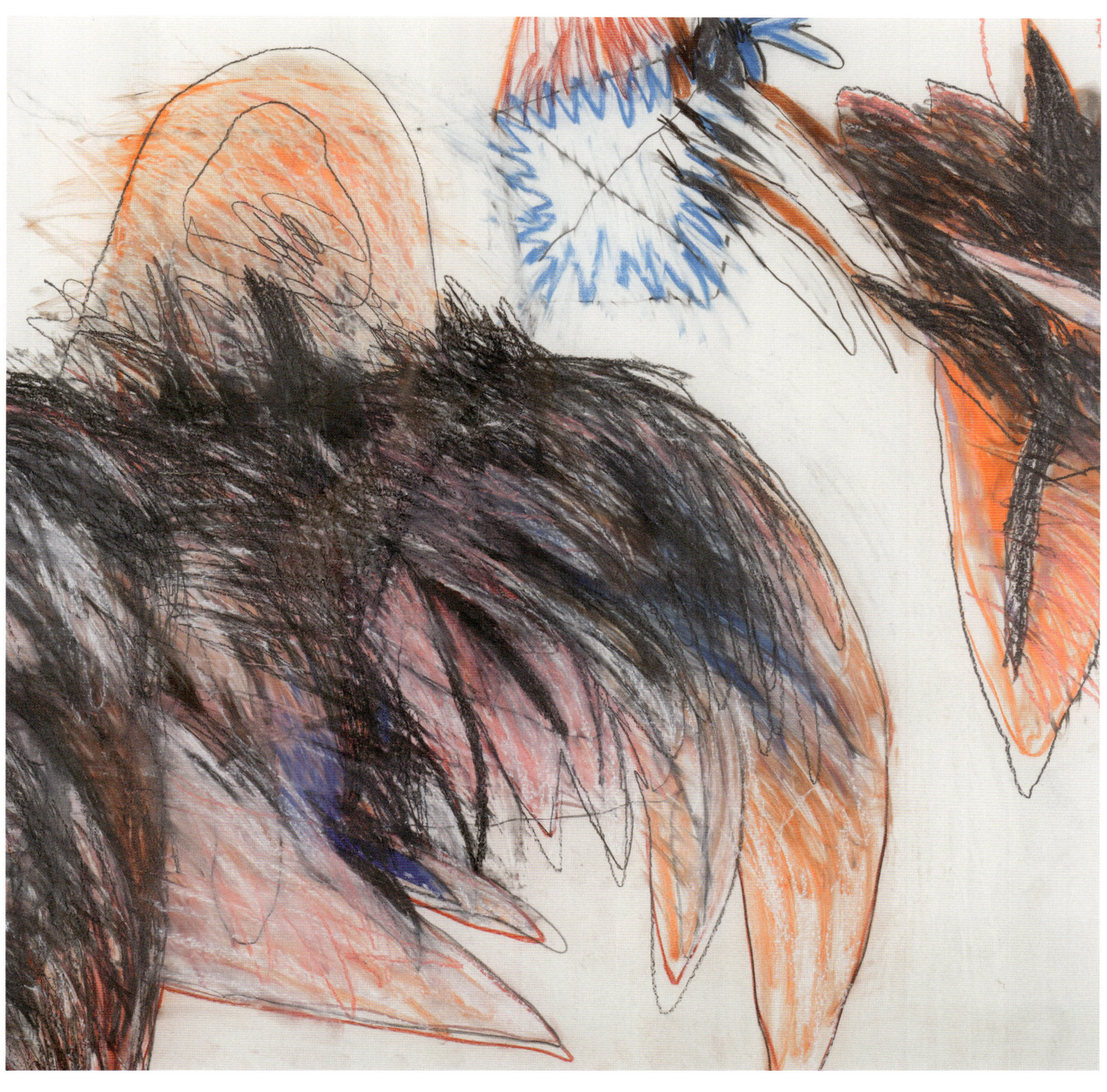

Untitled, n.d. (probably 1970s–80s)
pencil, coloured pencil and crayon on paper, 80 x 60cm

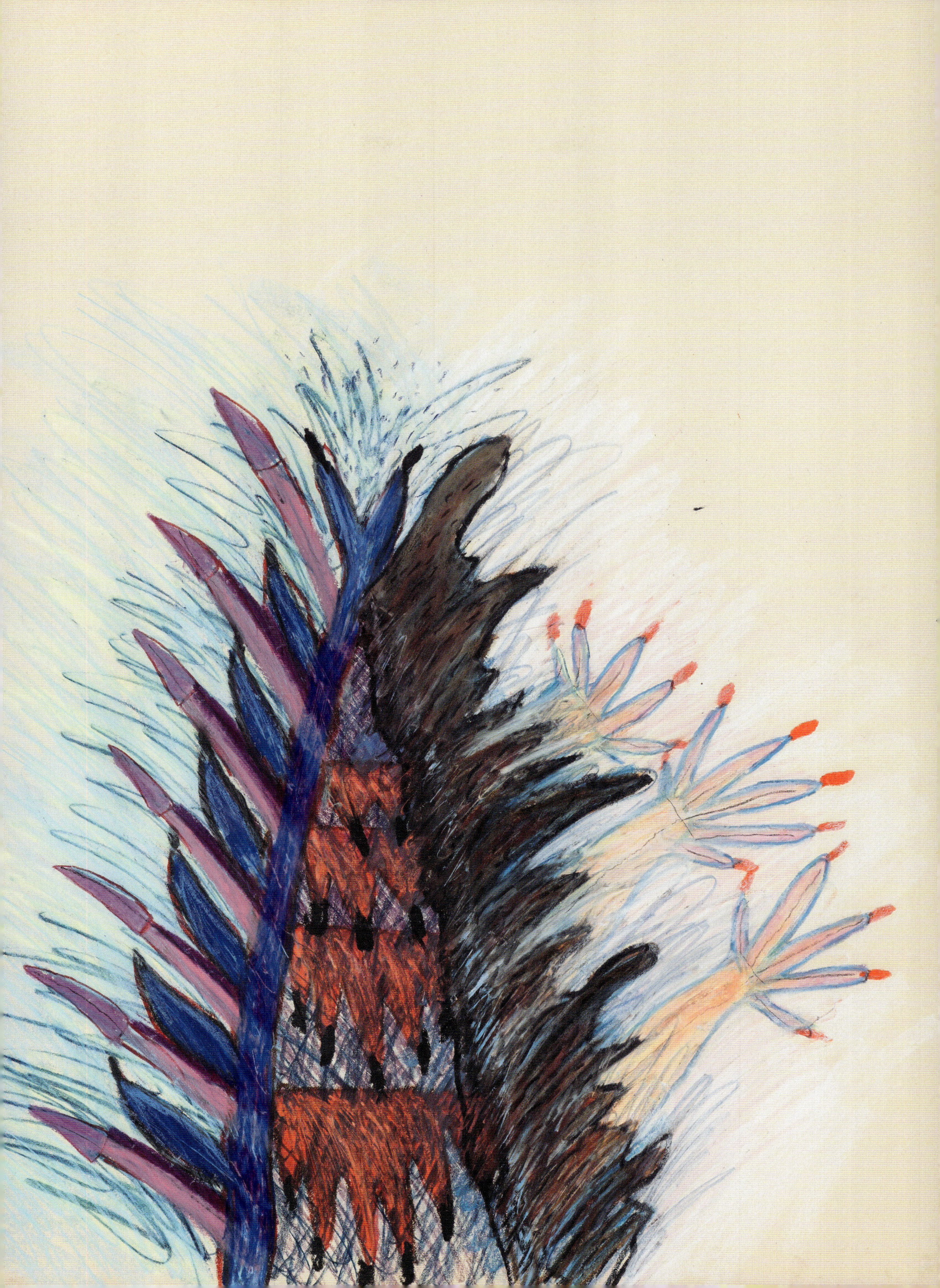

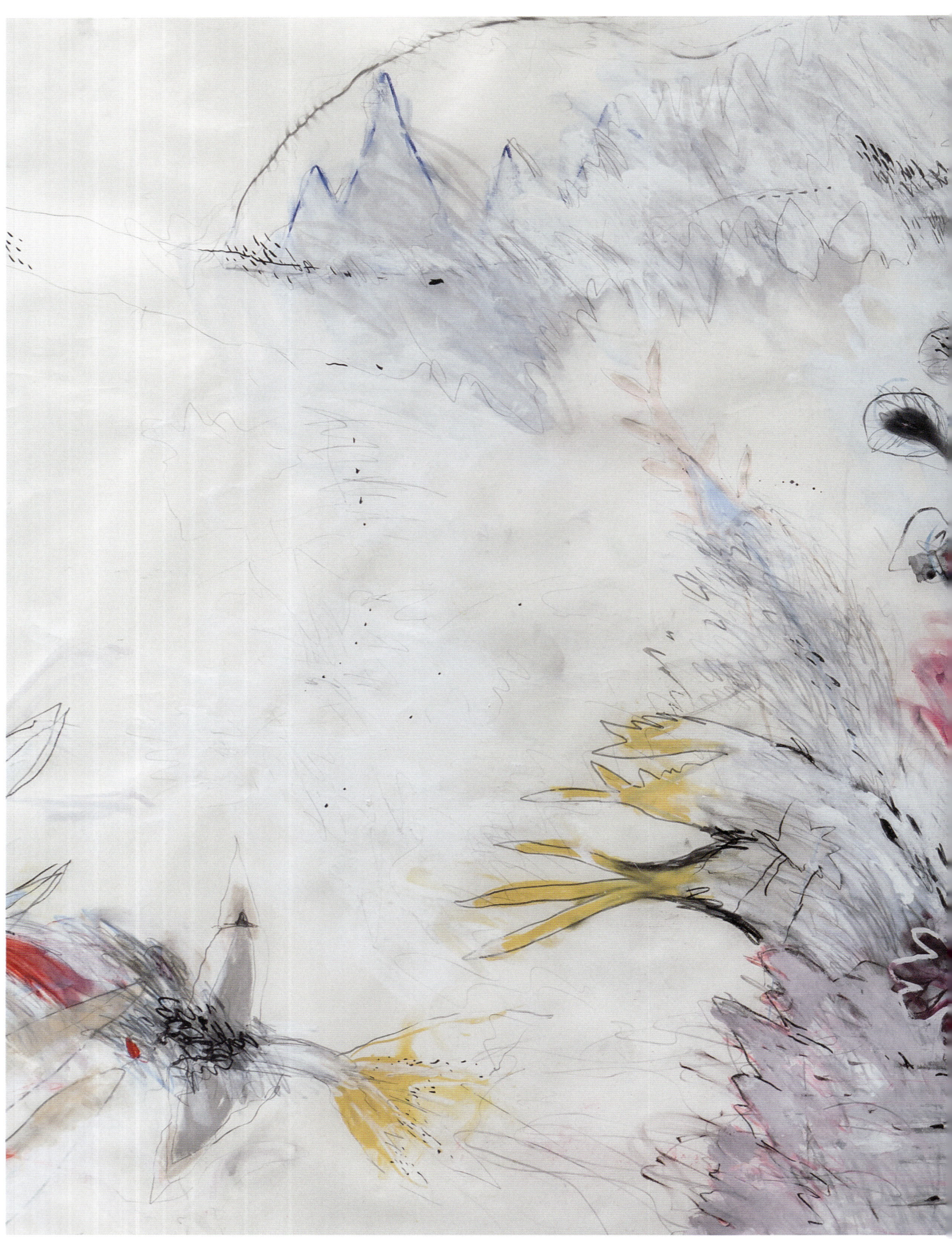

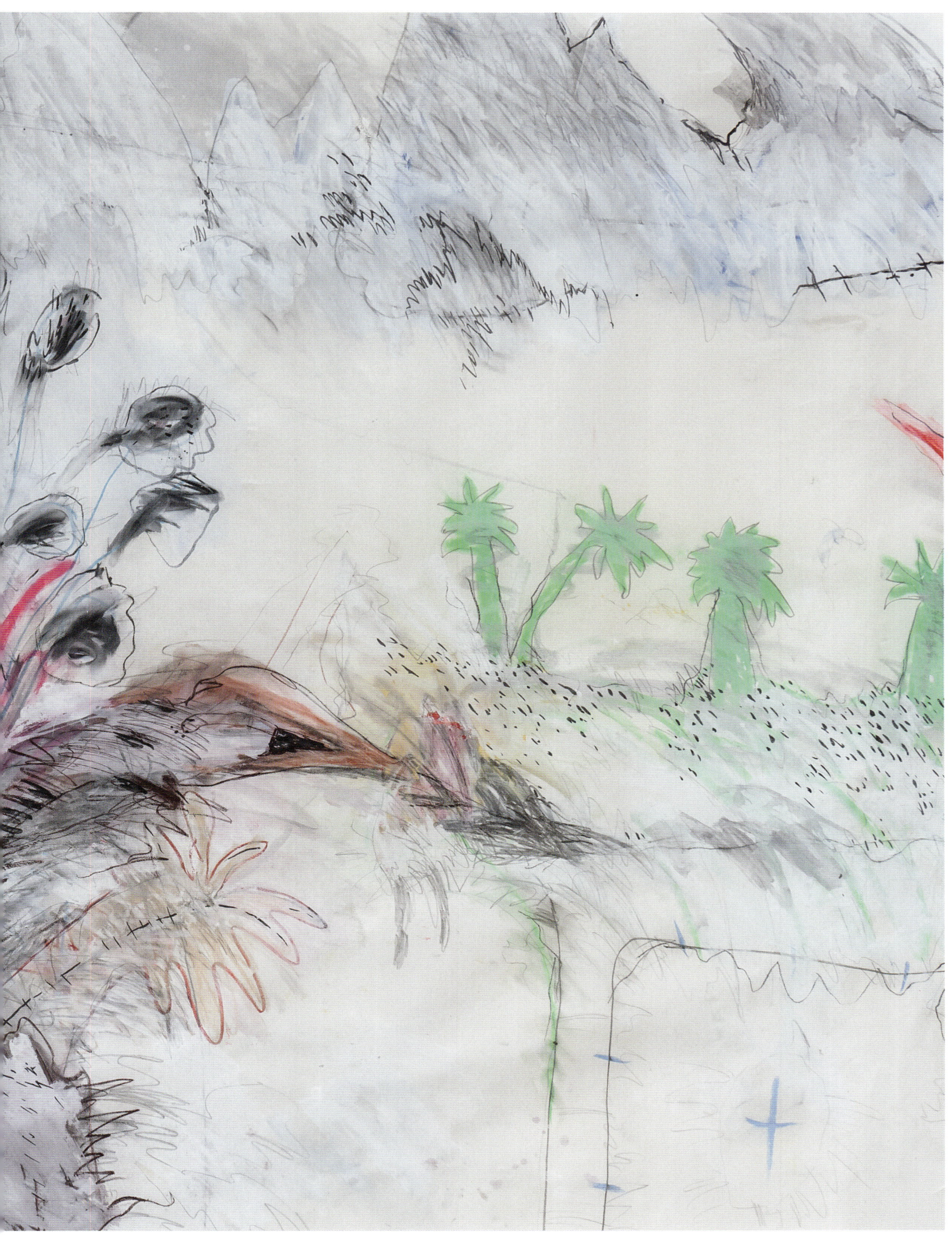

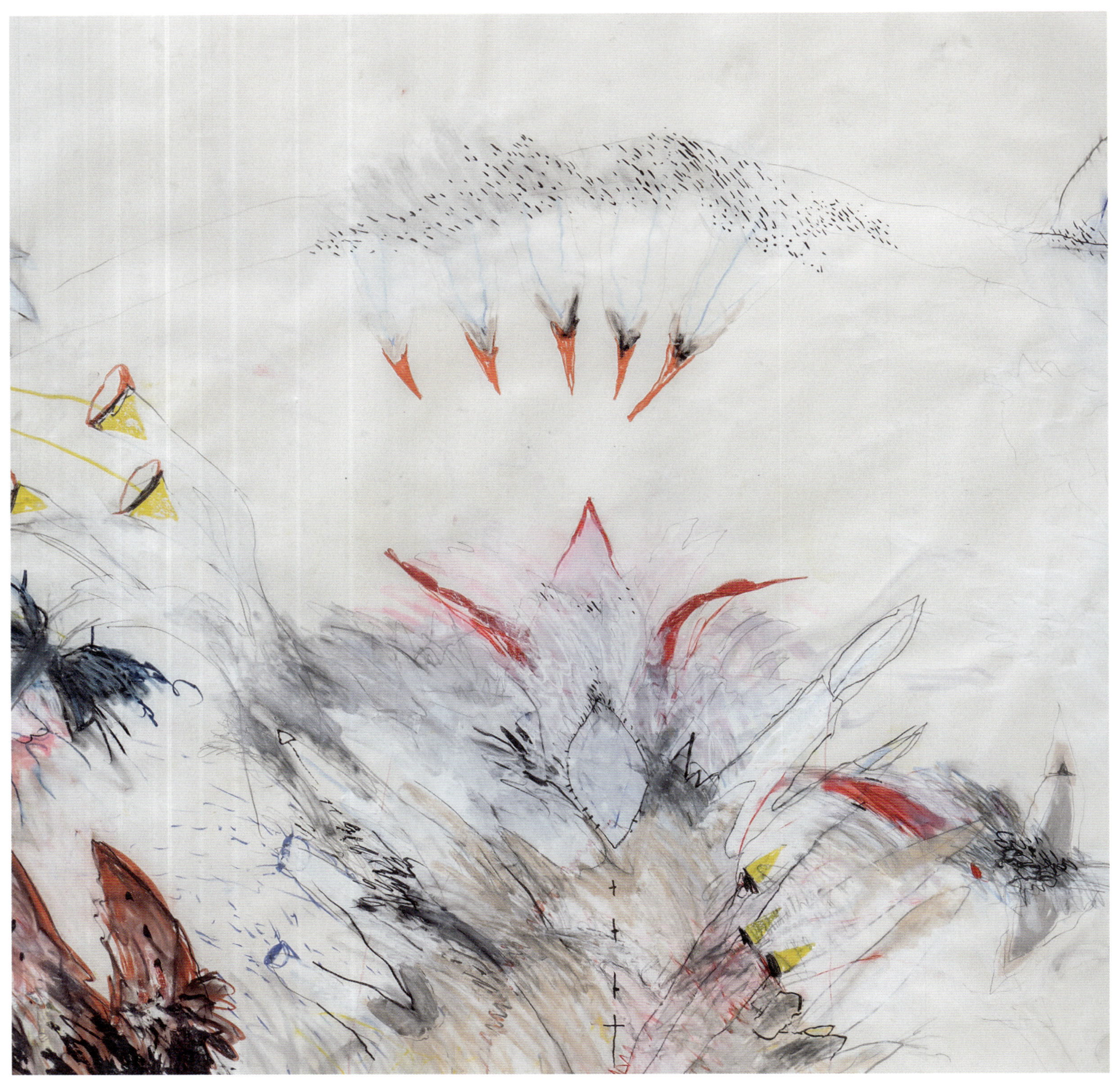

Previous page: *Untitled* (detail), c. 1976
wax crayon on paper, c. 150 x 1050cm

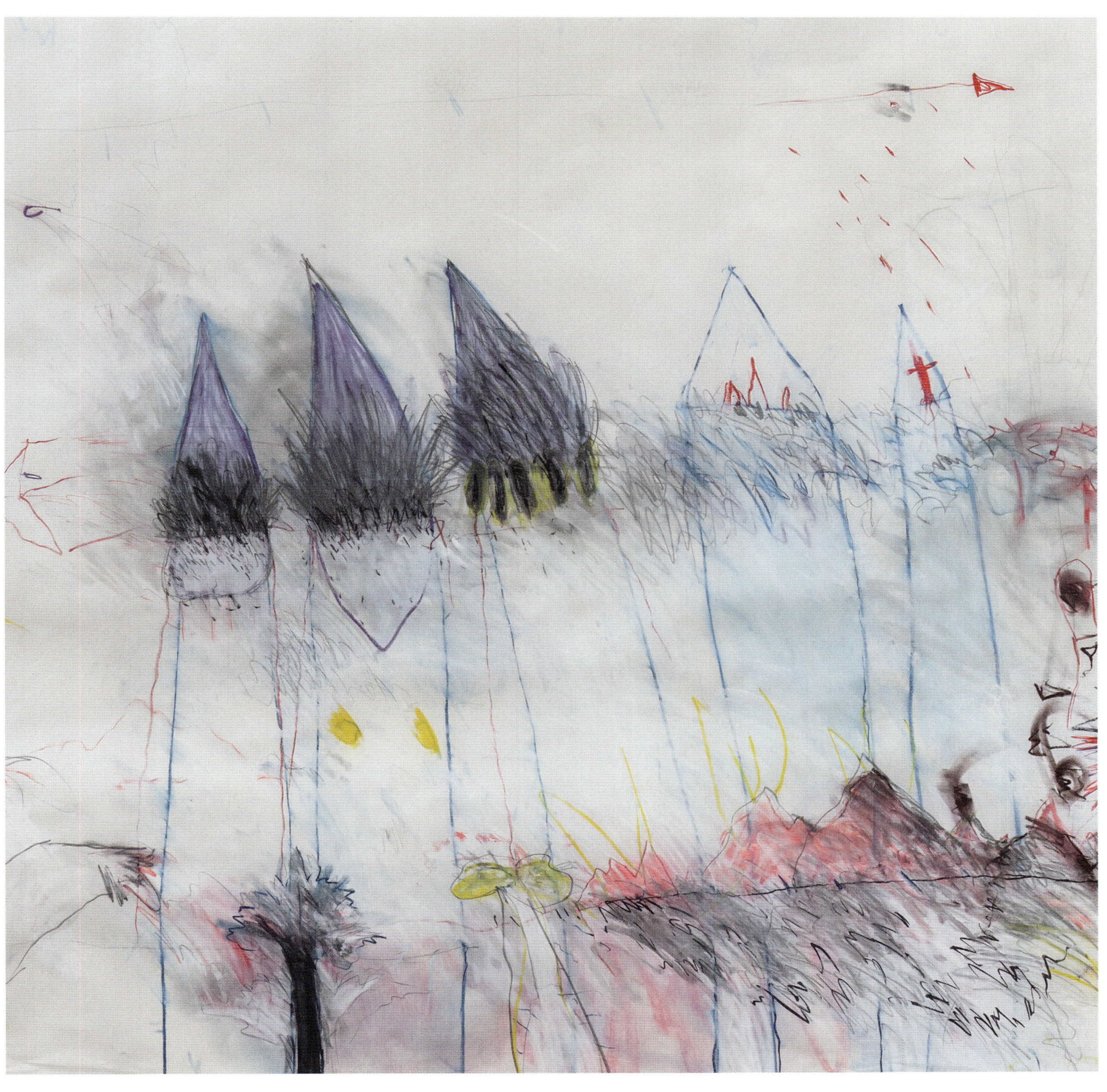

Untitled (detail), c. 1976
wax crayon on paper, c. 150 x 1050cm

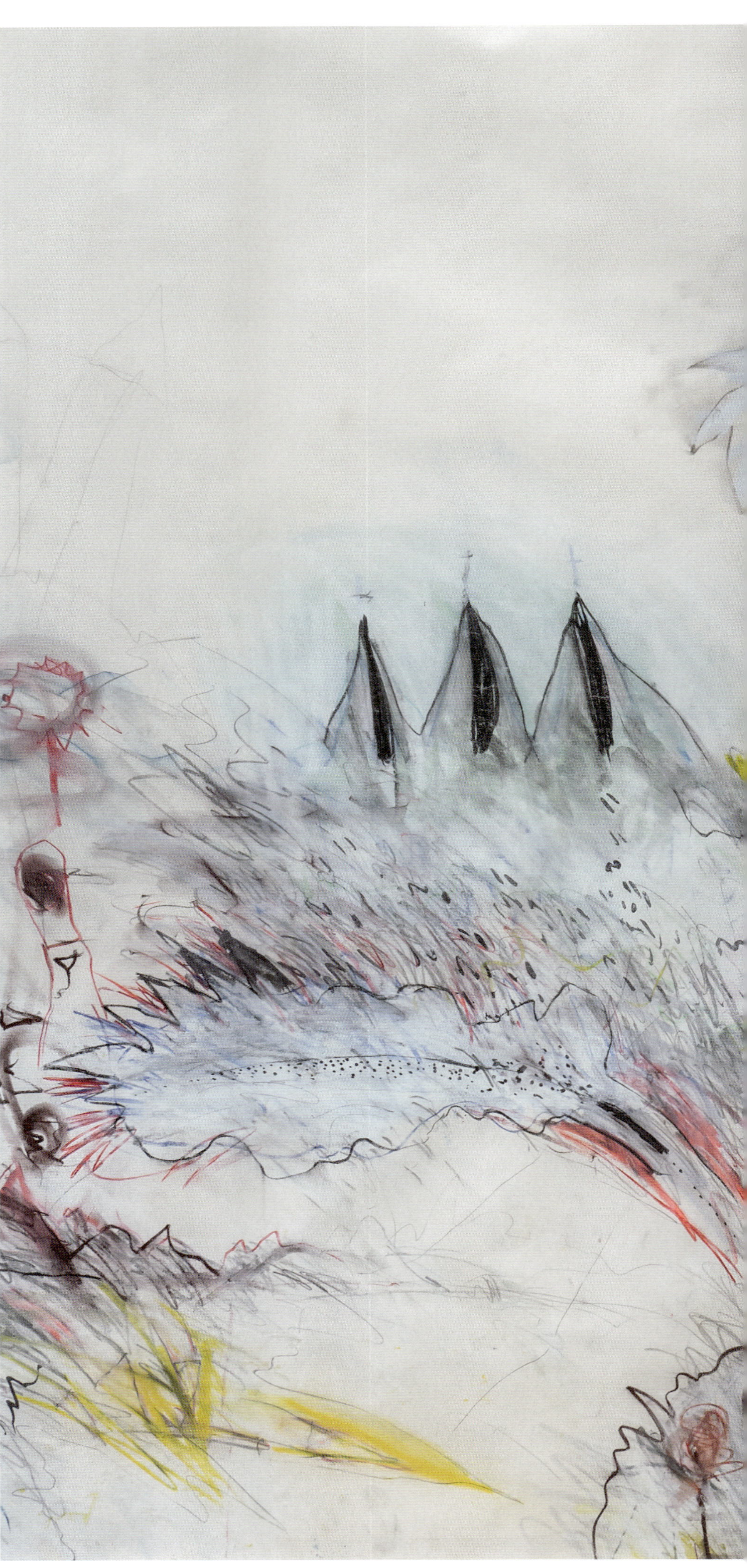

Untitled (detail), c. 1976
wax crayon on paper, c. 150 x 1050cm

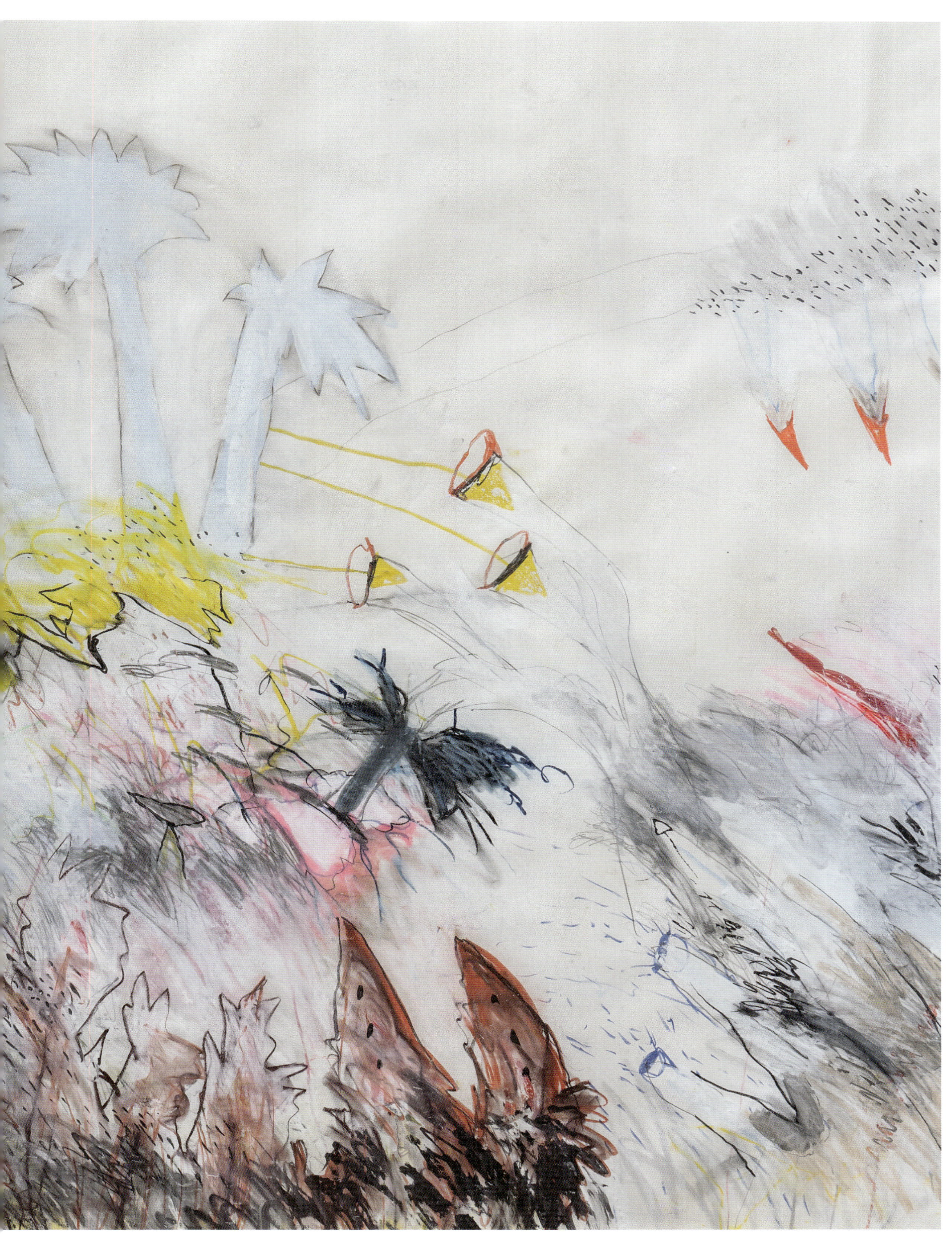

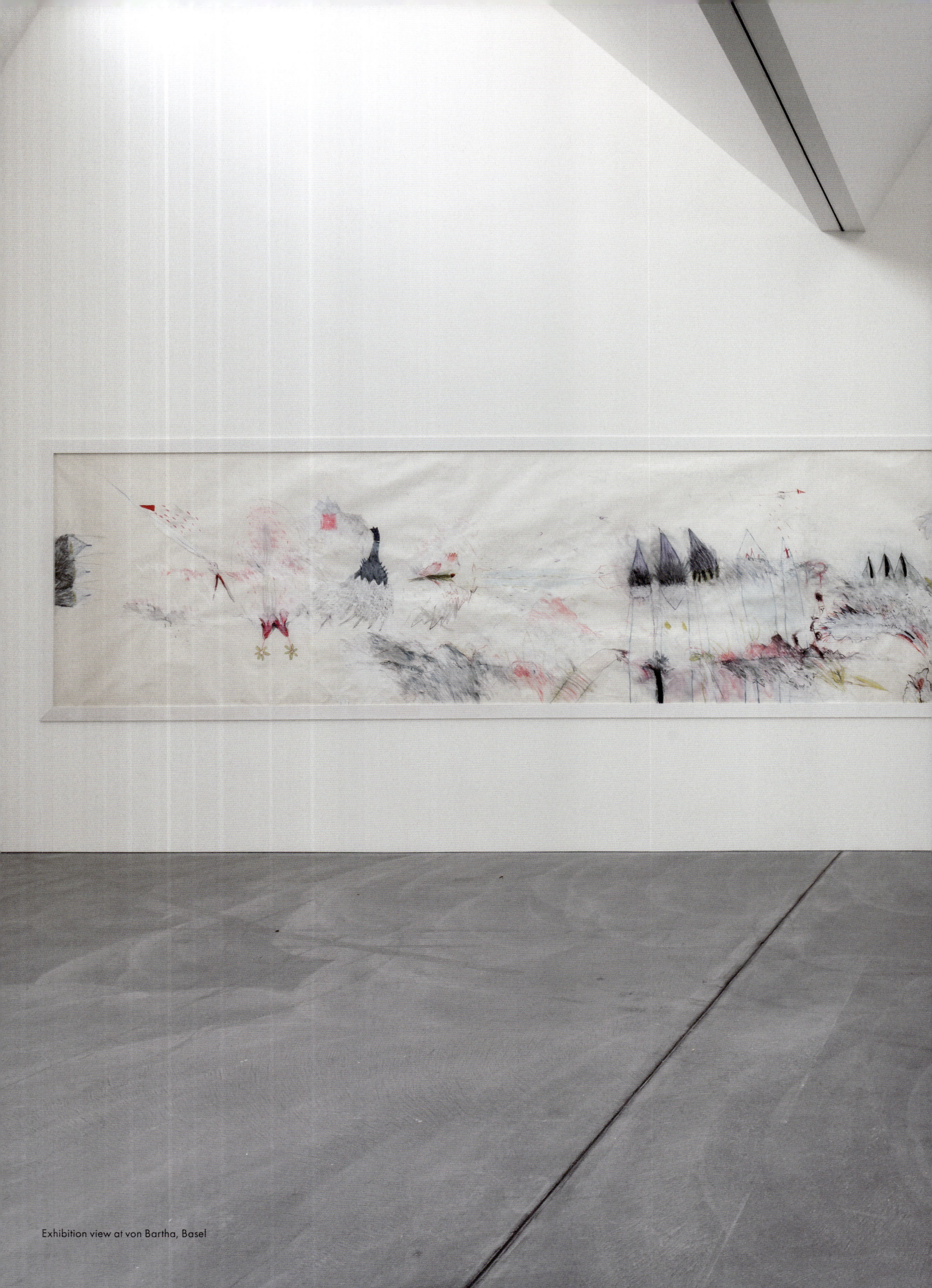

Exhibition view at von Bartha, Basel

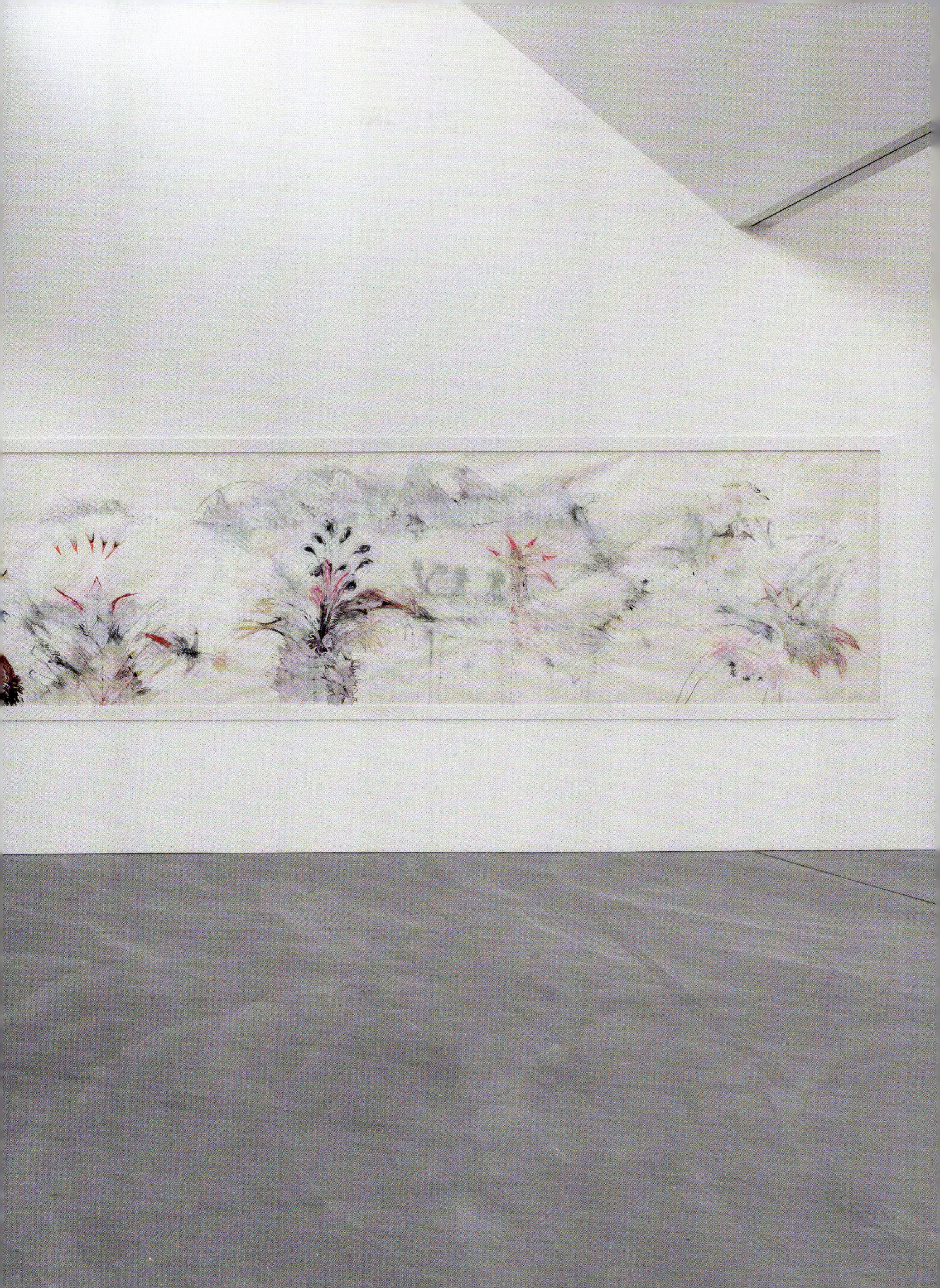

SPIDER WOMAN, IHRE UNENDLICHE GEDULD UND DAS LINIENGEFLECHT DER KUNST: GOD IS A DJ[1]

SPEECH BY MARIANNE EIGENHEER, HELD ON THE OCCASION OF THE OPENING OF HER FIRST EXHIBITION AT VON BARTHA, BASEL, IN MAY 2017.

Die Pueblo Kultur bezeichnete Spider Woman, die Schöpferin des Universums, mit Namen wie Kokyangwuti, Tsitsicinako, Sussistanako, Thought Woman, Thinking Woman.[2] Die Welt war ihr Kopf-Kind. Sie begann die Schöpfung mit dem Spinnen von zwei Fäden Ost-West und Nord-Süd. Sie schuf zwei Töchter: Sonne und Mond. Sie formte Menschen auf der Erde aus weissem, gelben, rotem und schwarzem Ton. Einige Male zerstörte sie die Welt und schuf sie neu, wie Spinnen es mit ihren Netzen tun.

„Nichts wird so fest geglaubt wie das, was wir am wenigsten wissen."[3]

Carl Gustav Carus, Leibarzt August des Starken, Mediziner, Künstler und Kunstwissenschaftler, schrieb zwischen 1819 und 1831 Neun Briefe über Landschaftsmalerei, mit einem Vorwort von Goethe.[4] Herr Carus fuhr mindestens einmal im Jahr mit der Kutsche von Dresden nach London, besuchte Freunde und tauschte alle Neuigkeiten aus. Er beschreibt z.B. die Entdeckung der Wolkenformationen durch Luke Howard, der 1802 darüber einen vielbeachteten Vortrag hielt.[5] Zur gleichen Zeit begann John Constable seine Wolkenstücke zu malen, ob er Herrn Howard kannte, wissen wir nicht.[6] In Dresden und London war man sehr froh über diesen Austausch per Kutsche, der persönliche Kontakt half, die Briefe lebendig zu halten.

Wir sind das Schiff / Wir sind der Kapitän / Wir sind das Wasser und die Luft, / Wir sind die Möven / und die Delphine, / die ums Schiff herumspielen[7]

Ist JETZT ein Ort? Wo ist die Vergangenheit? Als Kind war ich glücklich, einen Ort des Sein-Könnens gefunden zu haben, wenn ich Musik machte. Die Hände formten Töne und niemand konnte nachvollziehen, wo und wer ich selber war in diesen Augenblicken, für mich das unendliche, nicht bestimmbare JETZT.

In einer Ausstellung in Zürich beschrieb ein Professor der ETH, der sich mit künstlicher Intelligenz beschäftigte, meine Zeichnungen von 1986 so: „Sie bilden die Bewegungen Ihrer DNA ab, die vielen kleinen Veränderungen, die in den Blättern auftauchen, sich ausbreiten und dann wieder verschwinden." (Ich dachte damals an Zeichnungsreihen von Penck im Kunstmuseum Basel, da geschah sehr Aehnliches.)

Ab 1948/49 lesen, lesen, lesen: Deutsche Wochenzeitungen, *Life*-Magazin, etwas später C.G. Jung, Sven Hedin, Einsteins Theorien, niemand störte das. Daneben Kinderbücher, *Ivanhoe*,

SPIDER WOMAN, HER BOUNDLESS PATIENCE AND ART'S NETWORK OF LINES: GOD IS A DJ[1]

The Puebloans described Spider Woman, creator of the universe, with names such as Kokyangwuti, Tsichtinako, Sussistanako, Thought Woman and Thinking Woman.[2] The world was her brainchild. She began its creation with the weaving of two threads, east to west and north to south. She created two daughters, Sun and Moon. She moulded human beings on earth out of white, yellow, red and black clay. A number of times she destroyed the world and created it anew, as spiders do with their webs.

"Nothing is believed as firmly as that which we know least about."[3]

Between 1819 and 1831, Carl Gustav Carus – Augustus the Strong's private physician, medical practitioner, artist and art scholar – wrote *Nine Letters on Landscape Painting*, with a preface by Goethe.[4] At least once a year Carus went from Dresden to London by carriage and visited and exchanged news with friends. He describes, for example, the discovery of cloud formations made by Luke Howard, who gave a much-noted lecture on the subject in 1802.[5] At the same time John Constable began to paint his cloud studies; we do not know whether he knew Howard.[6] People were very happy in Dresden and London about this exchange by carriage; the personal contact helped to keep correspondences alive.

We are the ship
We are the captain
We are the water
and the air,
We are the seagulls
and the dolphins
playing around the ship[7]

Is NOW a place? Where is the past? As a child I was happy to have found a place where I was able to

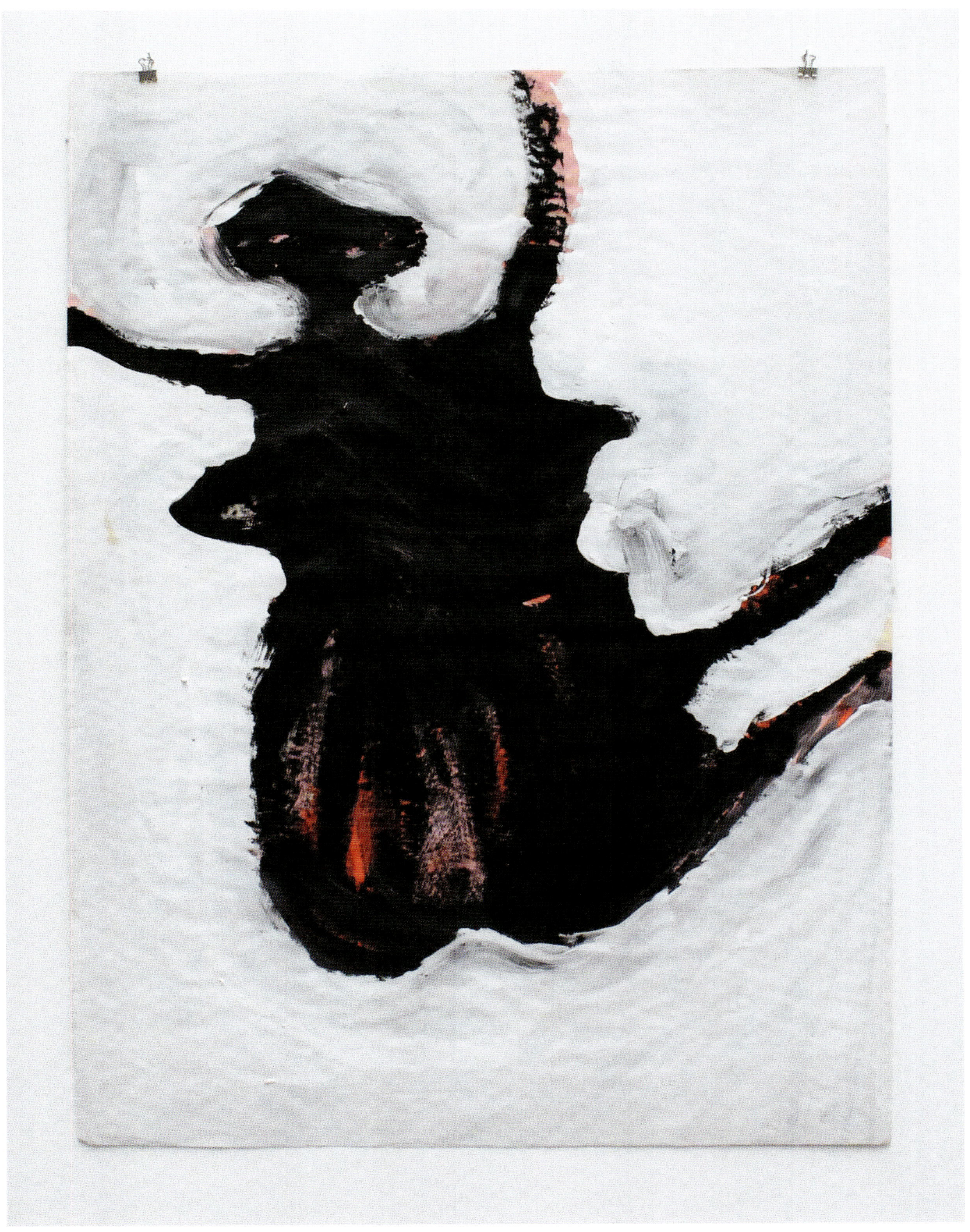

What is behind that curtain?, n.d. (probably 1984)
acrylic on paper, 79.8 x 59.6cm

"For more than 60 years now, I have
not done much aside from try to float
in endless water, without beginning
or end; ideas, images, impressions
simply pass through me like arrows
from all sides, and sometimes I can
imagine that this rotating in the water
will go on infinitely just as it began
in infinity, perhaps"

„Ich habe nun über 60 Jahre
nicht viel anderes gemacht als zu
versuchen, im unendlichen Wasser
zu schweben, ohne Anfang oder
Ende, Ideen, Bilder, Eindrücke, die
einfach durch mich hindurchgehen,
wie Pfeile, von allen Seiten und
manchmal kann ich mir vorstellen,
dass dieses sich im Wasser-Drehen
endlos weitergehen wird wie es
auch im Endlosen angefangen
hat, vielleicht"

Prinz Eisenherz in Wien, *Tarzan*-Heftchen in Bern. Später Antonin Artaud, Georges Bataille, Pierre Klossowski, Jean Genet, sein Seiltänzer begleitet mich bis heute.[8] Hubert Fichte, Carlos Castaneda, das rote Mao-Büchlein, viel feministische Literatur und das Kursbuch und Vieles was sich auf verschiedenen Realitätsebenen abspielte. Serge Golowin in Bern, Timothy Leary in Luzern. Weiter lesen, lesen, lesen neben intellektueller Literatur auch Chicken Lit aus London, wunderbar. Rumi, Hafiz, Ramon Llull, Jörg Rheinberger, David Deutsch, Max Raphael, Gertrude Stein, Viktor Schklowskij immer weiter lesen und denken, nachdenken bis heute.

Einstein and Shakespeare
Sitting having a beer
Einstein trying to figure out the number that adds up to this
Shakespeare said, „Man it all starts with a kiss"

Einstein is scratching
Numbers on his napkin
Shakespeare said, „Man, it's just one and one make three
Ah, that's why it's poetry"[9]

All dies nahm ich mit in die Kunstgewerbeschule und zeichnete, wie ich Noten spielte, Raum, Zeit und den Linien nachhörend, sie klangen wie Musik. Anders ging es nicht. Bis heute weiss ich nicht, wenn ich zeichne oder schreibe, ob ich nicht doch immer Musik mache, also komponiere, was mir als Kind verboten wurde, da Frauen das nicht konnten, das Verdikt meiner Mutter, genau wie Mathematik.

„Oh du Feuerlilie" sagte Alice.
Denn eine solche wuchs da und schaukelte anmutig im Wind.
„Wenn du doch nur reden könntest!"
„Wir können schon" sagte da die Feuerlilie,
„solange jemand da ist, mit dem es sich lohnt".[10]

„Wie eine Forschungsarbeit nachzeichnen? Wie eine fixe Idee, eine beständige Obsession nachvollziehen? Wie eine Denkarbeit, die auf ein winziges Fragment des Universums ausgerichtet war, auf ein ‚System', das sich dabei endlos umdreht und hin und her gewendet wurde? Wie vor allem sich jenes Gefühl eines Labyrinths ohne Ausgang vergegenwärtigen, jene unablässige Suche nach einer Lösung, ohne darauf Bezug zu nehmen, was sich inzwischen als die Lösung erwiesen hat – ohne sich von ihrer Evidenz blenden zu lassen?"[11]

„Wenn Du erst fragen musst, was es ist, wirst Du es nie erfahren."[12]

„The female Bunraku puppets consist only of a head and a pair of hands. The body, legs, and feet are concealed within a long kimono, and so the operators need only to work their hands within the costume to suggest movements. To me this is the very epitome of reality, for a woman of the past did indeed exist only from the collar up and the sleeves out; the rest of her remained hidden in the darkness."[13]

Die Sonaten von Mozart sind einzigartig, zu leicht für Kinder und zu schwierig für Pianisten.[14]

„Ich brauche nicht Klavier zu spielen. Aber ich muss sicher sein, dass die Bar des Ortes ein Klavier hat, auf dem ich, bei Bedarf,

simply be when I made music. The hands fashioned sounds, and no one could understand where and who I was in these moments – for me, it was the unceasing, unidentifiable NOW.

At an exhibition in Zurich a professor at the Eidgenössische Technische Hochschule (ETH) who focused on artificial intelligence described my drawings of 1986 thus: "They portray the movements of your DNA, the many tiny alterations that materialise on the pages, spread out and then disappear again." (At that time, I was thinking of Penck's series of drawings at the Kunstmuseum Basel; something very similar happened there.)

From 1948–49 on, reading, reading, reading: German weekly newspapers, *Life* magazine, somewhat later Carl G. Jung, Sven Hedin, Einstein's theories – that didn't bother anyone. In addition: children's books, *Ivanhoe*, *Prince Valiant* in Vienna, *Tarzan* comics in Bern. Later on: Antonin Artaud, Georges Bataille, Pierre Klossowski, Jean Genet (to this day his tightrope walker has stayed with me).[8] Hubert Fichte, Carlos Castañeda, Mao's "Little Red Book", lots of feminist literature and the coursebook and many things that unfolded on different planes of reality. Sergius Golowin in Bern, Timothy Leary in Lucerne. Further reading, reading intellectual literature alongside chick lit from London, wonderful. Rumi, Hafez, Ramon Llull, Jörg Rheinberger, David Deutsch, Max Raphael, Gertrude Stein, Viktor Shklovsky, on and on reading and thinking and contemplating to the present day.

Einstein and Shakespeare
Sitting having a beer
Einstein trying to figure out the number that adds up to this
Shakespeare said, "Man, it all starts with a kiss"

Einstein is scratching
Numbers on his napkin
Shakespeare said, "Man, it's just one and one make three
Ah, that's why it's poetry"[9]

All of this I took with me to art school and drew the way I played notes, listening to space and time and lines: they sounded like music. It wouldn't work any other way. To this very day, when I draw or write, I don't know whether I am not always making music, whether I compose – which I was forbidden to do as a child, since women weren't able to do that, just like mathematics (my mother's verdict).

"Oh, you tiger lily," said Alice
(Because there was one such growing there and swaying gracefully in the wind).
"If only you could talk!"
"We can already," the tiger lily said then,
"As long as there is someone there worth talking to."[10]

"How to portray a research paper? How to reproduce an idée fixe, a constant obsession? How to do so with brain activity which was aimed at a tiny fragment of the universe, at a 'system' which endlessly turns around and

herumklimpern könnte. Na gut, wenn ich ehrlich bin, einmal im Monat muss ich im wahrsten Sinne des Wortes ein Klavier anfassen, sonst kann ich nicht mehr richtig schlafen. Das stimmt wirklich."[15]

Ein sehr einschneidendes Ereignis, der unerwartete Tod meines Lehranalytikers, stoppte meine akademische Karriere an der Uni und die Ausbildung zur Psychoanalytikerin und schmiss mich buchstäblich in die Bilder zurück, grosse lange Bilderrollen, viele kleine Arbeiten, zuerst Tag und Nacht, mit viel Alkohol. Jede Nacht dann anschauen, was entstanden war, in den alten Räumen des Kunstmuseums, ich konnte die auf dem Boden liegenden Arbeiten nicht sehen zuhause. Viel Lesen, viel Schreiben und Zeichnen, daneben immer Geldverdienen, so sollte es nun viele Jahre weitergehen. Intensive langjährige Dialoge mit sehr guten Freunden und Freundinnen waren die Rettungsanker um nicht abzutauchen.

Bilder für das Totenhaus eines sehr guten Freundes[16]
Baron Samedi et les guédés dansent[17]
Das Pferd der Madam Edwarda[18]
Madame Edwarda trifft Madame Thérèse
Robert und Schneewittchen im Wald[19]
Bilder zur Lage[20]
1 Linie
Objektive Malerei[21]
Hansel and Gretel are alive and well and they're living in Berlin[22]
Misere des Herzens[23]
What is behind that curtain?[24]
The Secret Life of Milton Bozo
Il sorriso di Don Giovanni[25]
The Dream of the Dolphin[26]
Peterchens Mondfahrt[27]
History is an Angel[28]
100 Tears of a Dolphin[29]
Das Buch der 5 Ringe des Musashi[30]
Mit Goethe nach Japan oder Johnny W. goes to Tokyo[31]
Schwarz
Lotte soll in Weimar bleiben or for Lotte it's better to stay at home[32]
Please forgive me, can't stop loving you[33]
East End

Sag nicht
Es sei die Schuld
Der Poesie
Es ist das Leben
Rhythmus der Dinge
Dies ewige Aufundab
Die neuen Erfahrungen
Helden gibt es nicht mehr
Wir sind Menschen
Menschen verstehst du
Schlecht und gut

Ausser den Spuren des Farbwildwechsels –
Nichts zu sehen, nichts das mir helfen könnte.
Regeln dieses Spiels zu begreifen.
Ein anderes Sehen entwickelt sich nur langsam
Aus vielen vielen Zeichen,
sicher wie die Flugbilder schwarzer Vögel
kalt und fremd vor den Fenstern.
Aus den Kinderwelten der drei Farben
rücken Gestalten immer deutlicher ins Bild,
leise steigen aus der Wand die Erinnerungen.

was turned forwards and backwards in the process? How, above all, to realise that feeling of a labyrinth without an exit, that incessant search for a solution, without reference to what has shown itself to be the solution in the meantime – without being blinded by its evidence?"[11]

"If you have to ask what it is, you will never get to know it."[12]

"The female Bunraku puppets consist only of a head and a pair of hands. The body, legs and feet are concealed within a long kimono, and so the operators need only to work their hands within the costume to suggest movements. To me this is the very epitome of reality, for a woman of the past did indeed exist only from the collar up and the sleeves out; the rest of her remained hidden in the darkness."[13]

Mozart's sonatas are unique: too easy for children and too difficult for pianists.[14]

"I don't need to play it. But I'm sure the local bar has got a piano I could noodle on if necessary. Well, to be truthful, once a month or so I've literally got to touch the piano or I stop sleeping properly. That really is true."[15]

A very drastic event – the unexpected death of my training analyst – ended my academic career at university and vocational training as a psychoanalyst. It literally threw me back into painting: big, long reels of pictures, lots of small works, day and night at first, with lots of alcohol. Then every night examining what had come into being in the old rooms of the Kunstmuseum. I couldn't see the works lying on the floor at home. Lots of reading, lots of writing and drawing, and always earning money at the same time; it was to go on this way for several years. Intense conversations over a period of several years with very good friends were the lifeline keeping submergence at bay.

Pictures for the mortuary of a very good friend[16]
Baron Samedi et les guédés dansent[17]
The Horse of Madame Edwarda[18]
Madame Edwarda meets Madame Thérèse
Robert and Snow White in the forest[19]
Images for a situation[20]
1 Line
Objective Painting[21]
Hansel and Gretel are alive and well and they're living in Berlin[22]
Misery of the heart[23]
What is behind that curtain?[24]
The Secret Life of Milton Bozo
Il sorriso di Don Giovanni[25]
The Dream of the Dolphin[26]
Little Peter's Journey to the Moon[27]
History is an Angel[28]
100 Tears of a Dolphin[29]
Musashi's Book of Five Rings[30]
To Japan with Goethe, or Johnny W goes to Tokyo[31]
Black
Lotte should stay in Weimar, or for Lotte it's better to stay at home[32]

Leben in verschiedenen Realitäten gleichzeitig und dies wahrnehmen zu können, „the fabric of reality" wie es David Deutsch in seinen Büchern beschreibt oder mein Freund Idan Segev aus Jerusalem davon erzählt, der Professor für Computational Neuroscience ist und Kunst gerade heute eminent wichtig findet, da einfach immer weiter Linien zu zeichnen, that's bliss![34] Dazu nun auch im Kunstbereich die Diskussion über den Ort der Zeit, wo ist Gegenwart, was Vergangenheit, oder geht es energetisch doch vielleicht nach dem Tod weiter, eventuell einfach im Speicher der weitergegebenen DNA? Post-Contemporary kann man auch richtig erleben, ganz direkt, beim Arbeiten, beim Vermischen von Intellekt und Sexualität. Ich habe nun über 60 Jahre nicht viel anderes gemacht als zu versuchen, im unendlichen Wasser zu schweben, ohne Anfang oder Ende, Ideen, Bilder, Eindrücke, die einfach durch mich hindurchgehen, wie Pfeile, von allen Seiten. Und manchmal kann ich mir vorstellen, dass dieses sich im Wasser-Drehen endlos weitergehen wird, wie es auch im Endlosen angefangen hat, vielleicht.

«I need your voice» says the man armoured in iron,
«sing me your song.»
Two marigolds glow in my hands, the angel stands by.
«I'm a dreamer», the man says.

«I shall sing your dreams that are also mine,
the grey wolf and the black leopard at my side.»

In einem Tropfen Wasser ist die ganze Welt zu sehen.

Please forgive me, can't stop loving you[33]
East End

Don't say
That it's the fault
Of poetry
It is life
Rhythm of things
This eternal up and down
The new experiences
No heroes any longer
We are people
People, you understand
Bad and Good

Apart from these traces of the animal-coloured spoors –
Nothing to see, nothing that could help me
To grasp the rules of this game.
A different vision emerges only slowly
Out of many, many signs,
Certain as the flight silhouettes of black birds
Cold and strange in front of the windows.
From the children's worlds of the three colours
Figures move into the picture ever more clearly,
The memories climb softly out of the wall.

To be able to live in various realities simultaneously and to perceive this, "the fabric of reality" as David Deutsch terms it in his books, or as my friend Idan Segev from Jerusalem tells it, who is Professor for Computational Neuroscience and finds art eminently important especially today, because simply drawing lines on and on – that's bliss![34] In addition, there is now, in the field of art, the discussion about the place of time, where the present is, what the past is, or whether energy perhaps continues on after death, eventually ending up simply in the memory of passed-on DNA? You can also experience the post-contemporary truly and quite directly while working in the intermingling of intellect and sexuality. For more than 60 years now, I have not done much aside from try to float in endless water, without beginning or end; ideas, images, impressions simply pass through me like arrows from all sides, and sometimes I can imagine that this rotating in the water will go on infinitely just as it began in infinity, perhaps.

"I need your voice," says the man armoured in iron,
"Sing me your song."
Two marigolds glow in my hands, the angel stands by.
"I'm a dreamer," the man says.

"I shall sing your dreams that are also mine,
the grey wolf and the black leopard at my side."

The whole world can be seen in a drop of water.

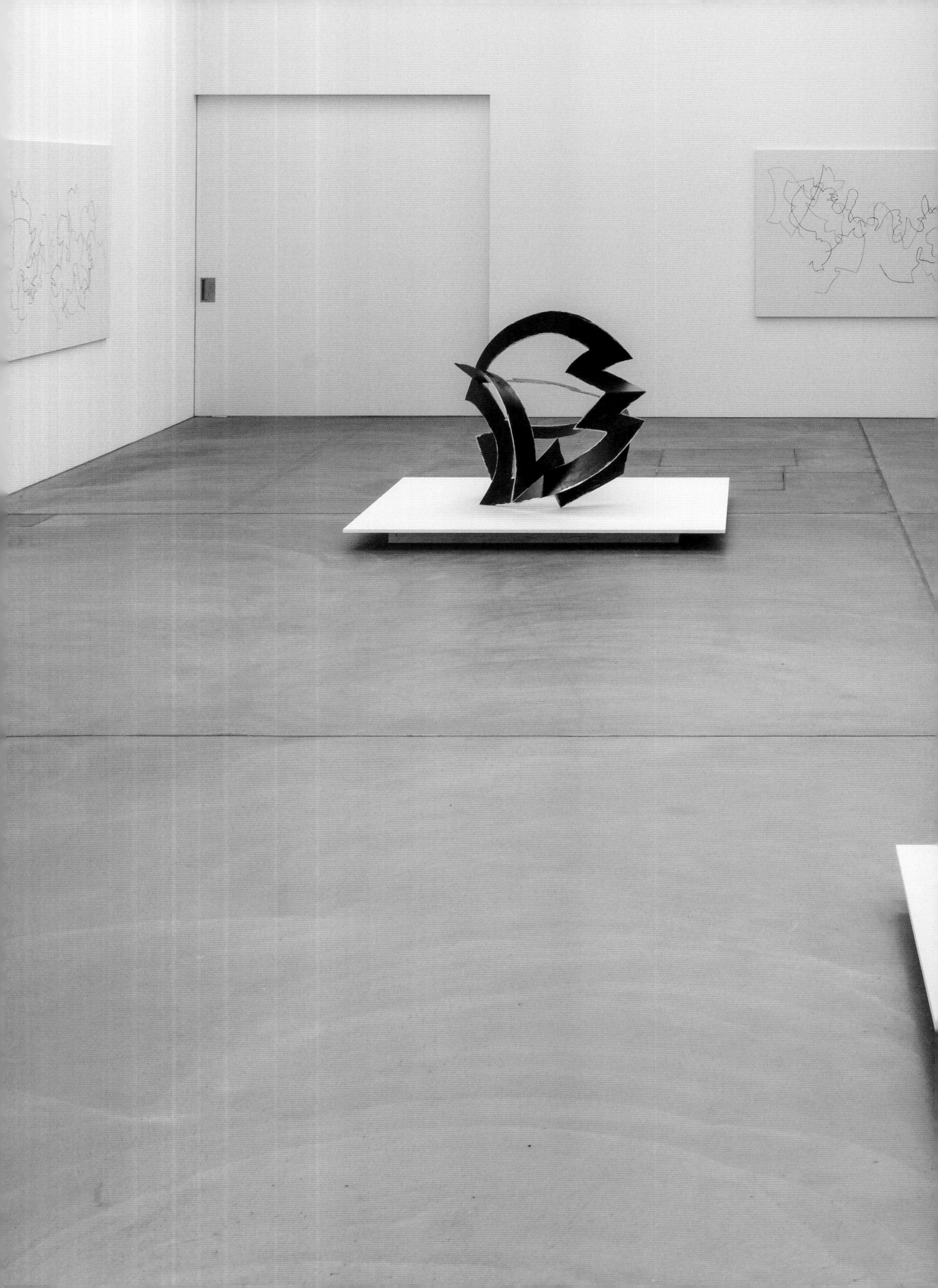

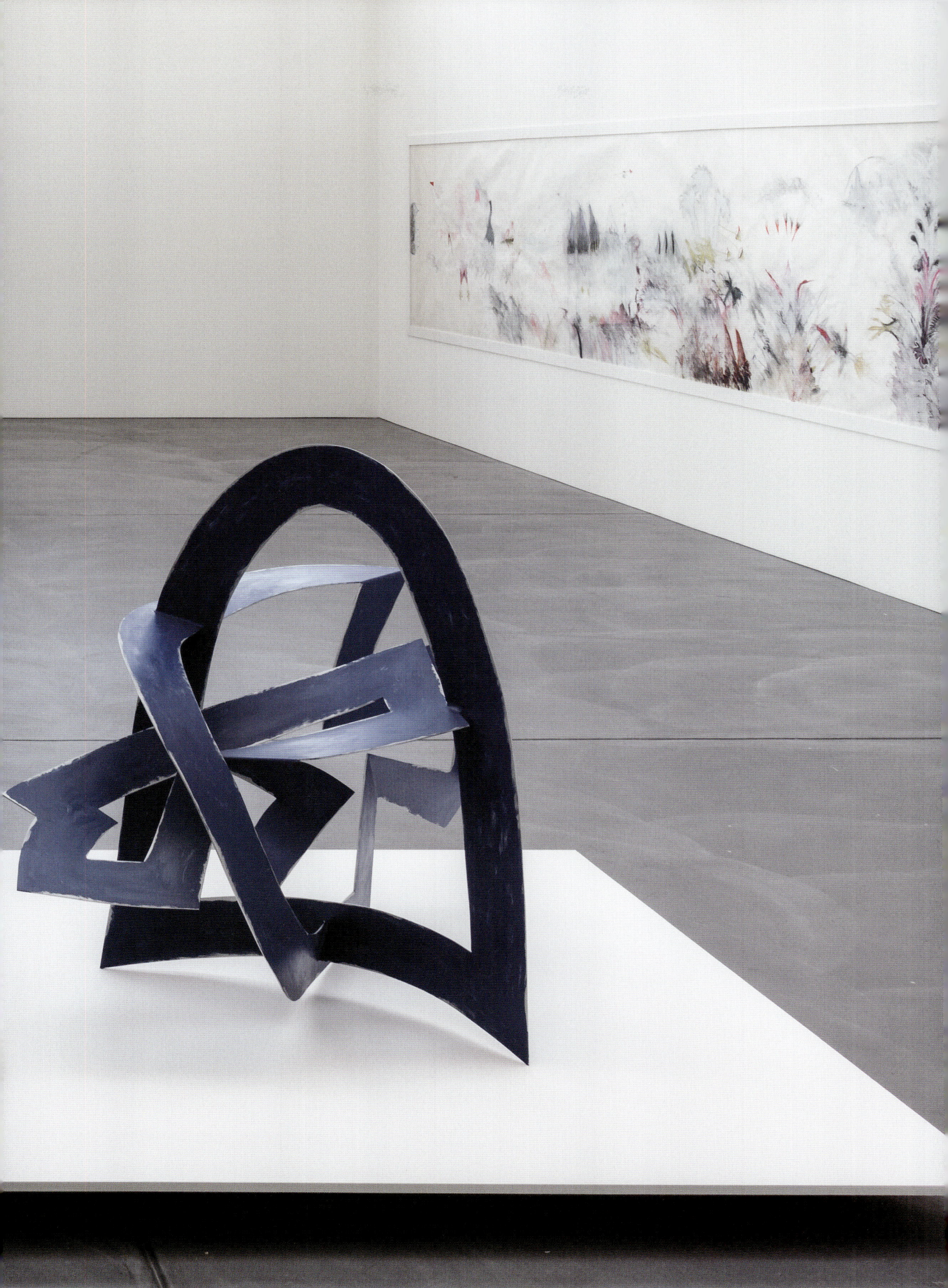

Previous page: Exhibition view,
2019 von Bartha, Basel

Untitled, 1998
aluminium, c. 100 x 150cm

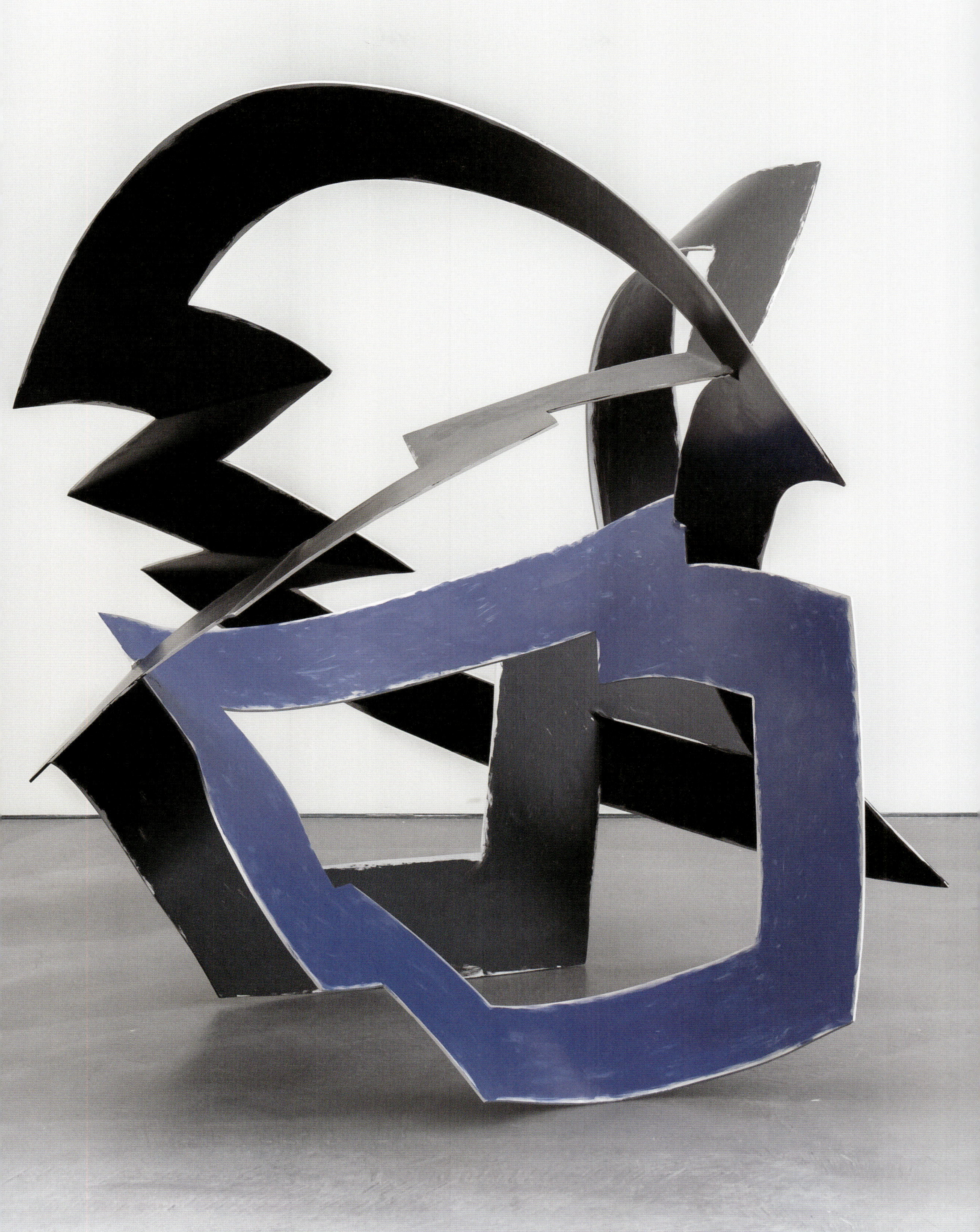

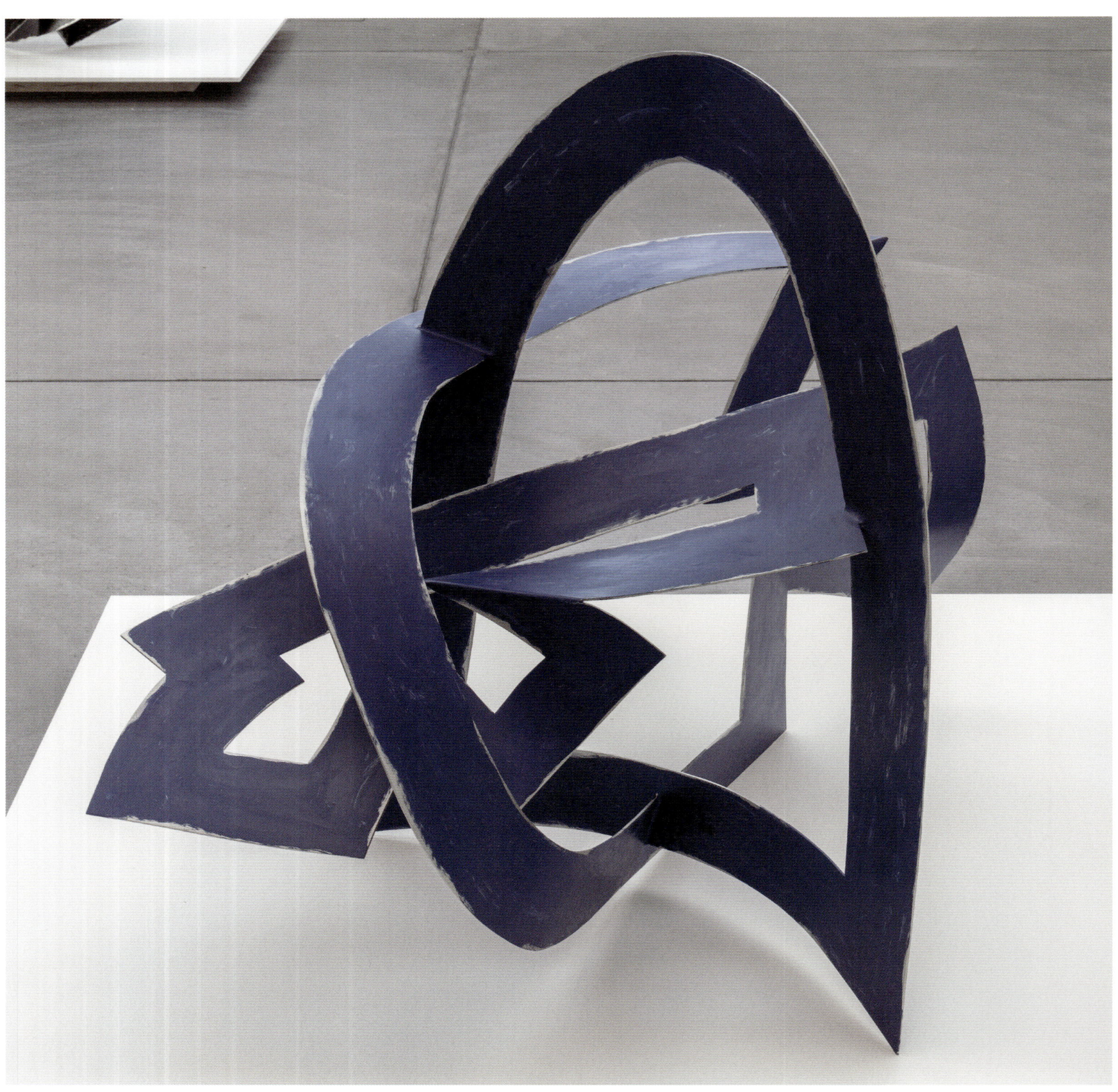

Untitled, 1998
aluminium, c. 100 x 150cm

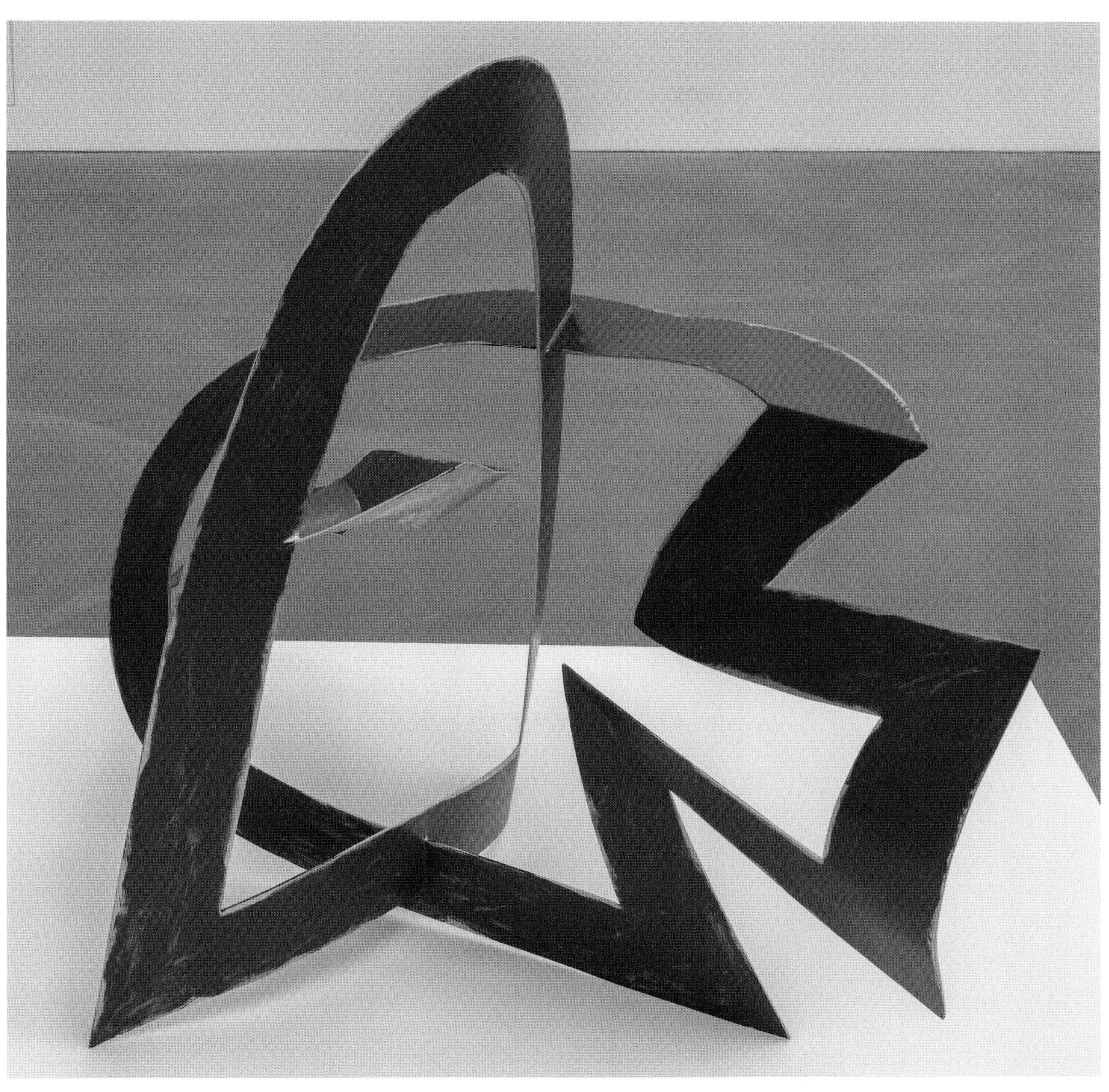

Untitled, 1998
aluminium, c. 140 x 170cm

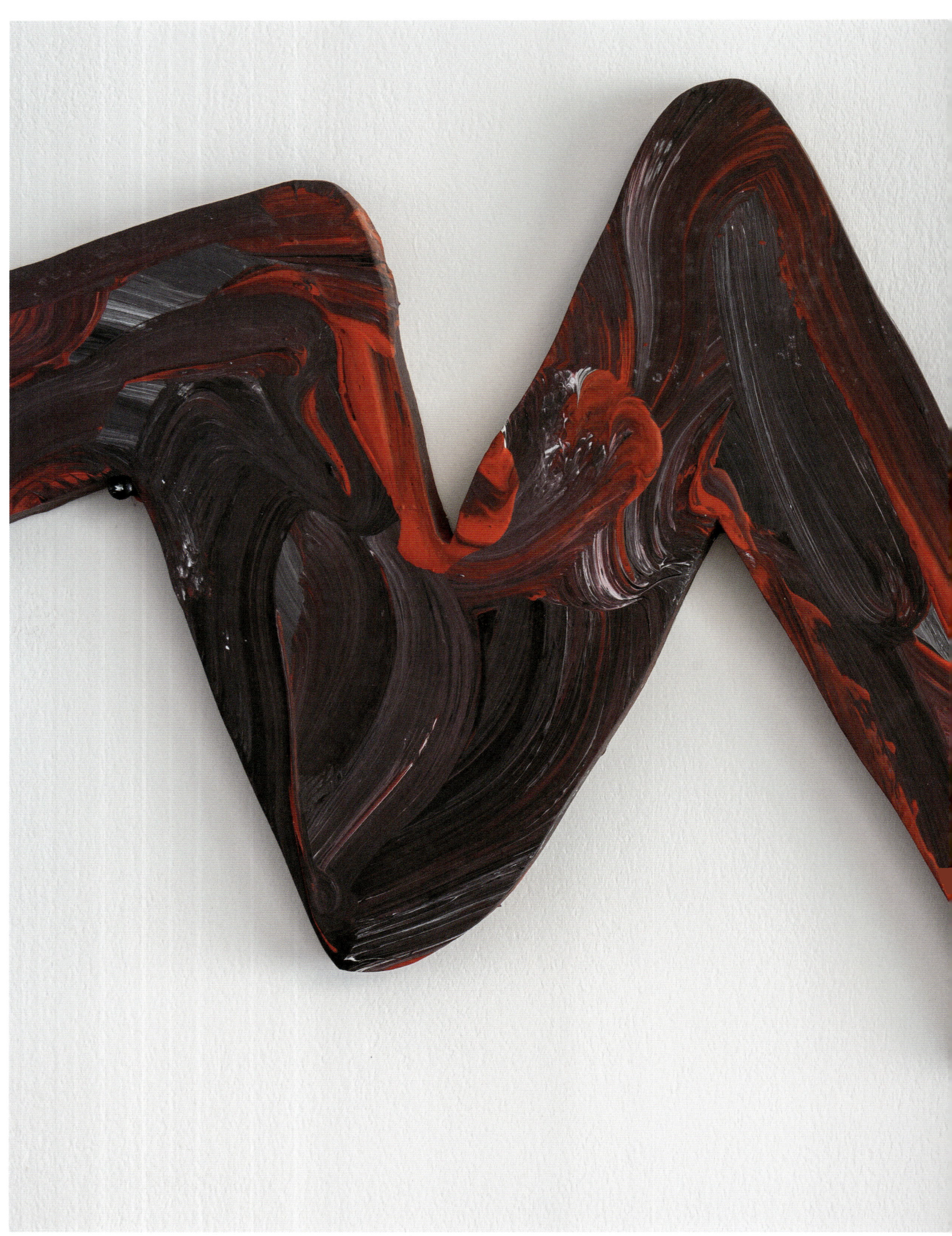

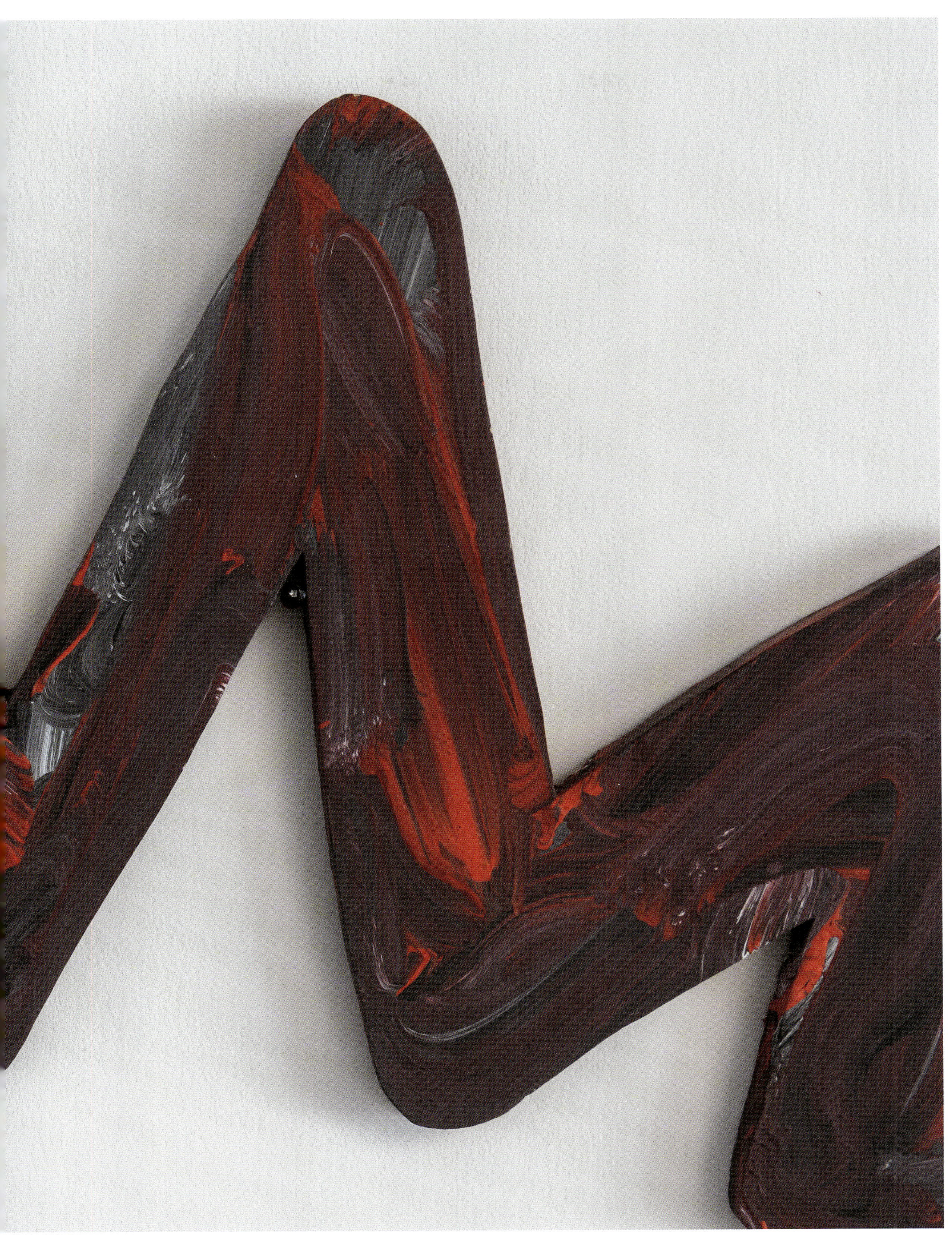

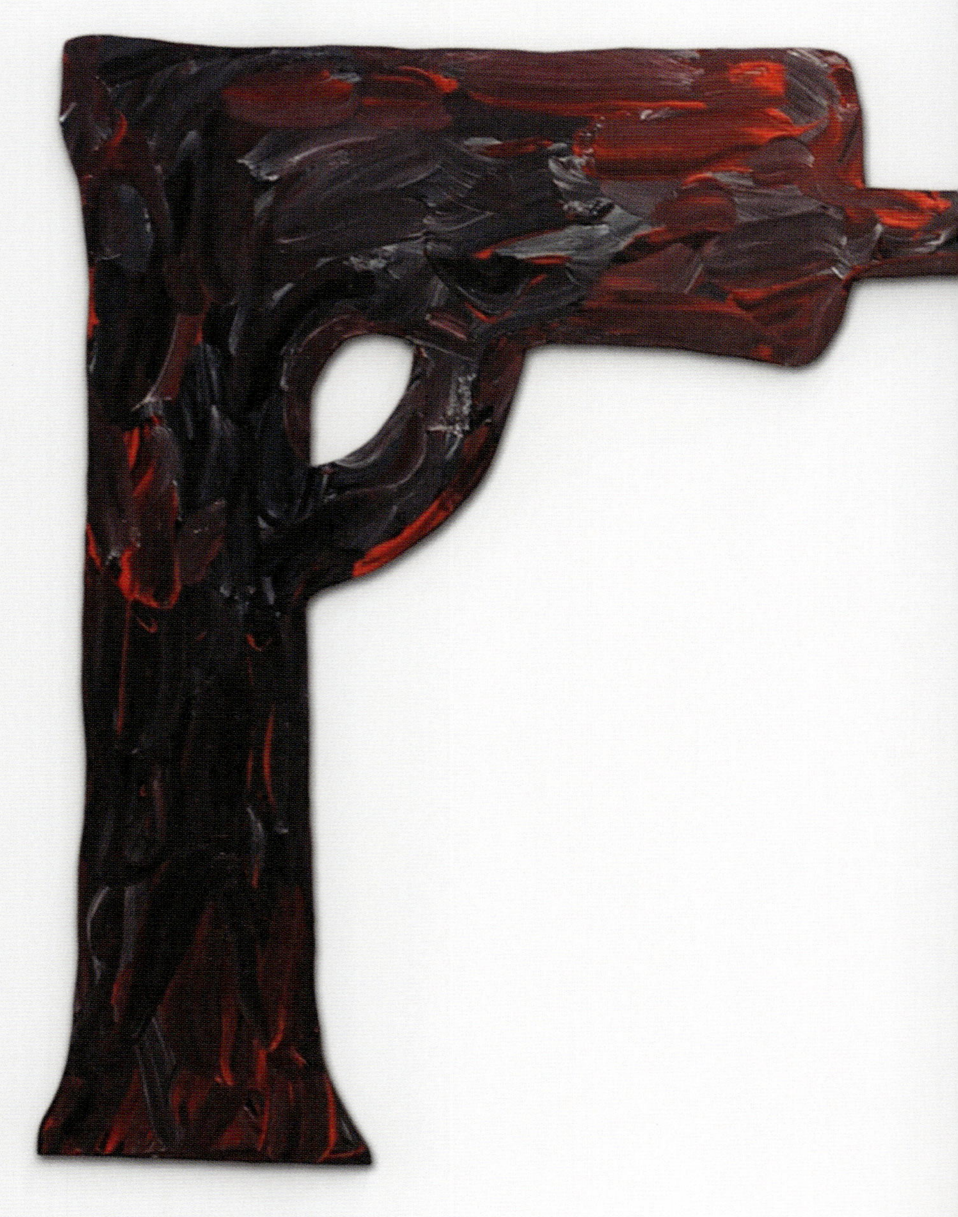

Objektive Malerei, 1982
acrylic on panel, 147 x 280 x 2.5cm

Previous page: detail

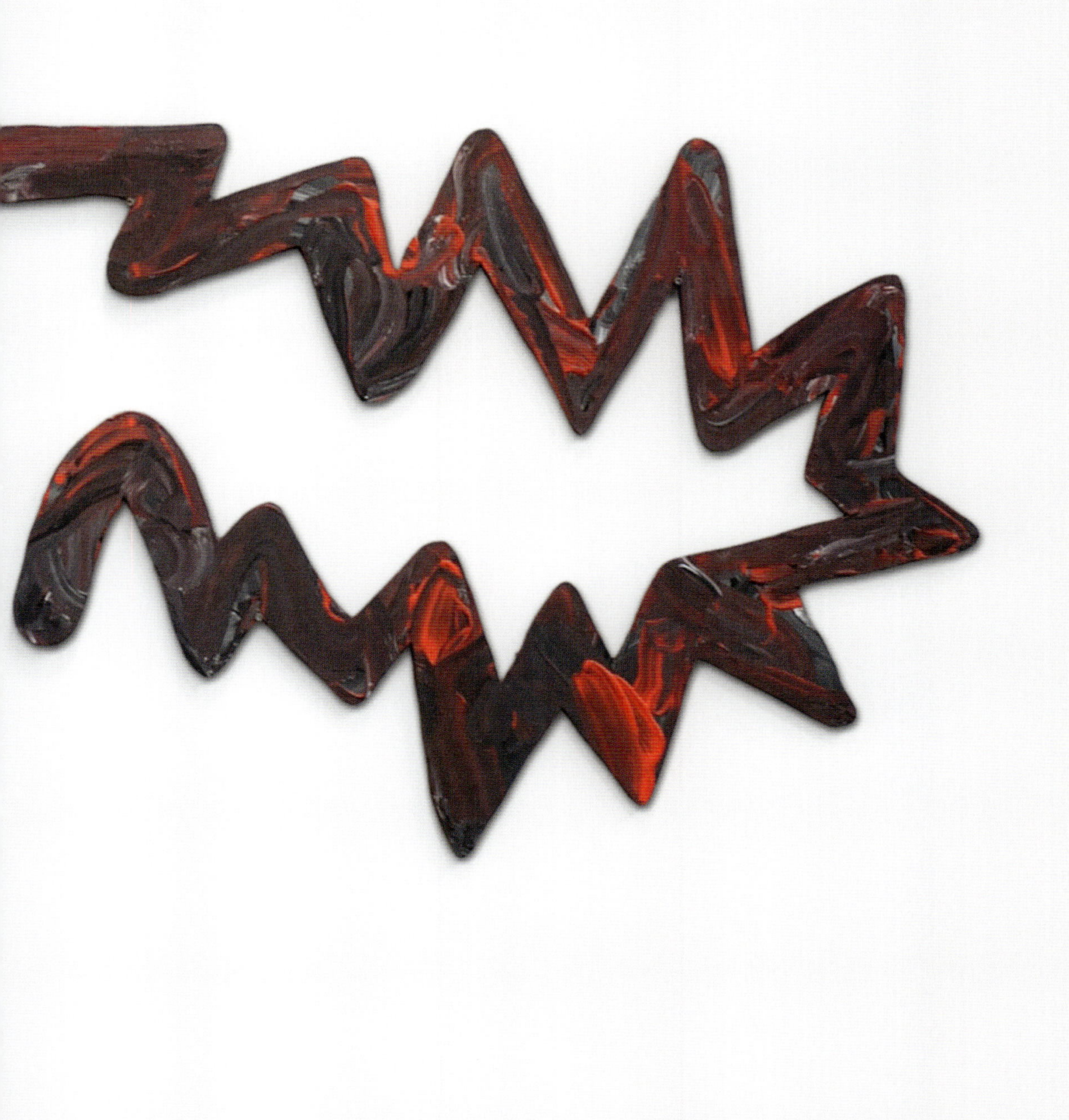

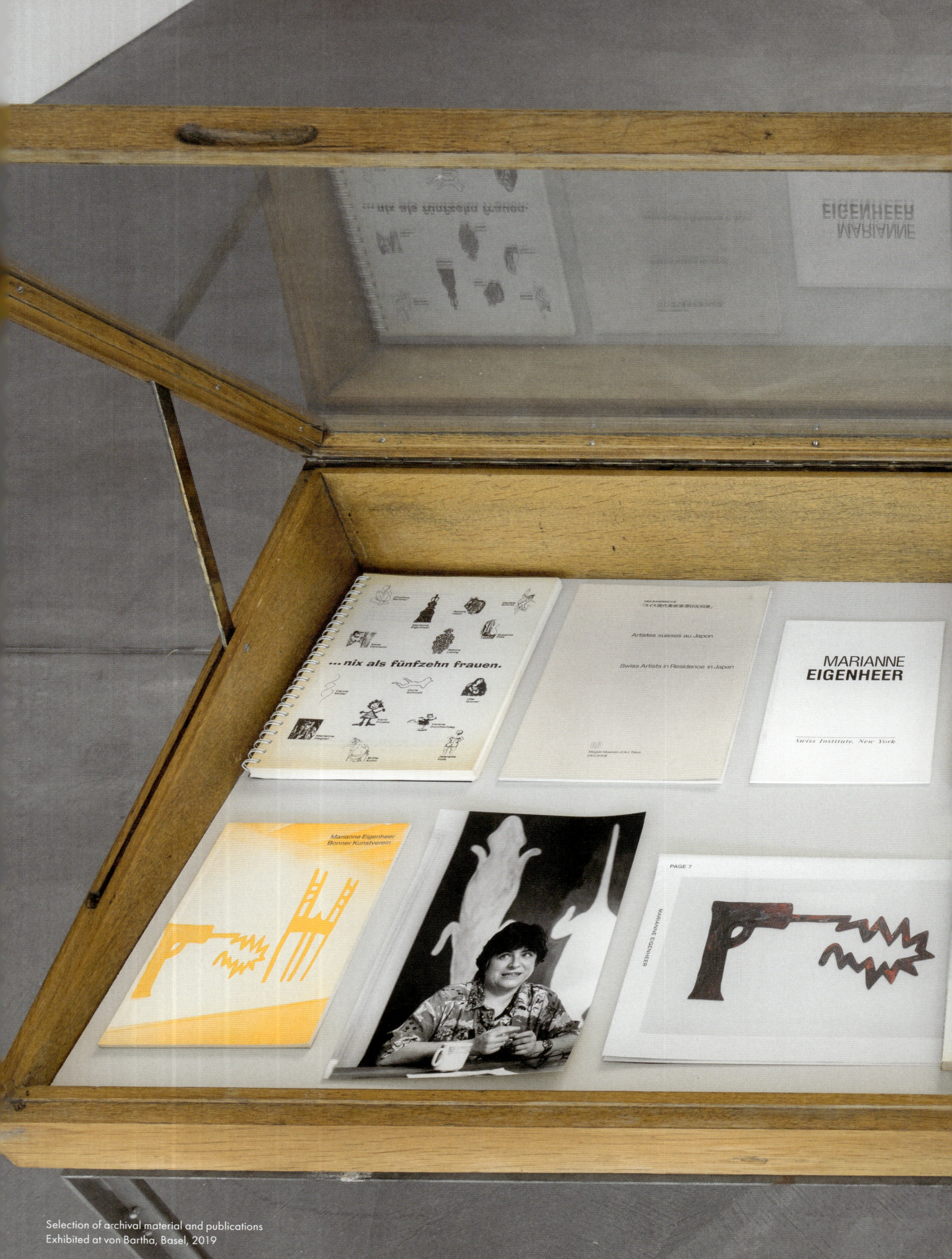

Selection of archival material and publications
Exhibited at von Bartha, Basel, 2019

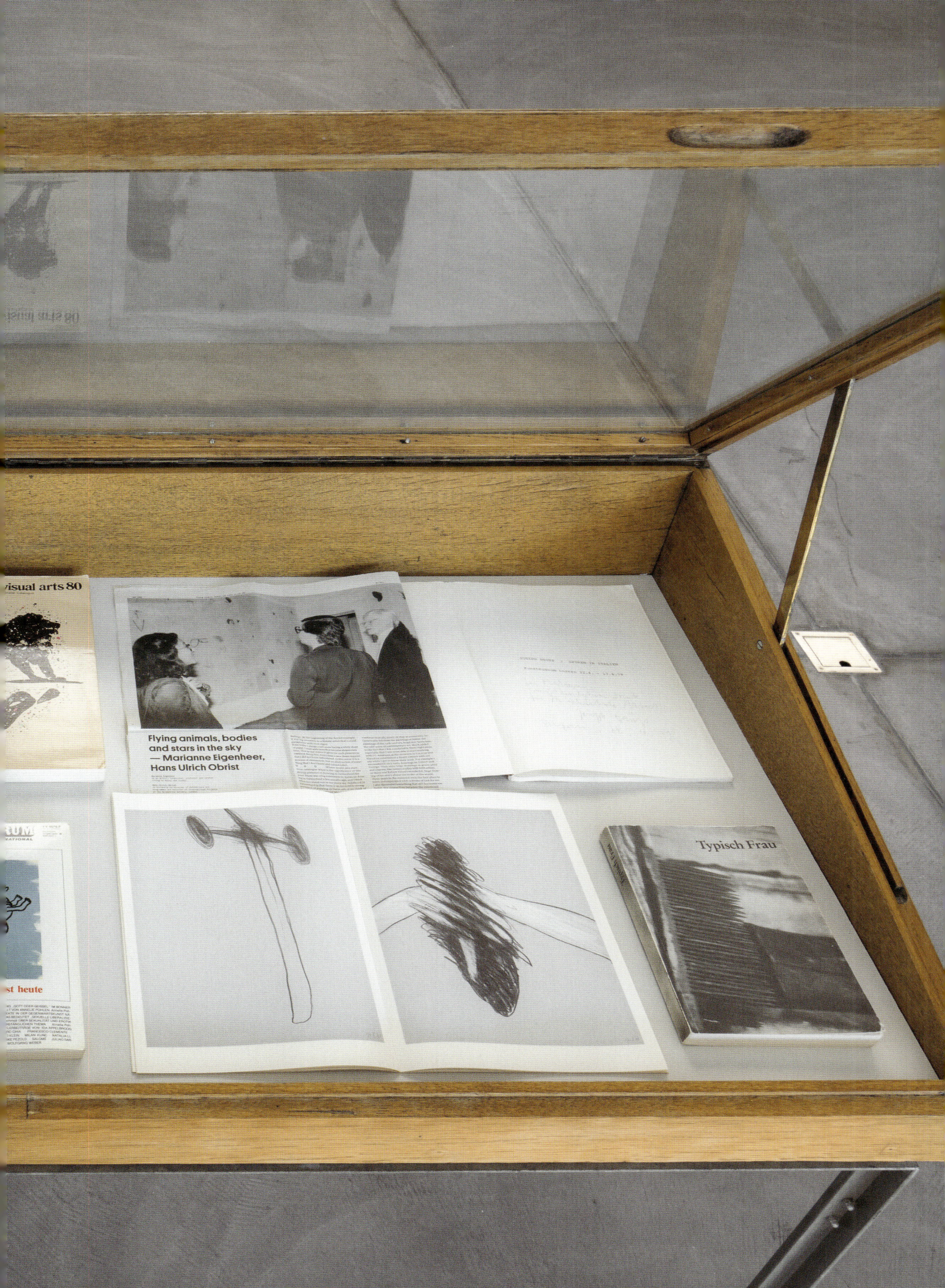

visual arts 80
Flying animals, bodies
and stars in the sky
— Marianne Eigenheer,
Hans Ulrich Obrist
Typisch Frau
st heute

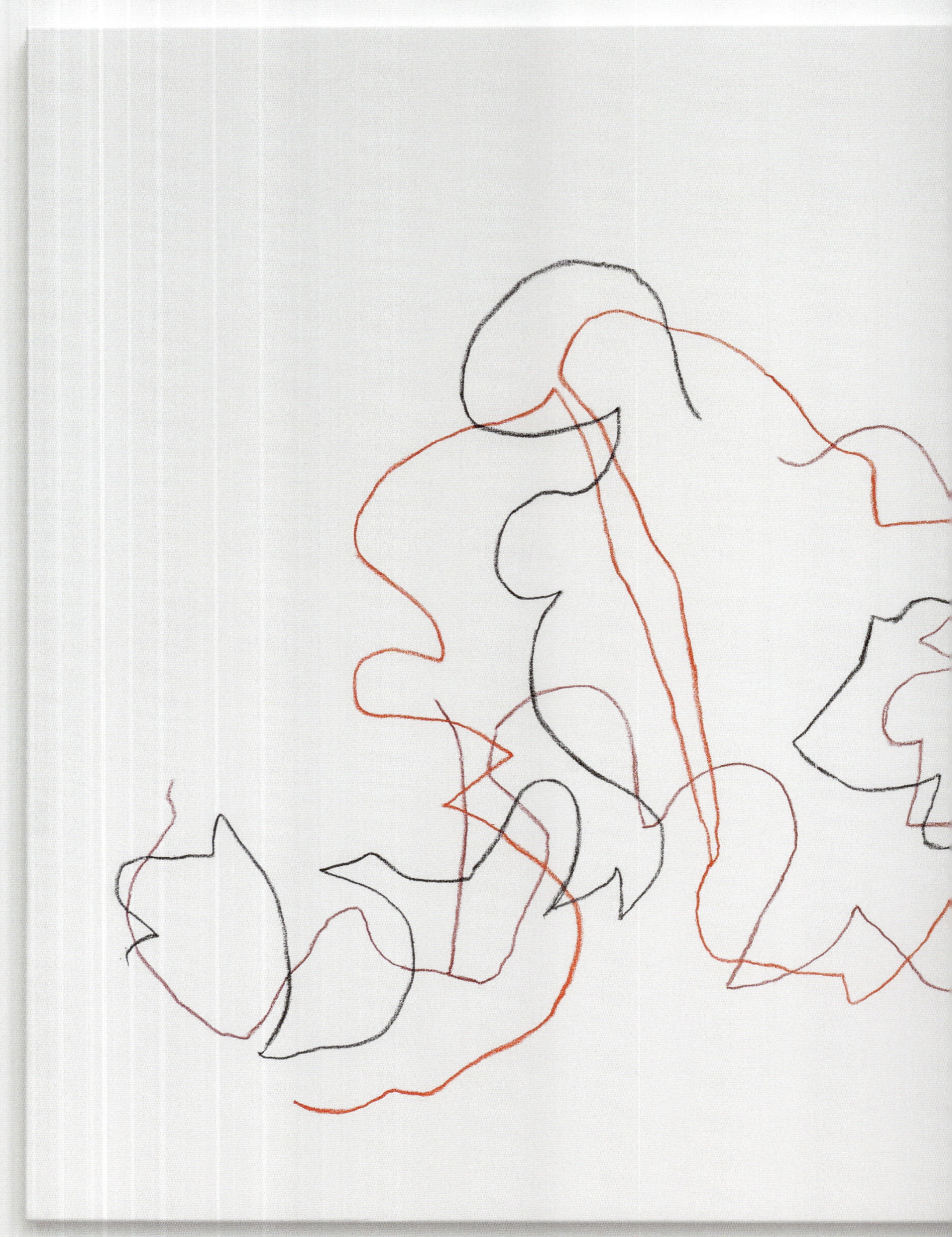

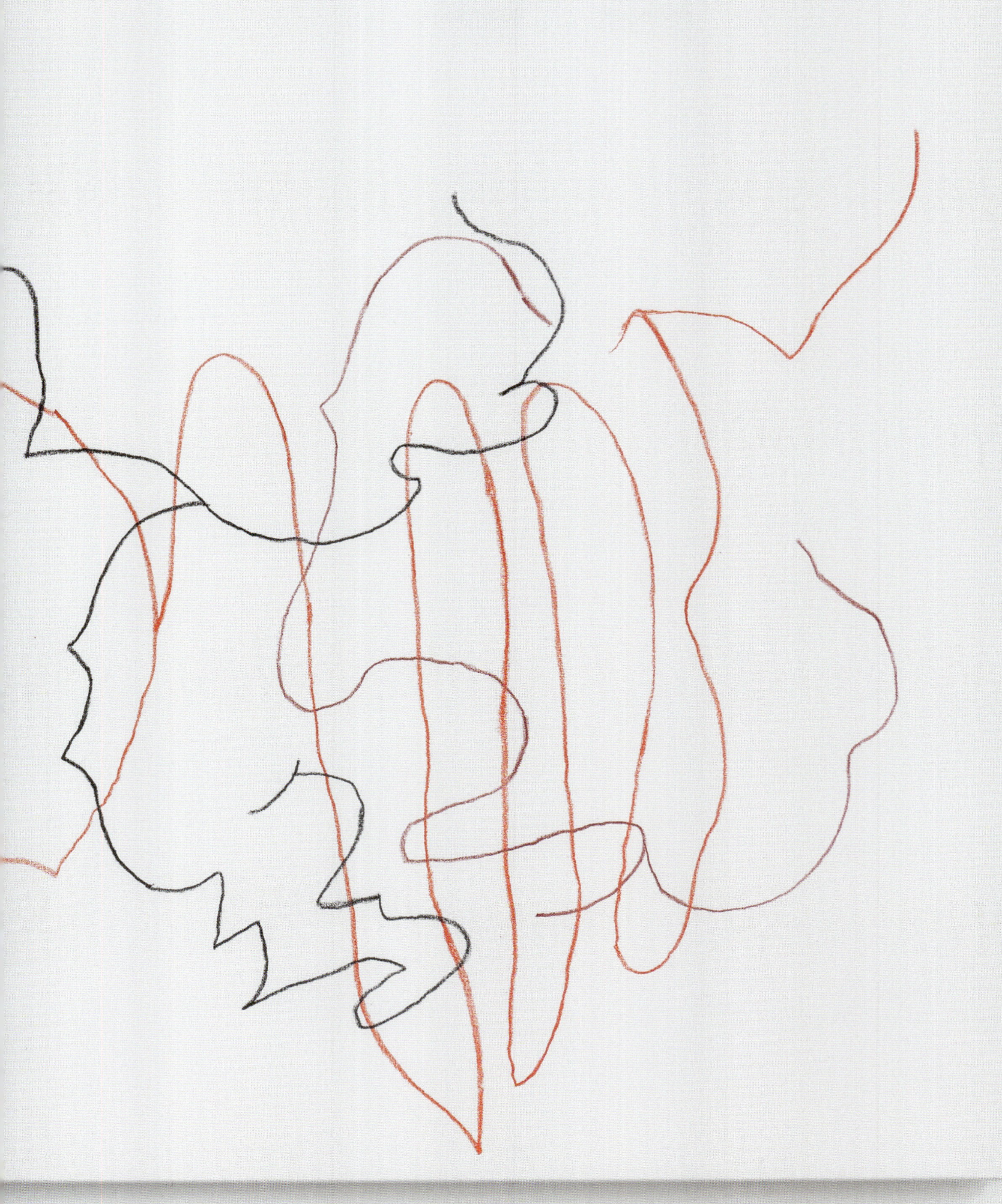

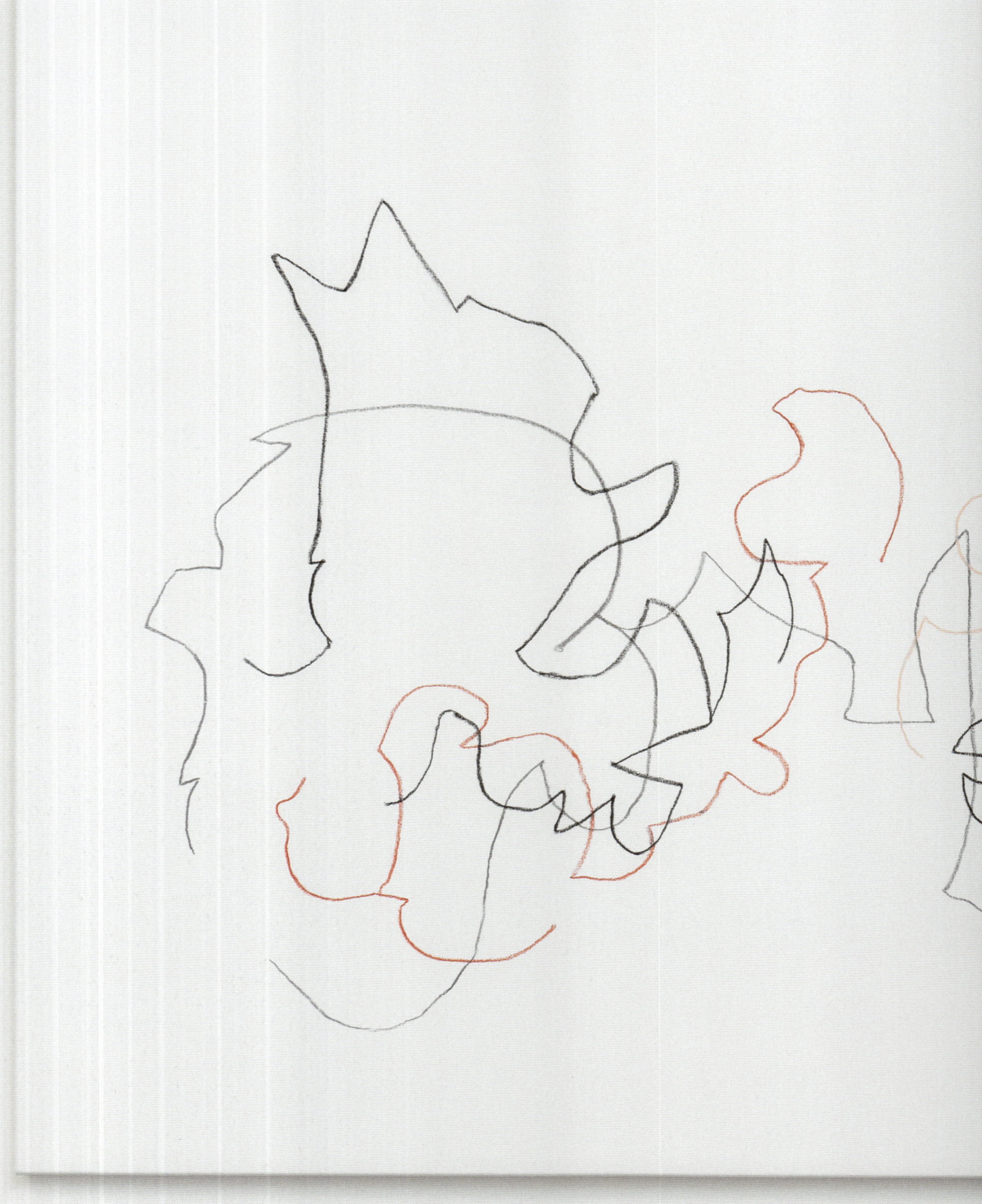

Untitled, 2013
oil pastel on canvas, 145 x 248cm

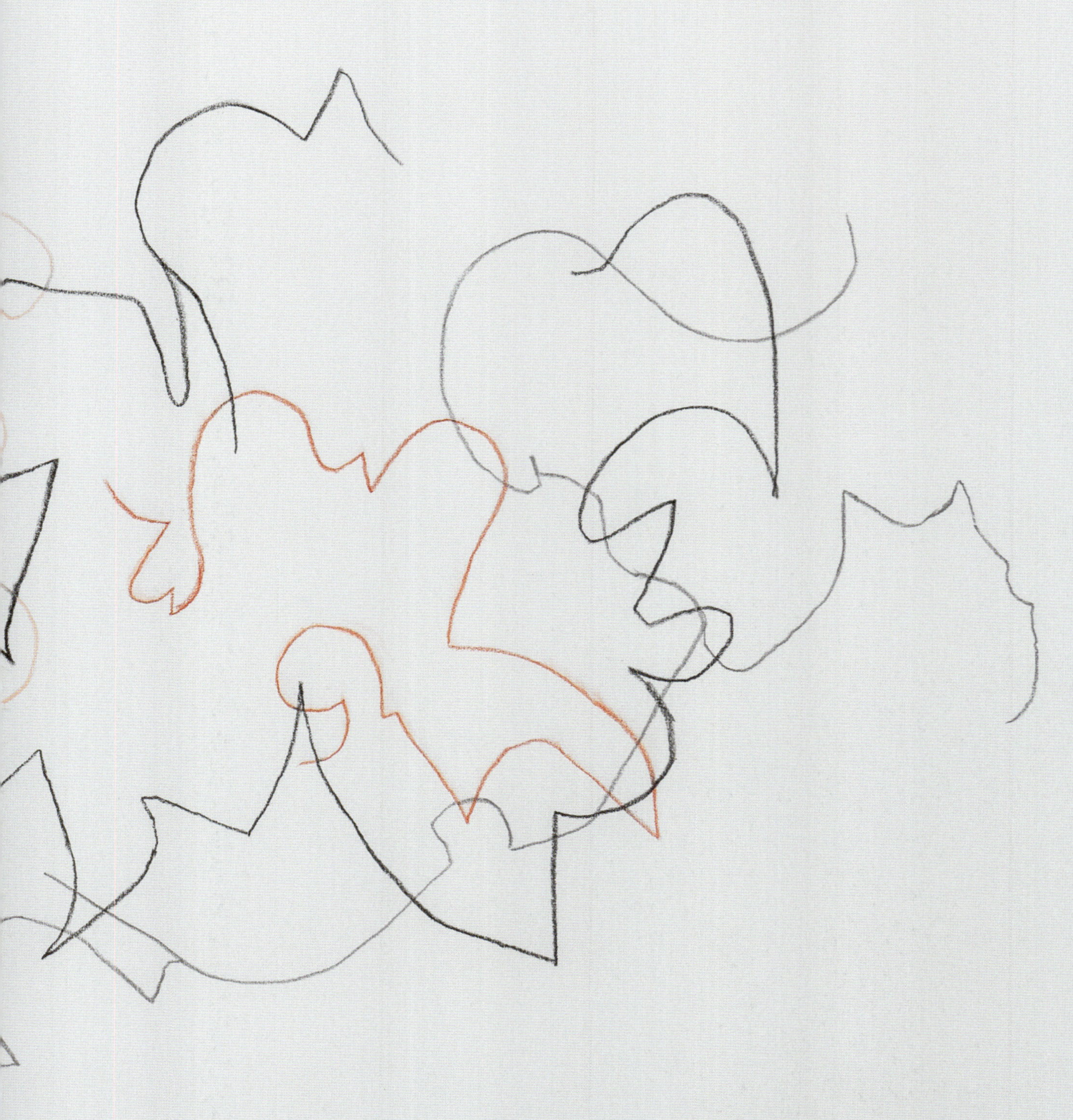

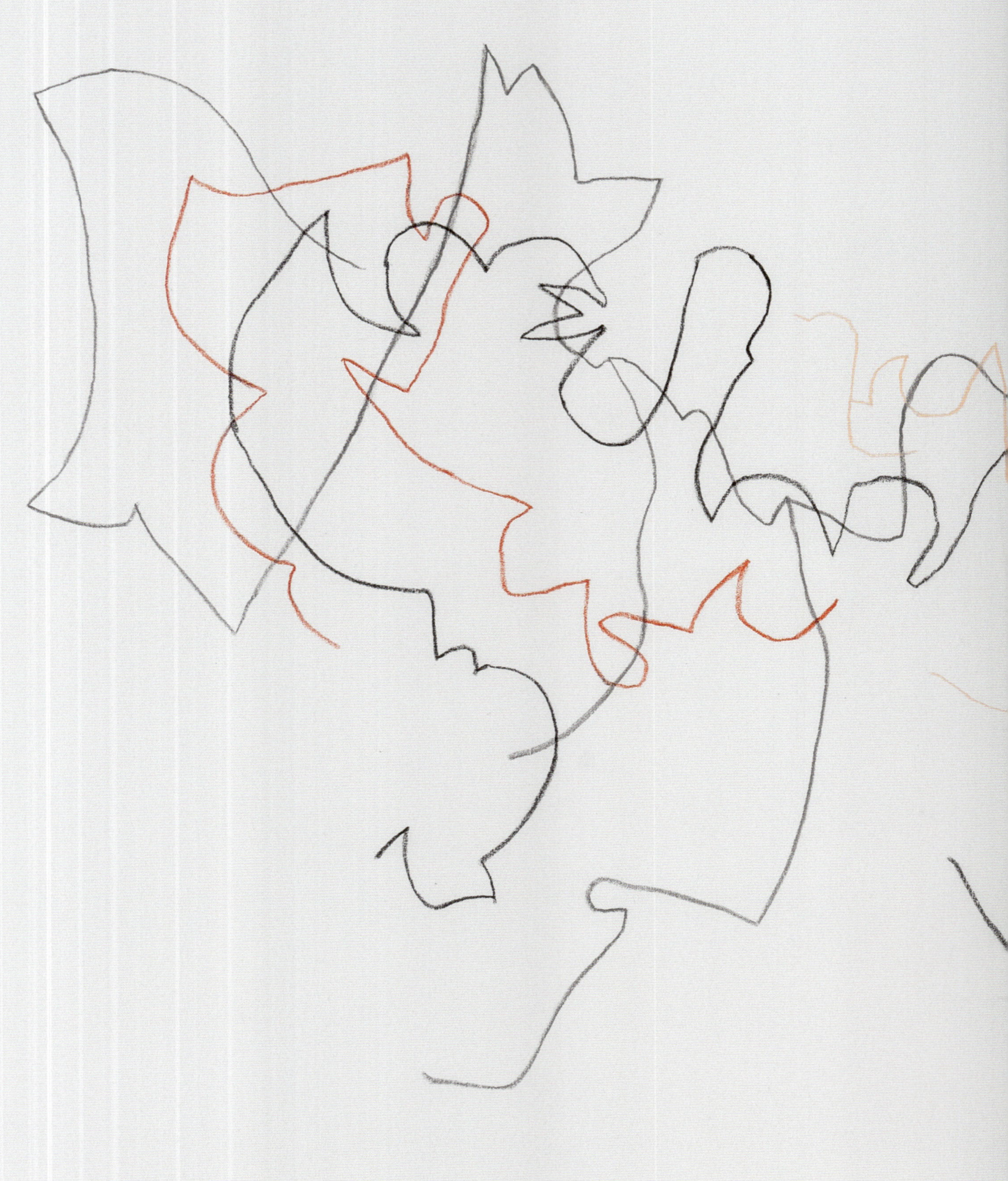

Untitled, 2013
oil pastel on canvas, 145 x 235cm

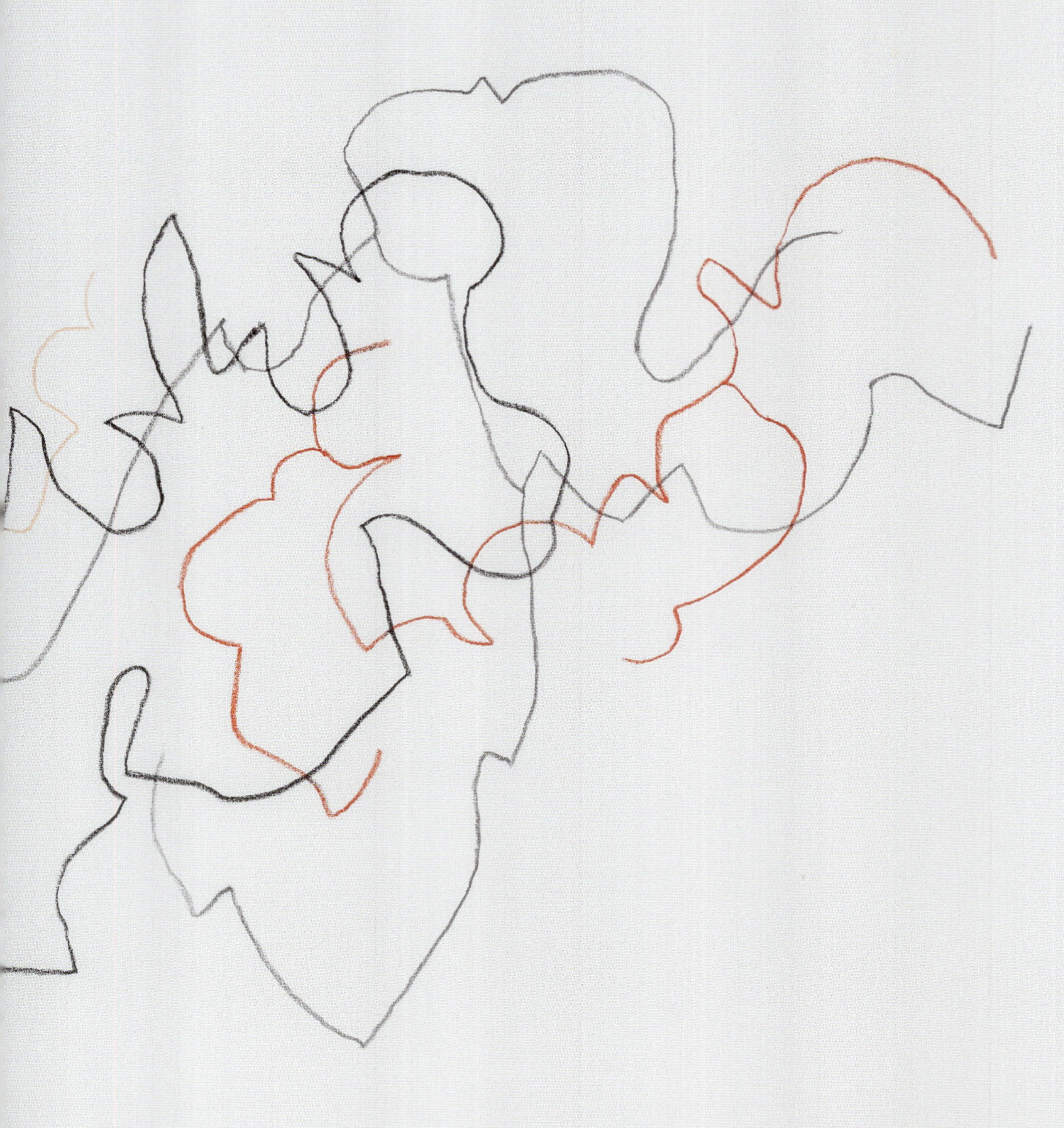

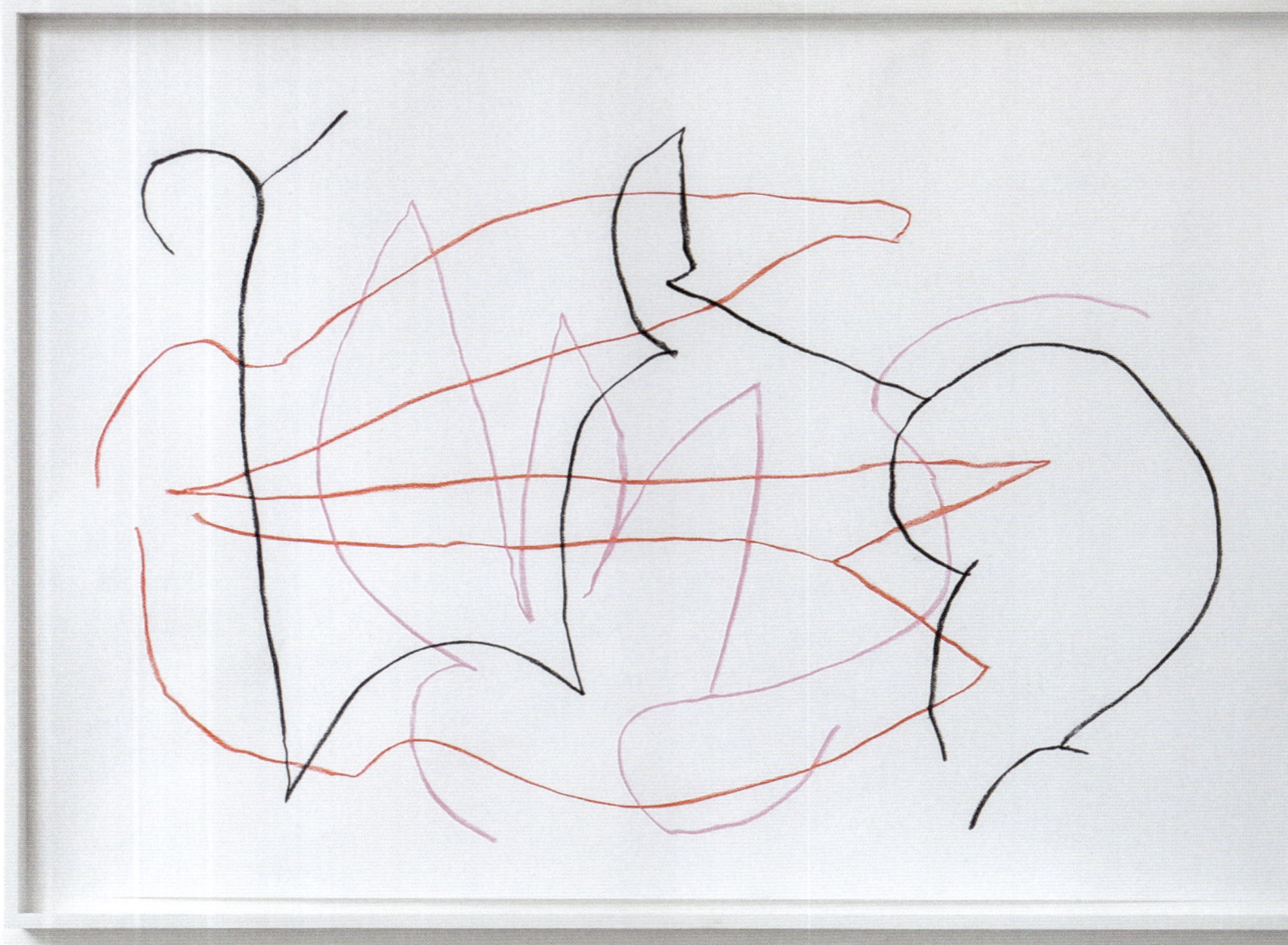

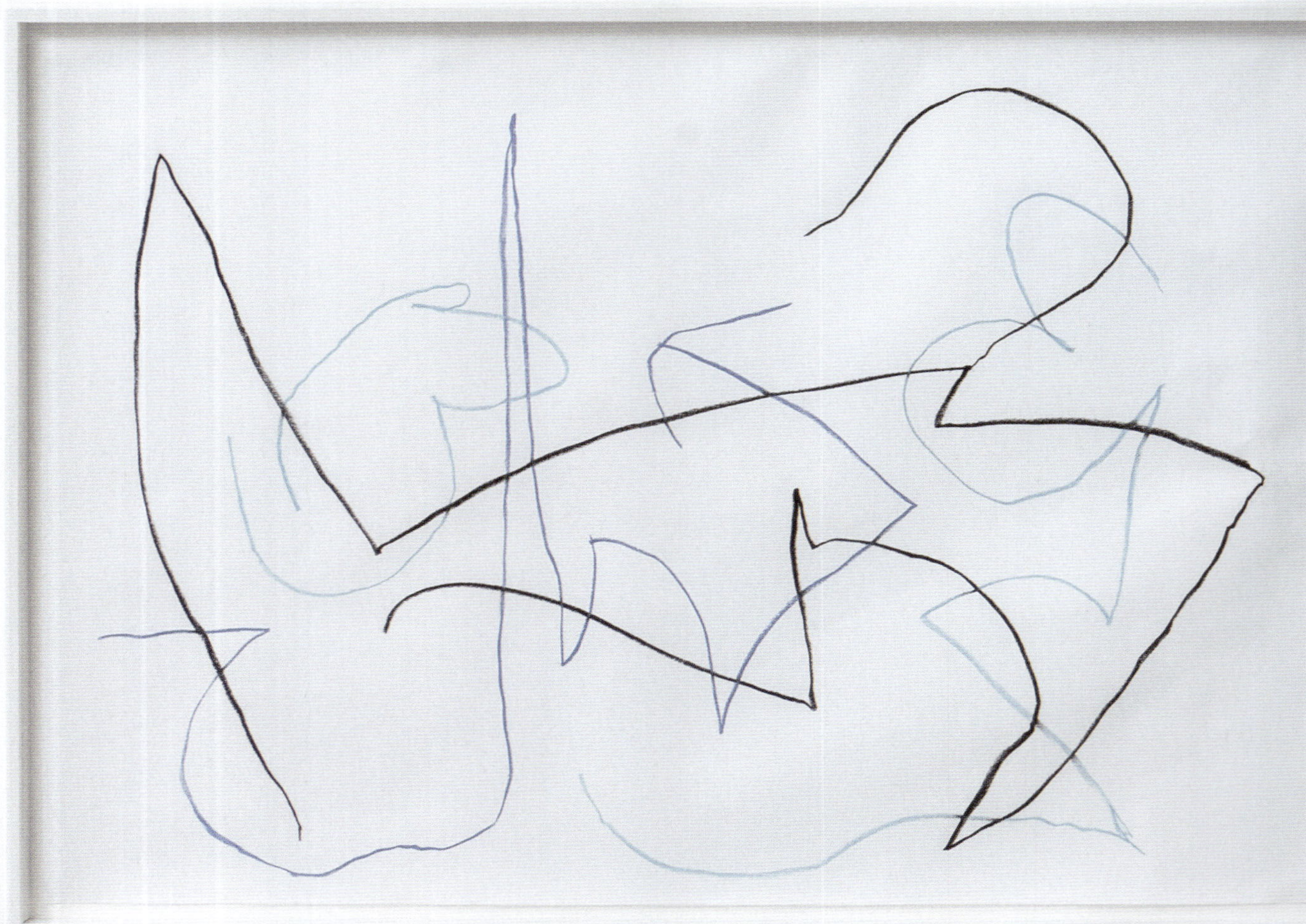

Exhibition view, 2019
von Bartha, Basel

Each: *Untitled*, 2014
oil pastel on paper
70 x 100cm

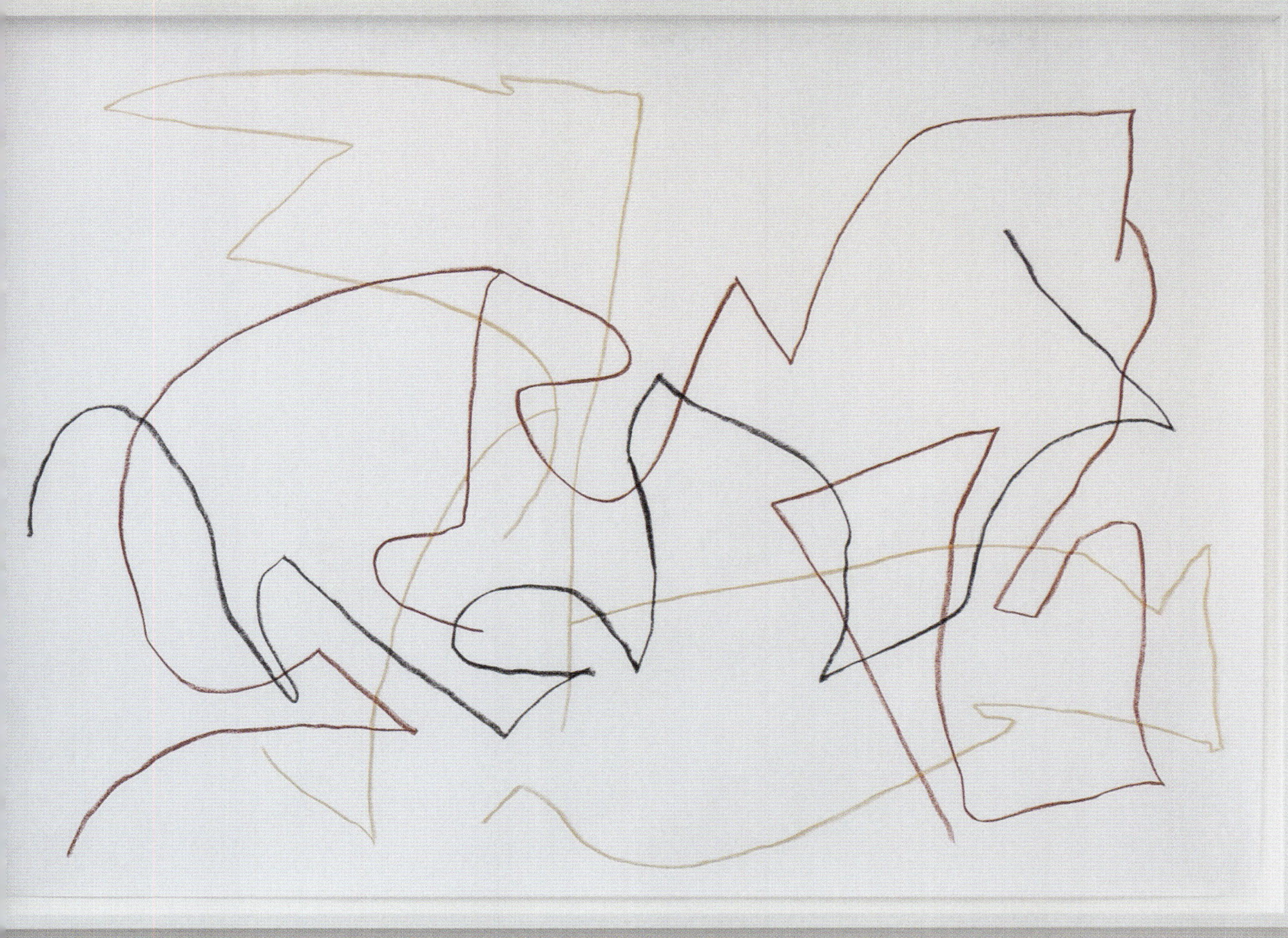

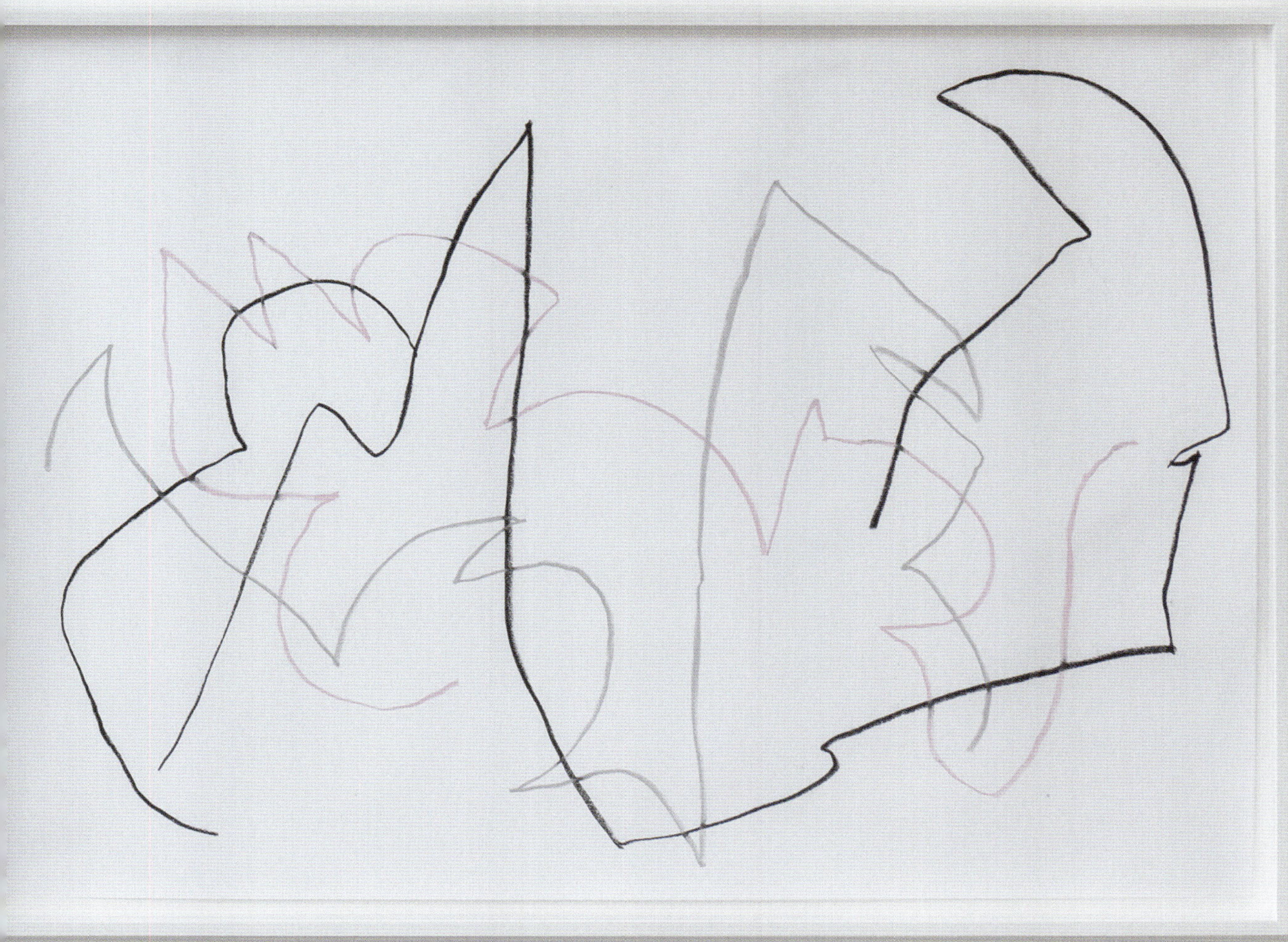

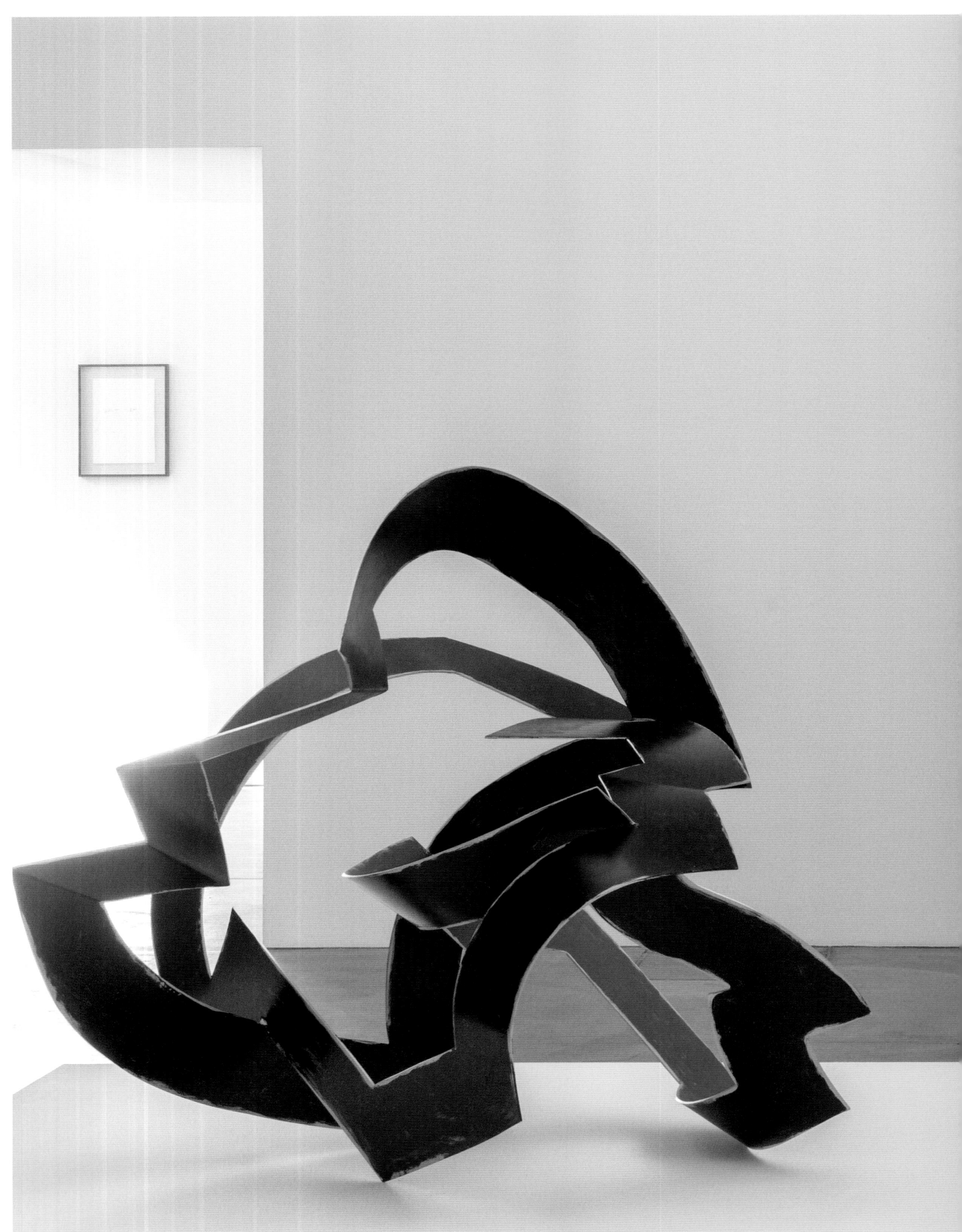

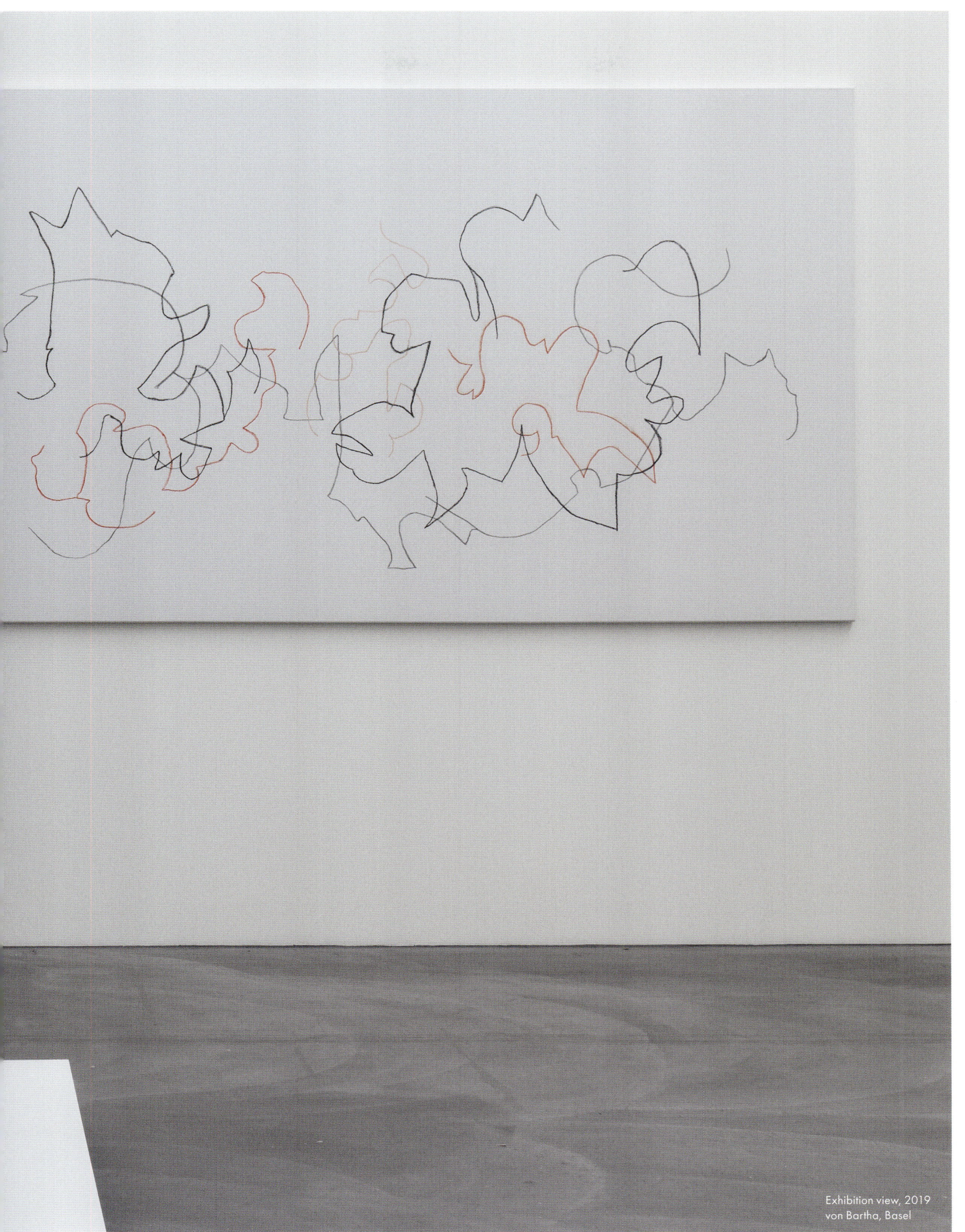

Exhibition view, 2019
von Bartha, Basel

Being Part and Counterpart

By Klaus Honnef

Marianne Eigenheer is one of those remarkable artists who stepped out of the shadows of the male-dominated art world and into the public eye in the 1970s. And it was with such vigour, as if they had been suppressed for far too long under a suffocating canvas of ignorance. Suddenly they were present, shredding with aplomb the prevailing male prejudices that women could not create art by presenting strikingly independent artistic stances and coming up with works that were defiantly unlike any of the gutted clichés of the avant-garde.

The fact that Marianne Eigenheer worked as a painter also represented a break with the then prevailing aspirations towards conceptually-oriented art. The way she painted and what she painted were precisely the opposite of ideas, rationality and control. That is to say: her work was spontaneous, seemingly impulsive and boisterous, unpredictable, lively and incredibly sensuous. At the same time, she confidently broke with the rigid conventions of painting. In her work, a tangible representational quality made a comeback – however, not through the traditional forms of illustrative representation, but as an echo or evocation taking shape as silhouettes. Even so, like many of her fellow artists, she imbued painting with a long-lost sense of corporeality. This new and refreshing physicality seized upon the emotional state of the viewer even at the first fleeting glance. She relied on a new immediacy of forms and colours. And she did so with the finest sense of ambivalence, and therefore also in the spirit of modernist art. But also going back to the beginning, as it were, and working from a fresh perspective.

In Eigenheer's *Il sorriso di Don Giovanni*, 1986–87, lines are transformed into colour networks. They are either loosely or more tightly interwoven, sometimes on their own and sometimes in dialogue with others, ultimately finding their way to tenuous colour formations. They remain permanently *in statu nascendi* (in a nascent state), and are never fully realised. The act of conclusive realisation is left to the viewer, with the proviso that the creative process is never finished. Don Giovanni's smile lends a touch of modern melancholy to the Kore of Euthydikos' immortal grin.

The self-contained colour fields in the series *Misere des Herzens*, 1984, on the other hand, are transformed into powerful and, at the same time, feather-light silhouettes. They are drawn from a realm where we find the most diverse environments and realities, human beings, half-human beings, animals and things. Owing to a fluid and subtle treatment of colour, however, they shed their shadowy existence in favour of vibrating, opaque corporeality. The cinema comes to greet us. As apparitions from an interstitial world, they float, swing and tumble over the mostly monochrome but never uniform painting surfaces, which are often considerable in scale. The given limits of picture formats neither impress nor constrict them; they refuse to be pinned down to a specific position. Weightless, and regardless of whether they are birds, elephants or animal-humans, they triumph over the constraints of the real world. Real, but not realistic. These two-dimensional and, due to their colourful staging, compact creatures conquer the large canvas fields. Eventually, this even extends to walls and entire rooms, where they create their own universe. If you came across them unexpectedly, you could feel a little uneasy. Around humans, they are able to awaken buried memories of the vast, repressed world of non-humans, similarly to the birds in Alfred Hitchcock's masterpiece. Yet they are the wonderful and mysterious creatures of a great artist.

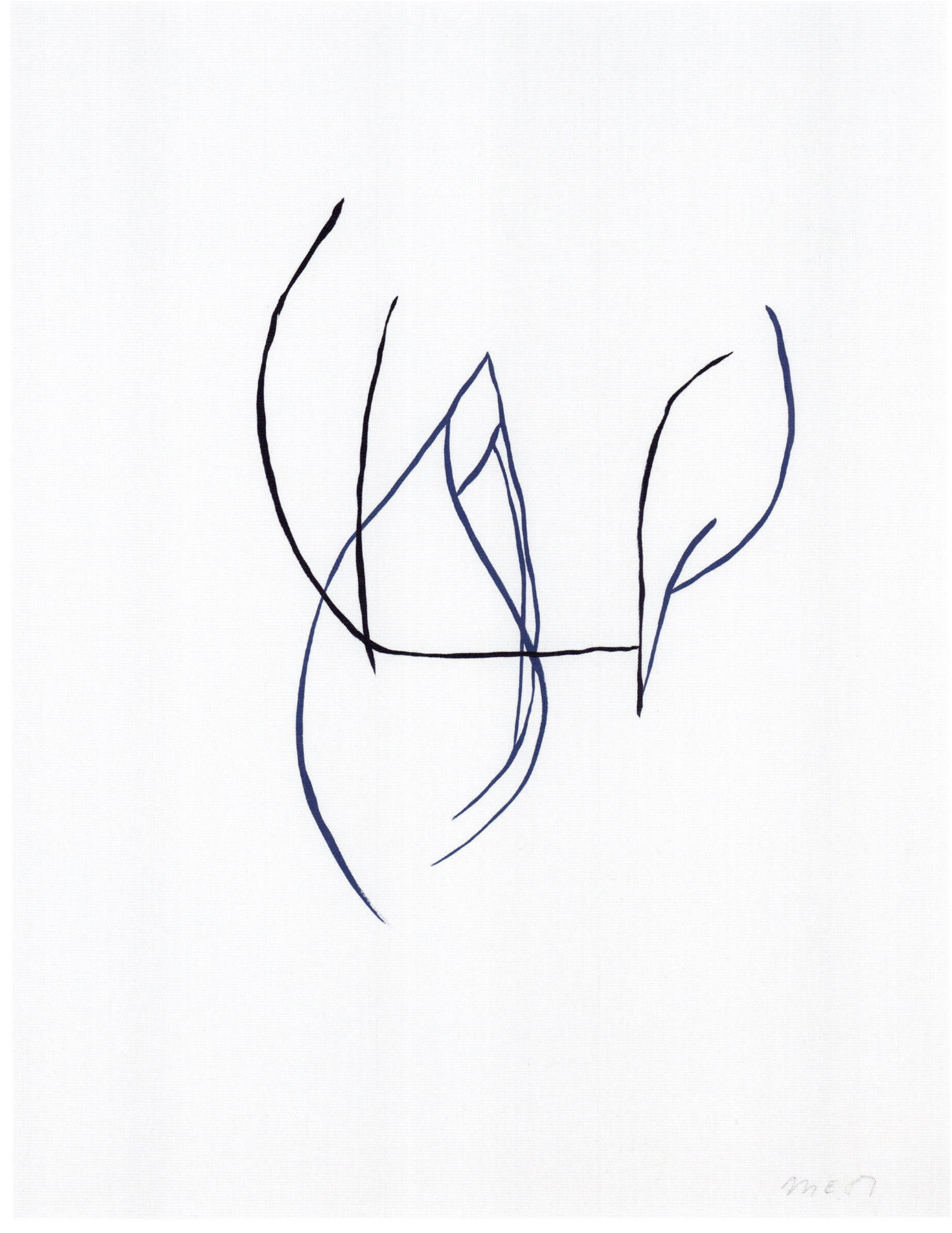

Untitled, 1987
gouache on paper, 110 x 75cm

The formal language of this work corresponds with the series *7 Tage, 7 Träume*.

Untitled, c. 2001/2
watercolour on paper, 41 x 29.5cm

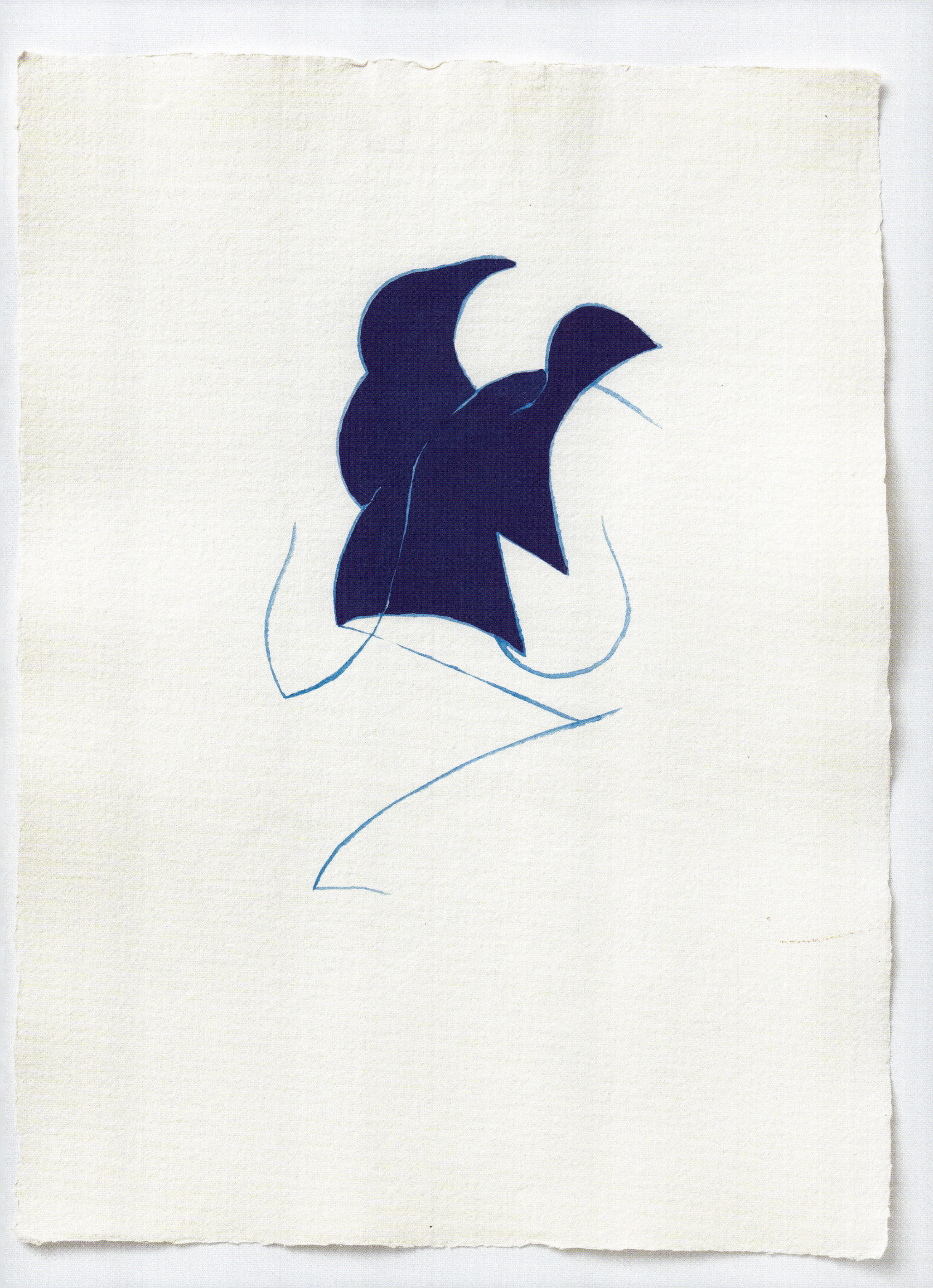

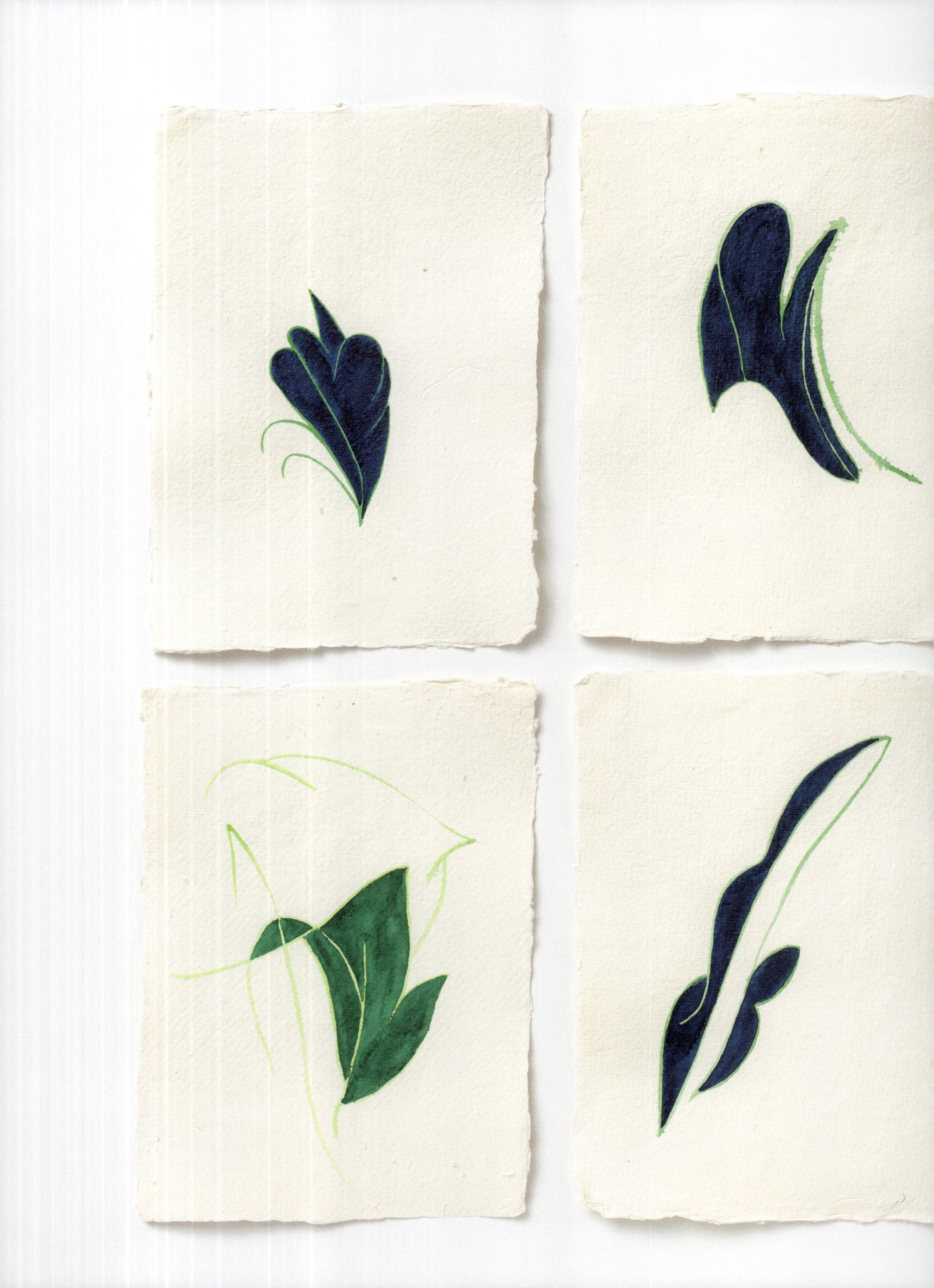

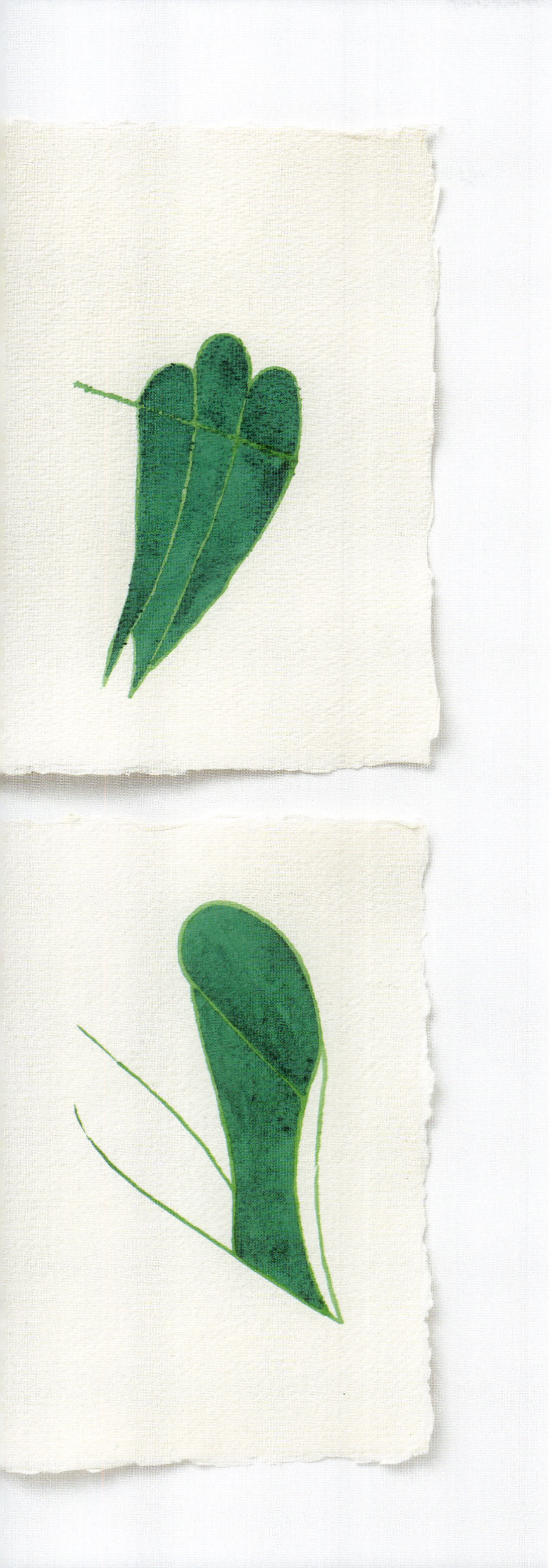

Each: *Untitled*, c. 2002
watercolour on paper, 22 x 15cm

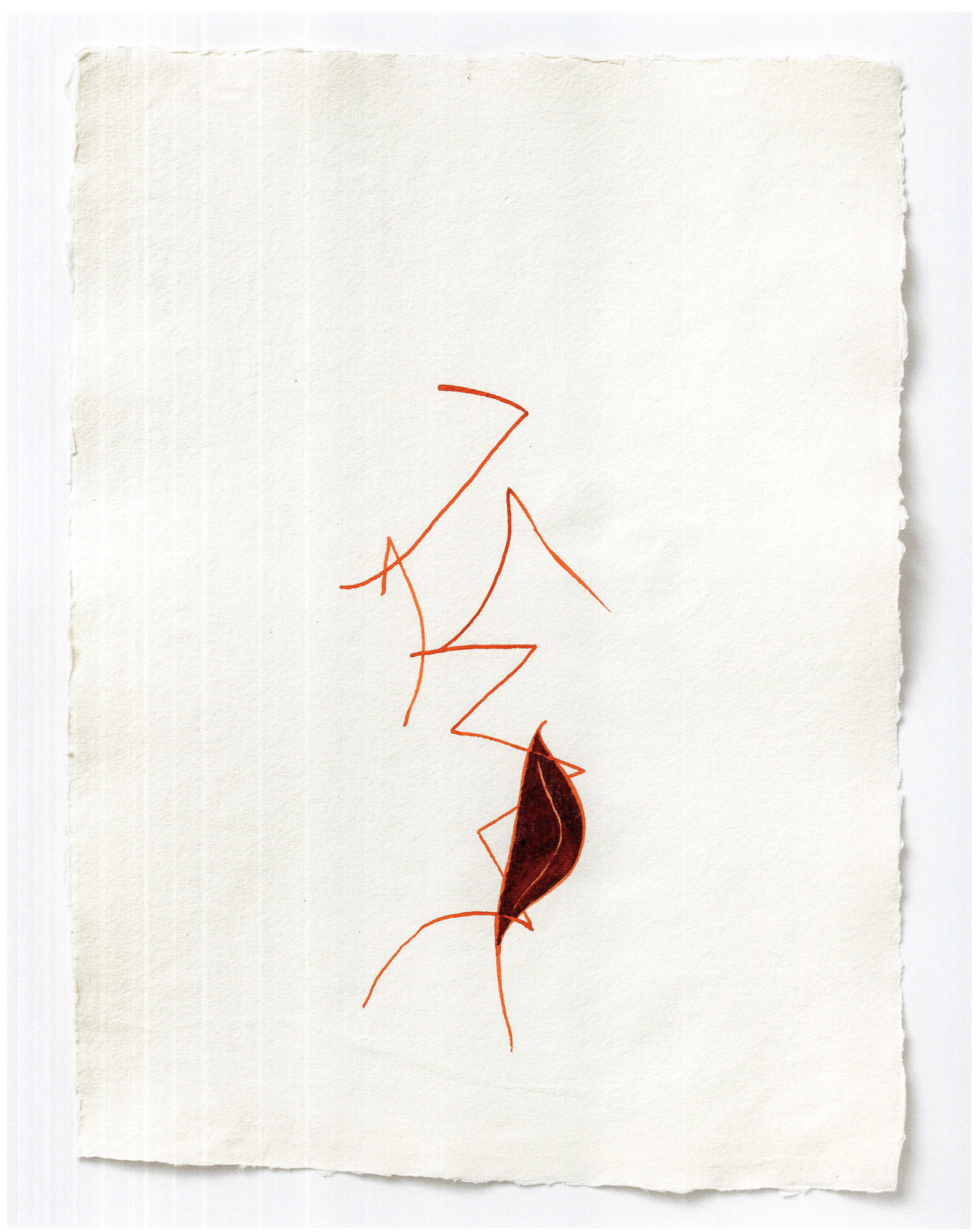

Untitled , c. 2002
watercolour on paper, 40 x 29cm

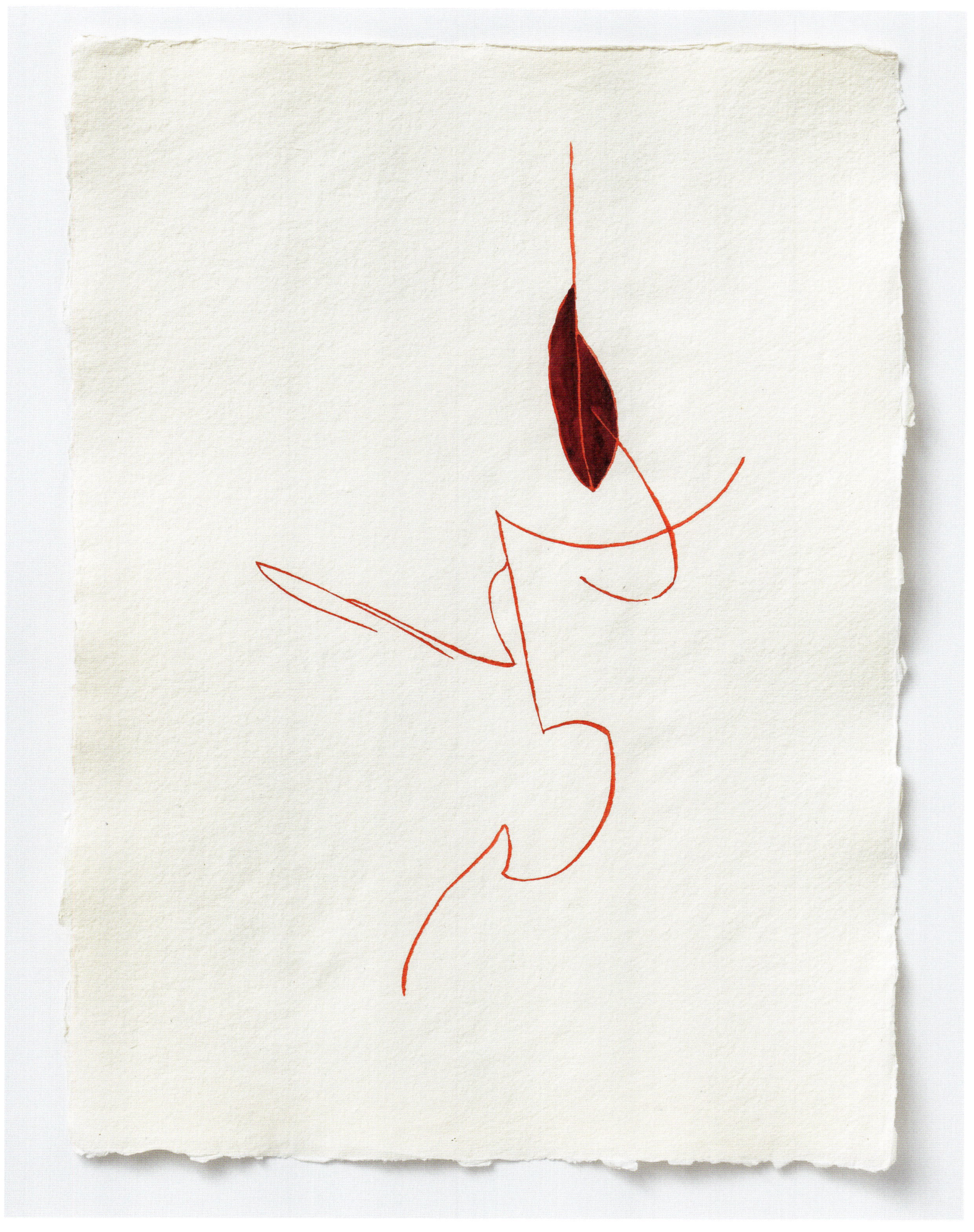

Untitled, 2002
watercolour on paper, 41 x 29.5cm

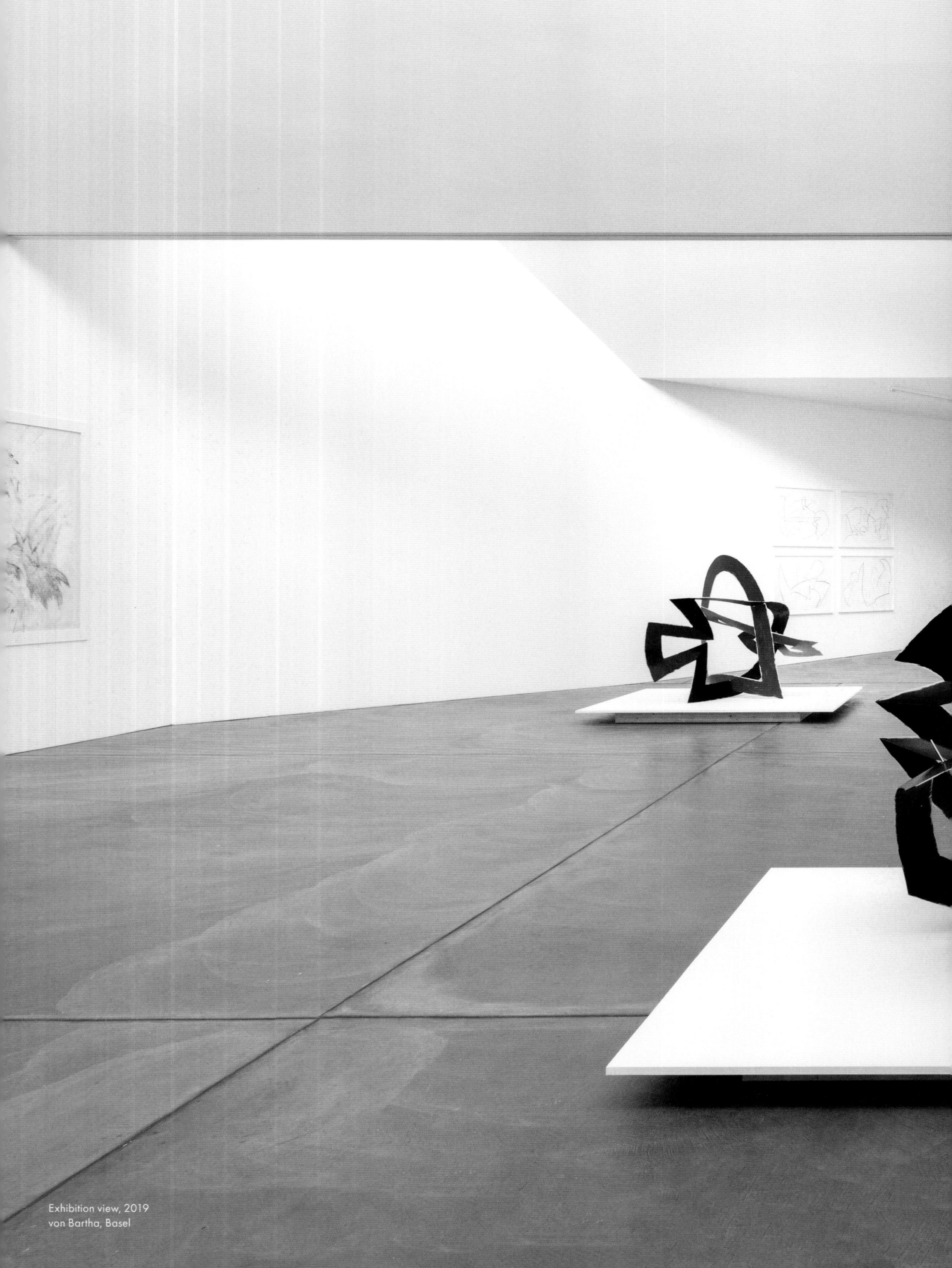

Exhibition view, 2019
von Bartha, Basel

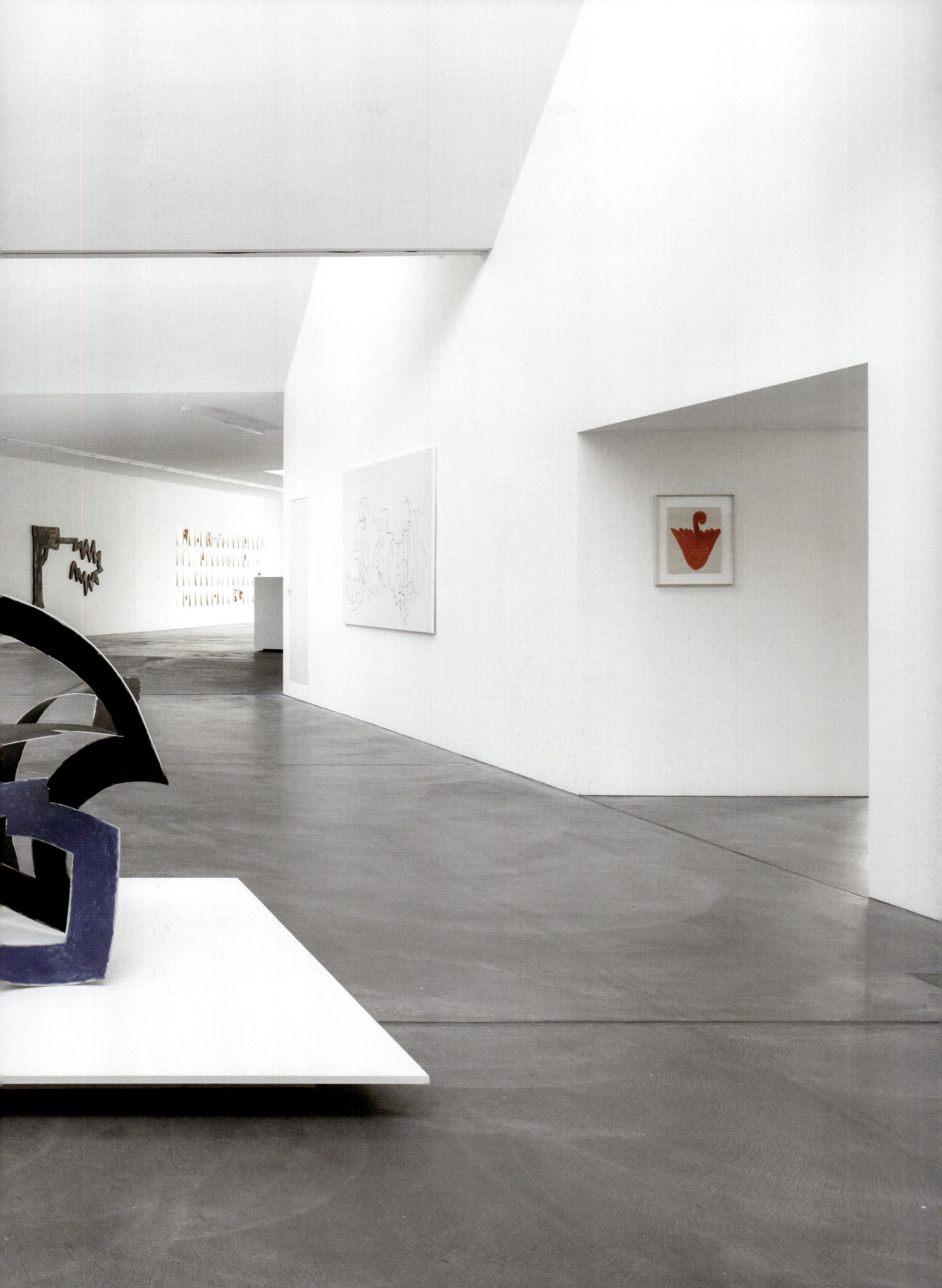

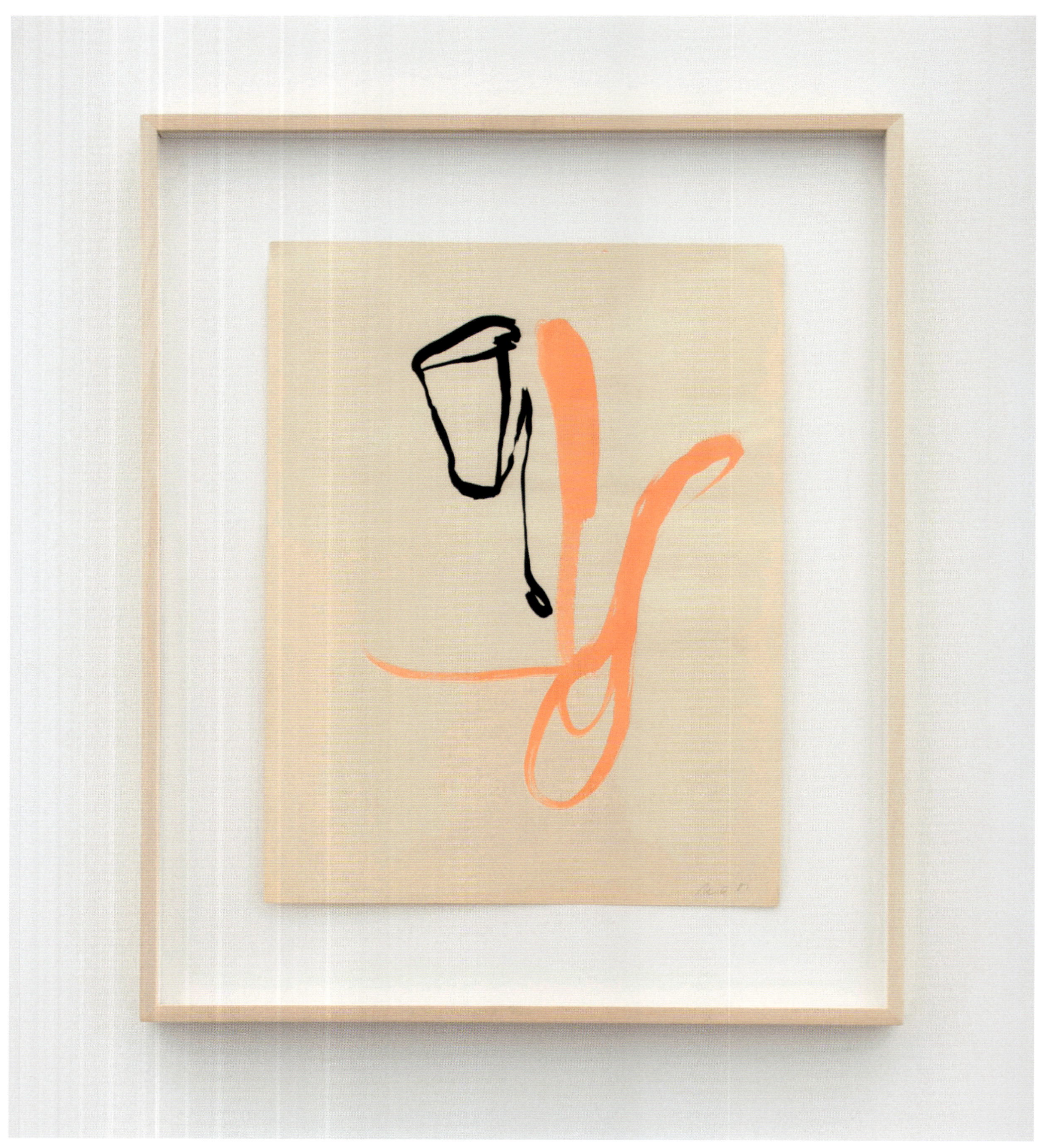

Untitled, 1981
mixed media on paper, 40 x 30cm

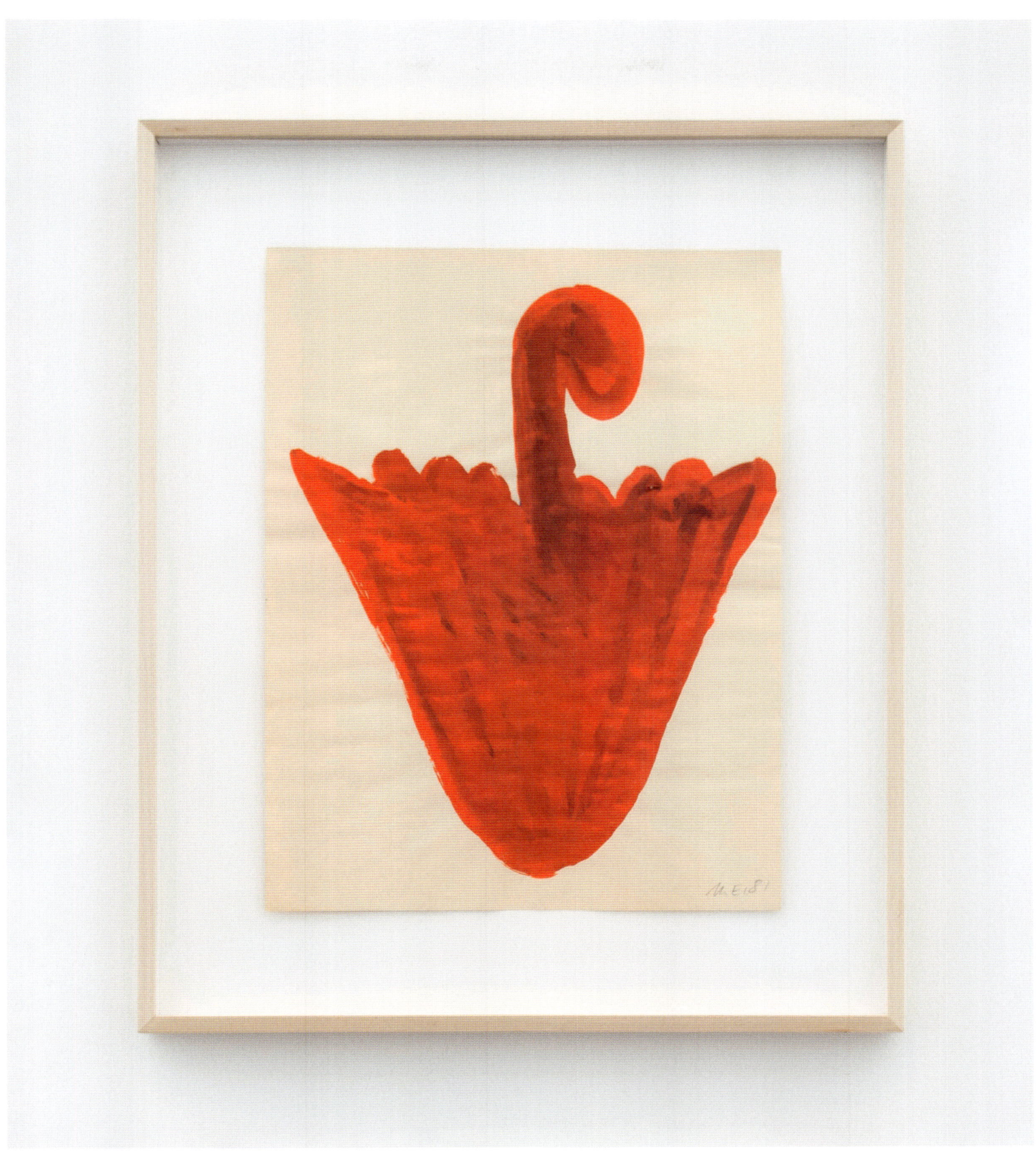

Untitled, 1981
mixed media on paper, 40 x 30cm

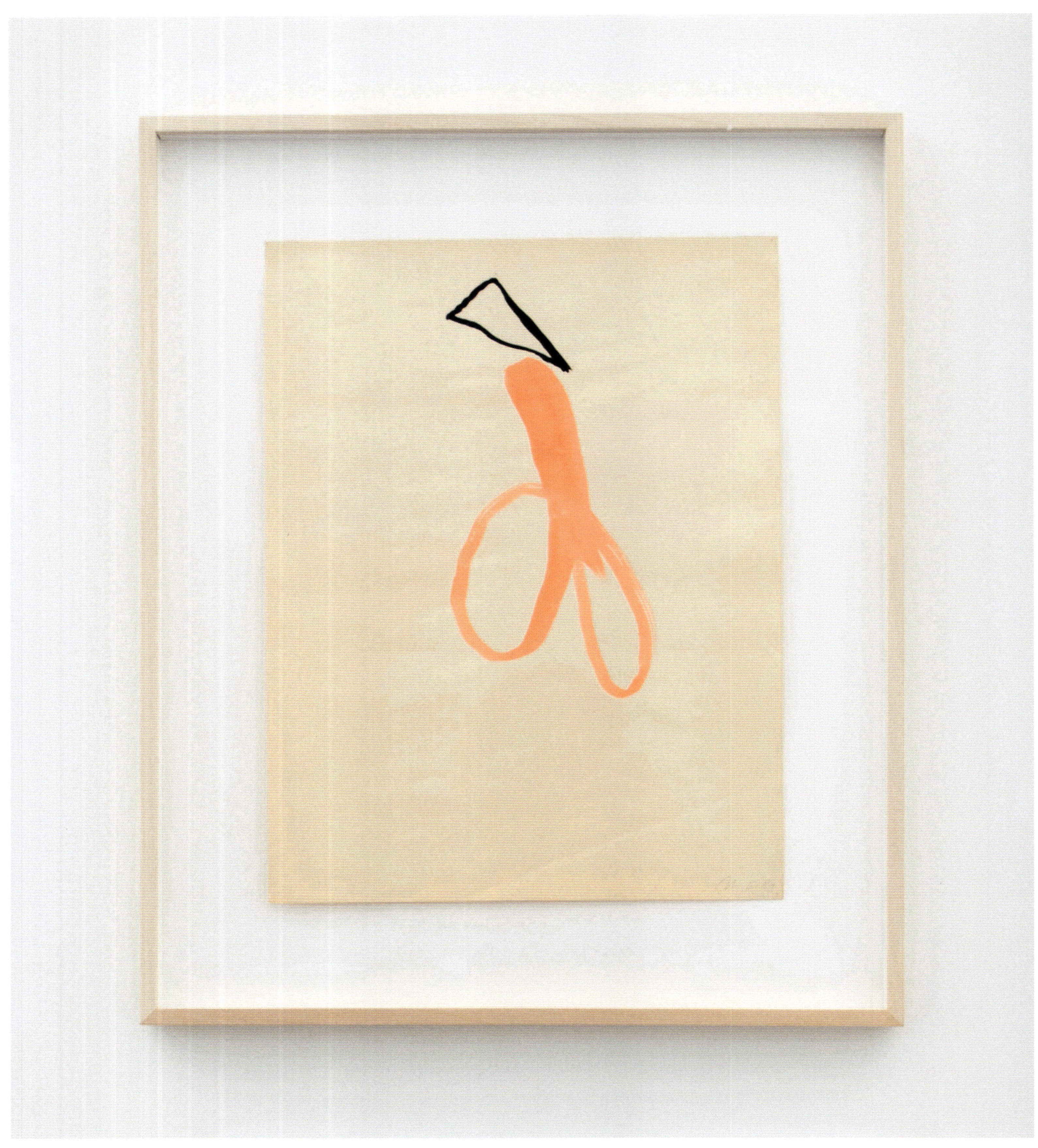

Untitled, 1981
mixed media on paper, 40 x 30cm

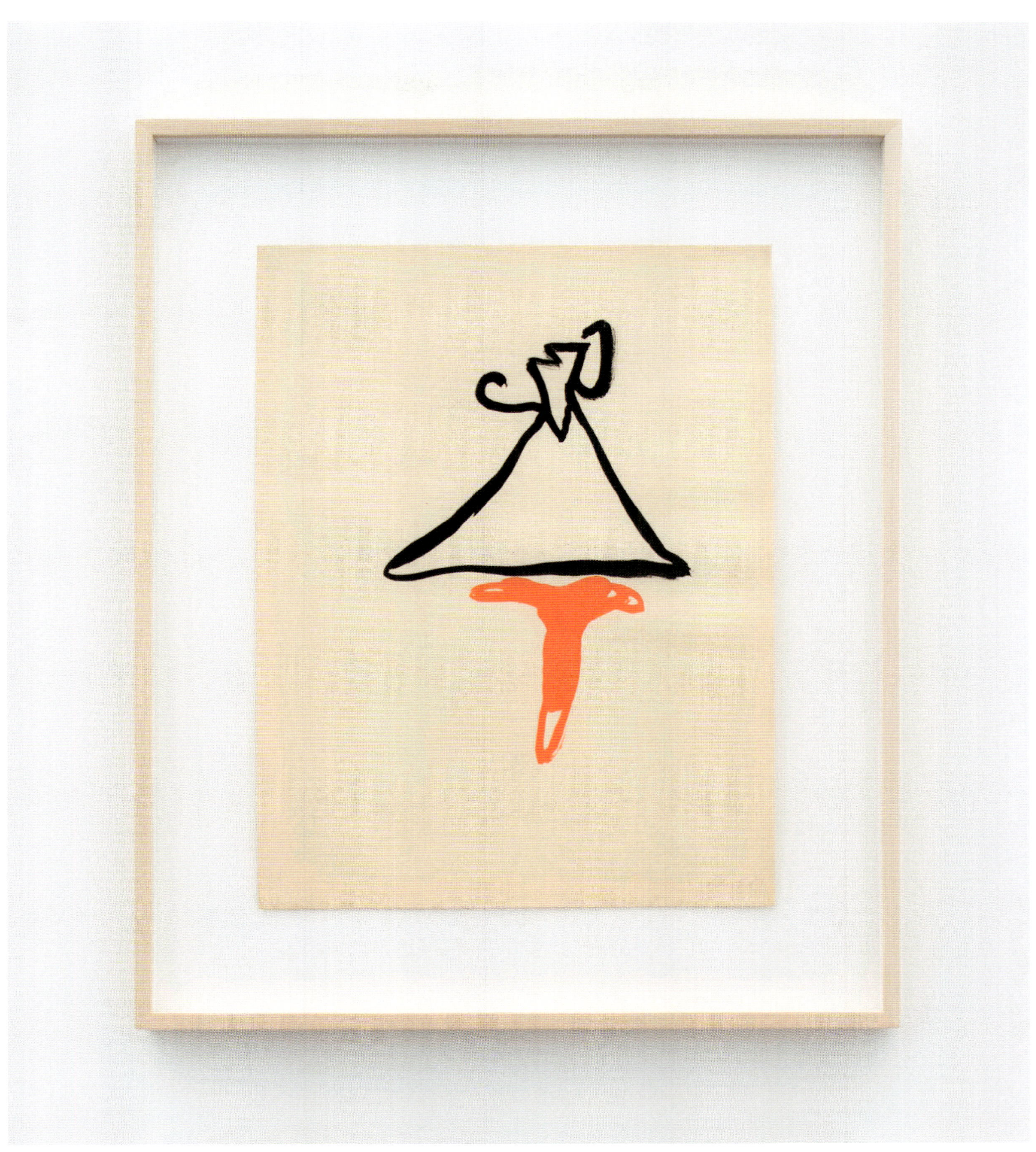

Untitled, 1981
mixed media on paper, 40 x 30cm

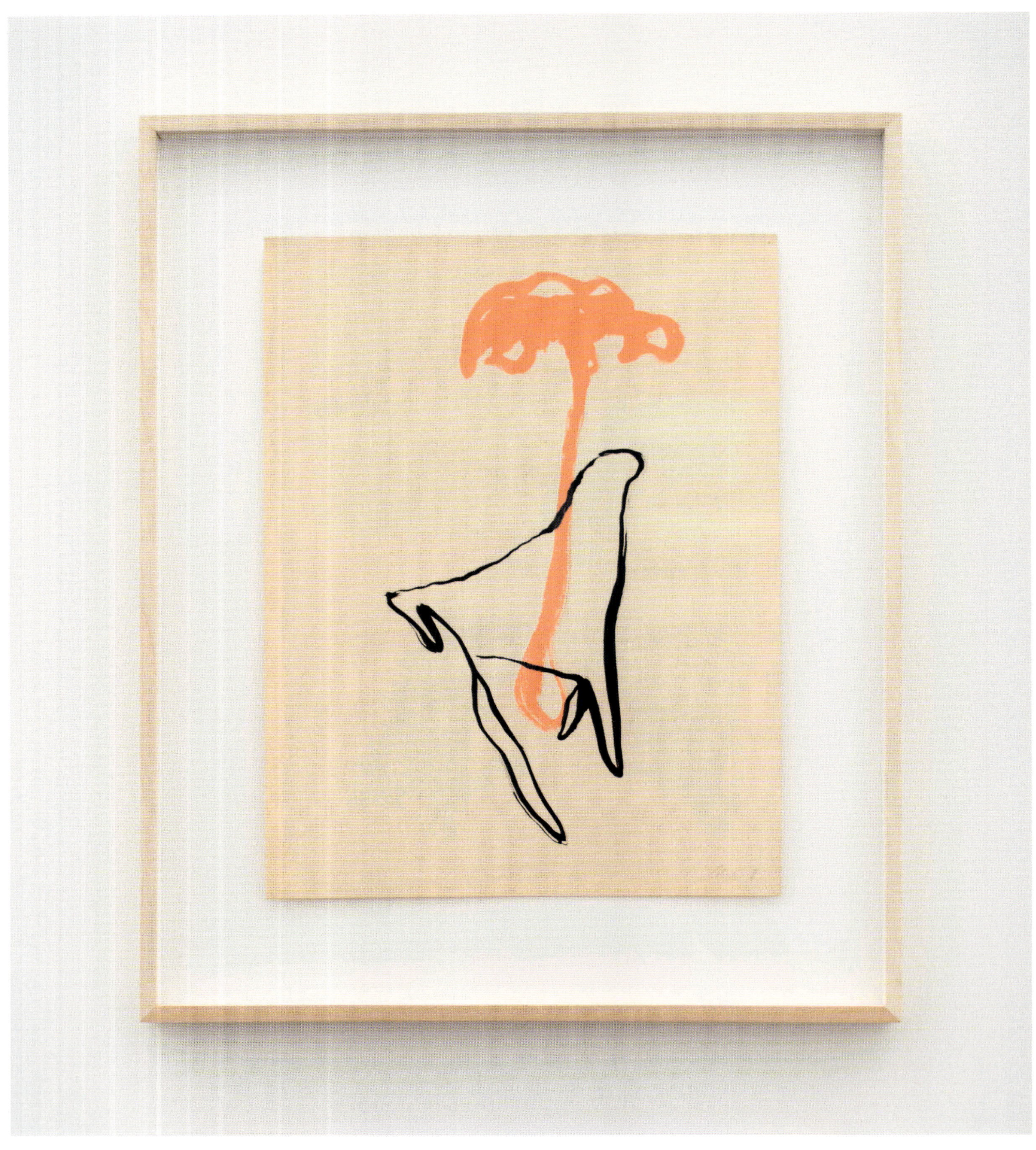

Untitled, 1981
mixed media on paper, 40 x 30cm

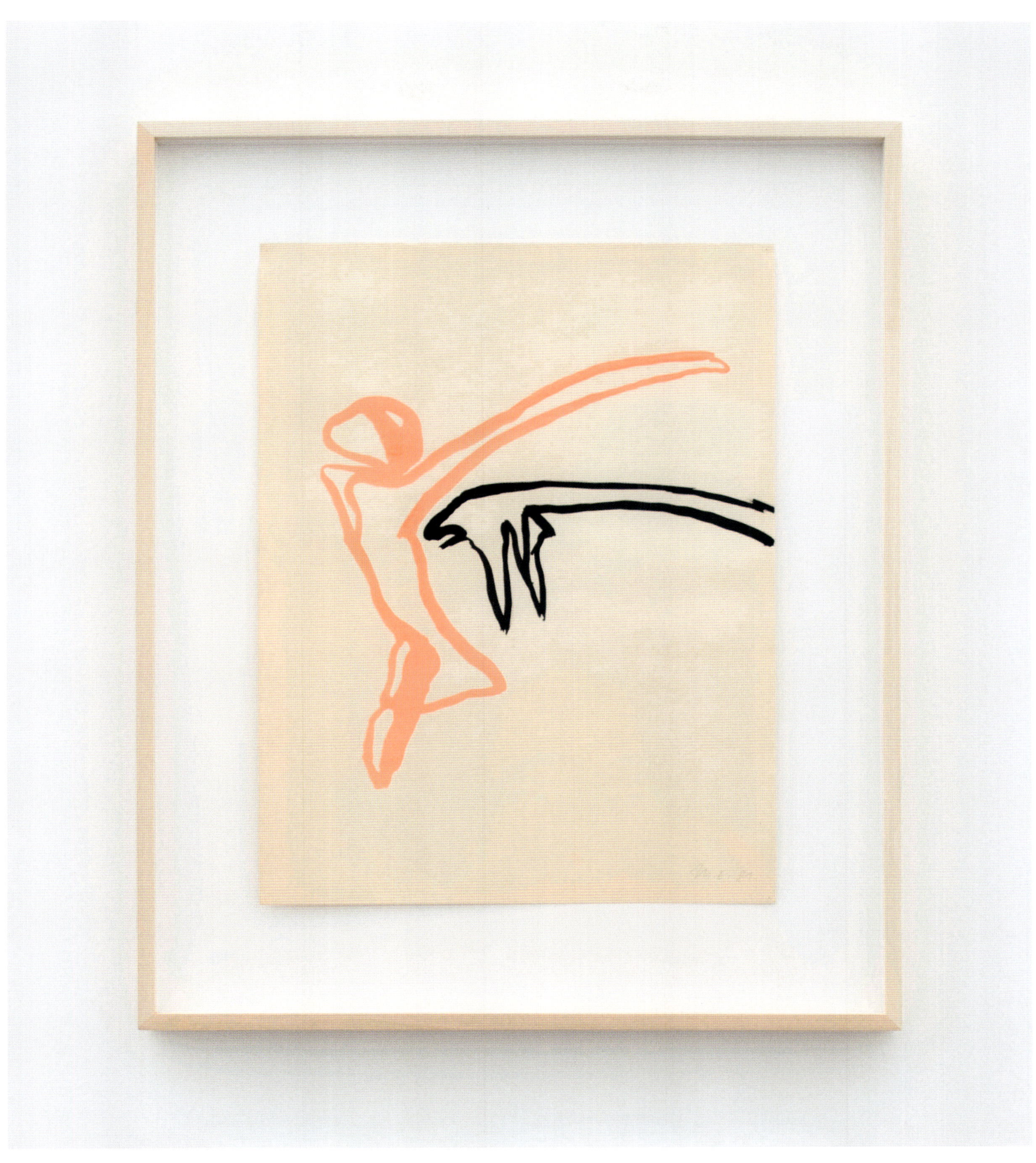

Untitled, 1981
mixed media on paper, 40 x 30cm

VIELLEICHT AUCH EIN LIEBESBRIEF...

BY MARIANNE EIGENHEER

Die beiden rotschwarzen Katzen, von Autos überfahren, auf der gelben Fläche die spinnenlangen Glieder angespannt, zum Sprung bereit ... Du sagst, dass Du nicht weisst, was ich damit will. Es ist nur, weil mein Jagdgebiet grösser wird. Es dehnt sich aus bis in die äussersten Regionen meiner Haut, besonders auf Gängen durch die grosse Stadt sitze ich nicht mehr hinter meinen Augen, das Sehen ist jetzt überall. Immer mehr Tiere fange ich ein, finde sie im weissen Bildraum wieder. Ich jage mit dem Fangnetz der Farbigkeit, das der Berührung ihren Zauber lässt, wie das zeitlose Meer die Körper umhüllend schützt. Den dunkelschwarzen Elefanten mit rosaroten Stosszähnen würde ich mit Buntheit, die sich begreifbar gibt, in die Leere der Stühle fallen lassen, er lebt aber nur dazwischen, immer. – „Aber das ist ja nur ein Hund, flüsterte das Einhorn, ein hungriger unglücklicher Hund, der nur einen Kopf und fast kein Fell hat, der Ärmste. Wie können sie ihn für einen Zerberus halten? Sind sie alle blind? Sieh genau hin, sagte der Zauberer.“ (Peter E. Beagle)[1] – Ich lasse mich nicht gern auf bereits bekannte Wege ein, auch nicht auf solche, die mir gestattet sind. Ich liebe das Jagen ohne Ziel.

Der grosse blauschwarze Vogel hängt ins Gelbweiss herunter, warum, darf ich nicht wissen, sonst falle ich in die Unbeweglichkeit, erobere ungewollt die Grenzen des Vorher mir zurück, wandle die Raum-Zeit des Bildes und der ekstatisch obszönen Ruhe in eine Szene um. Der Vogel bildet sich in meinem Körper nur ab, hört auf, sich wirklich zu bewegen, sobald die Schimmer des Zweifels auftauchen. Pulcinella tanzt auf dreckig blutrotem Grund um sein Leben. „Für die Körperlichkeit ist die Angst das Memento zu leben.“ (Giorgio Cesarano)[2] – Jeden Tag möchte ich aus der Starrheit der Furcht herauskommen, die Angst leben, auf die Welt kommen, immer wieder die Ordnung meines Lebens herstellen. – „Die Ratio, die Produktion, der Wert, die Akkumulation, die auf Armut erbaute Herrschaft, das Elend: das ist die Unordnung. Die Herrschaft dessen, was tot ist, über das, was lebt. Die Gefangenschaft des Wunsches, die Sklaverei des verdrehten Bedürfnisses, die grausame Verstümmelung der Kinder, das Gesetz des Machtmissbrauchs, des Opfers, des Mordes, der Krieg, das Grauen der Demütigung und der Lüge: dieses allgemein verbreitete Schicksal der gewalttätigen Unordnung ...“ (Giorgio Cesarano)[3] – dies einmal auch in mir selbst aufzulösen, darum jage ich die Tiere, versuche ich mich der Angst auszusetzen, der Angst, einmal die Sprache doch

MAYBE A LOVE LETTER TOO...

Both the red-black cats, run over by cars, their spidery limbs stretched out across the yellow surface, ready to pounce... You say that you don't know what I want with it. That's only because my hunting ground is getting larger; it extends outwards to the outermost regions of my skin. Particularly on walks through the big city, I no longer sit behind my eyes, now vision is everywhere. I capture more and more animals, find them again in white pictorial space. I hunt with a net of colours that on contact passes on their magic, as the timeless sea enfolds bodies and protects them. The dark black elephant with its rosy tusks I would drop, with its faux-comprehensible colourfulness, into the blankness of chairs but it only lives between them, always. "'It's only a dog,' (whispered the unicorn), 'a hungry and unhappy dog with only one head and hardly any coat at all, poor thing. How could they ever take it for Cerberus? Are they all blind?' 'Look again,' the magician said." (Peter E. Beagle)[1] – I don't much enjoy embarking on paths that are already well-known, not even the permitted ones. I love hunting aimlessly. The large blue-black bird hangs down onto the yellow-white – I mustn't know why, or else I'll fall into inflexibility, inadvertently reclaim the borders of before, transform the image's space-time and the obscene, ecstatic calm into a tableau. The bird only forms its likeness in my body, stops truly moving as soon as a flicker of doubt appears. Pulcinella dances for dear life on filthy, blood-red ground. "For physicality, fear is the memento to live." (Giorgio Cesarano)[2] – Every day I wish to emerge out of the stupor of fear, to live anxiety, to be born into the world, to restore the order of my life over and over. "Reason, production, value, accumulation, domination built on poverty, misery: That is disorder. Domination of that which is dead over that which is alive. The confinement of desire, the servitude of twisted needs, the gruesome mutilation of children, the law of the abuse of power, of the victim, of murder, of war, the horrors of indignity and of lies: the widespread destiny of violent disorder..." (Giorgio Cesarano)[3] – to unloose this all one day in myself

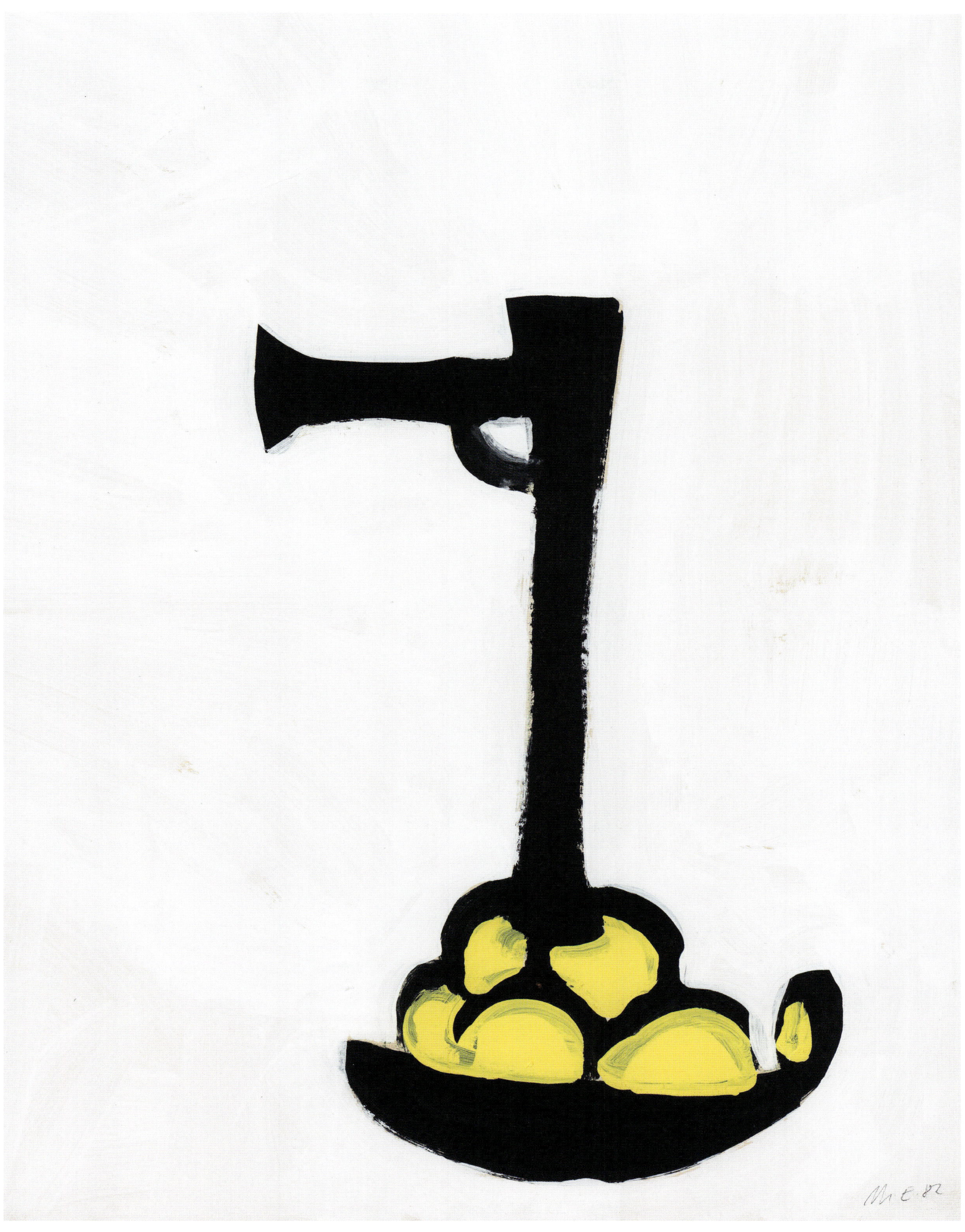

Untitled, 1982
acrylic on canvas, c. 80 x 60cm

"And since for the moment I'm just painting pictures, not writing books, you will have to force yourself simply to look, as I have no desire to explain anything to you. It doesn't matter whether you understand me"

„Und da ich im Augenblick eben Bilder male, keine Bücher schreibe, wirst Du Dich bequemen müssen, einfach zu sehen, denn eigentlich habe ich keine Lust, Dir was zu erklären. Es ist egal, ob Du mich verstehst"

nicht wiederfinden zu können, vielleicht. Wie lange ich das durchhalte, weiss ich nicht, es gibt immer wieder das letzte Bild. Morgen schon könnte sein, dass ich fischen gehe, ich muss ordentlich sein, wenn Du nun spürst, was ich damit meine. Und da ich im Augenblick eben Bilder male, keine Bücher schreibe, wirst Du Dich bequemen müssen, einfach zu sehen, denn eigentlich habe ich keine Lust, Dir was zu erklären. Es ist egal, ob Du mich verstehst. Würdest Du mich wirklich begreifen, müsste ich ja die Jagd aufgeben, denn es wäre Schonzeit. – „Alle kimmerischen Bücher sind unvollständig ... seufzt der Professor, denn alle gehen sie drüben weiter, in jener anderen Sprache, in jener schweigenden Sprache, auf welche all die Worte verweisen, die wir in den Büchern zu lesen glauben." (Italo Calvino)[4]

too, that's why I hunt the animals, I try to expose myself to fear, the fear of not being able to find the language again, one day, perhaps. I do not know how long I can bear it, there is always one last picture. It could be that I go fishing tomorrow, I must be neat – if you feel what I mean by that. And since for the moment I'm just painting pictures, not writing books, you will have to force yourself simply to look, as I have no desire to explain anything to you. It doesn't matter whether you understand me. If you did, I would have to give up the hunt, it would be the closed season. "All Cimmerian books are incomplete (sighed the professor) because they continue beyond... in the other language, in the silent language to which all the words we believe we read refer." (Italo Calvino)[4]

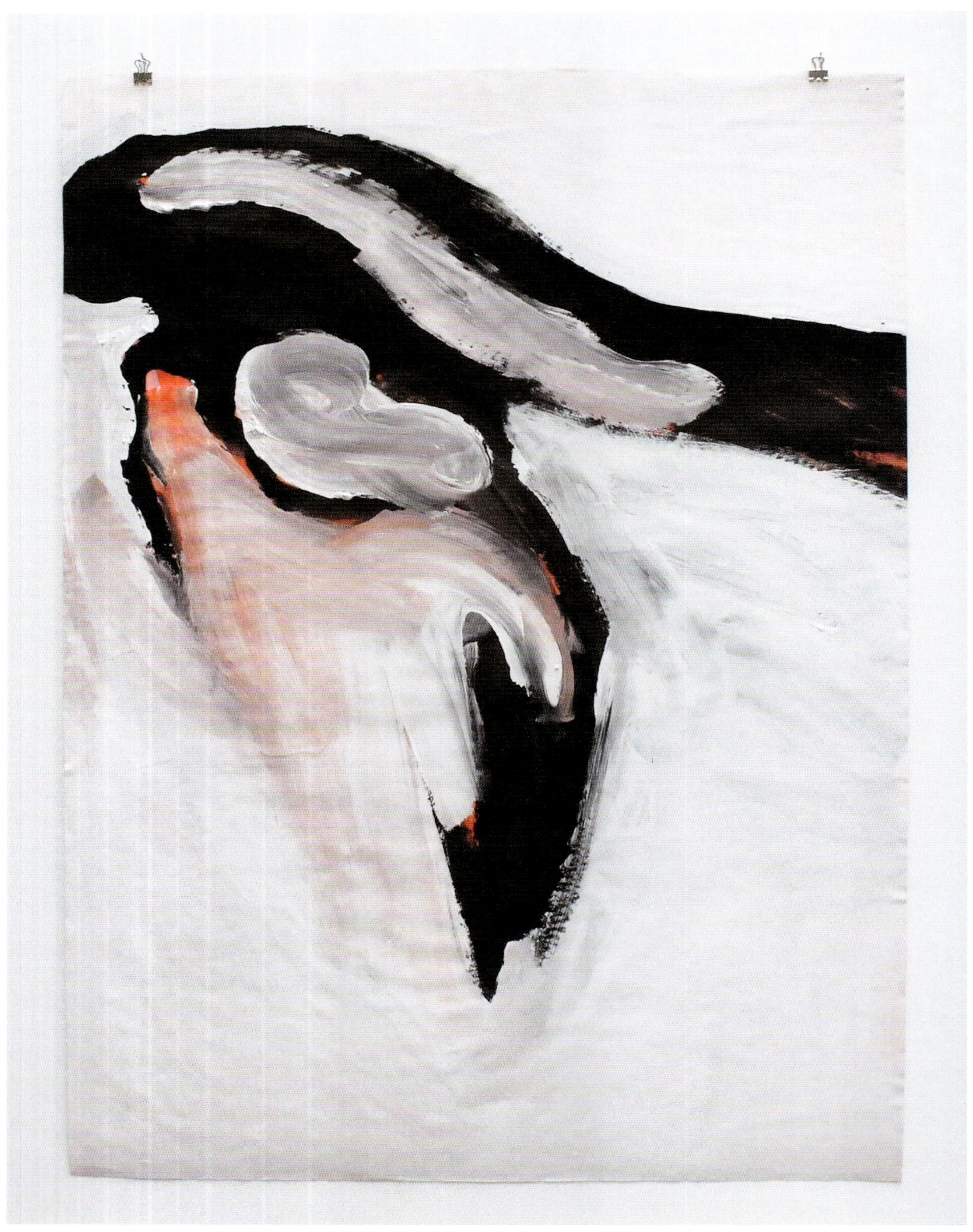

What is behind that curtain?, 1984
acrylic on paper, 79.8 x 59.6cm

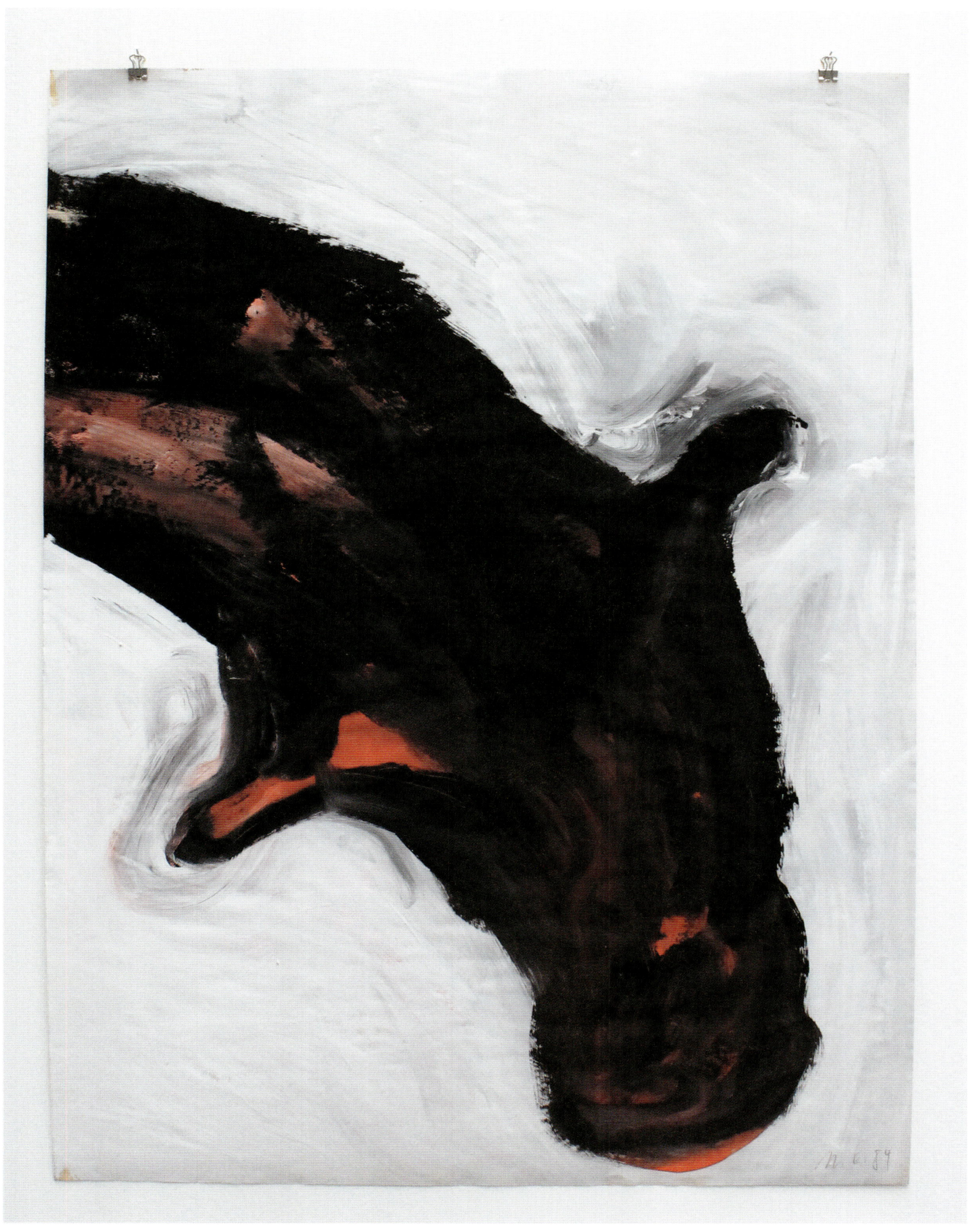

What is behind that curtain?, 1984
acrylic on paper, 79.8 x 59.6cm

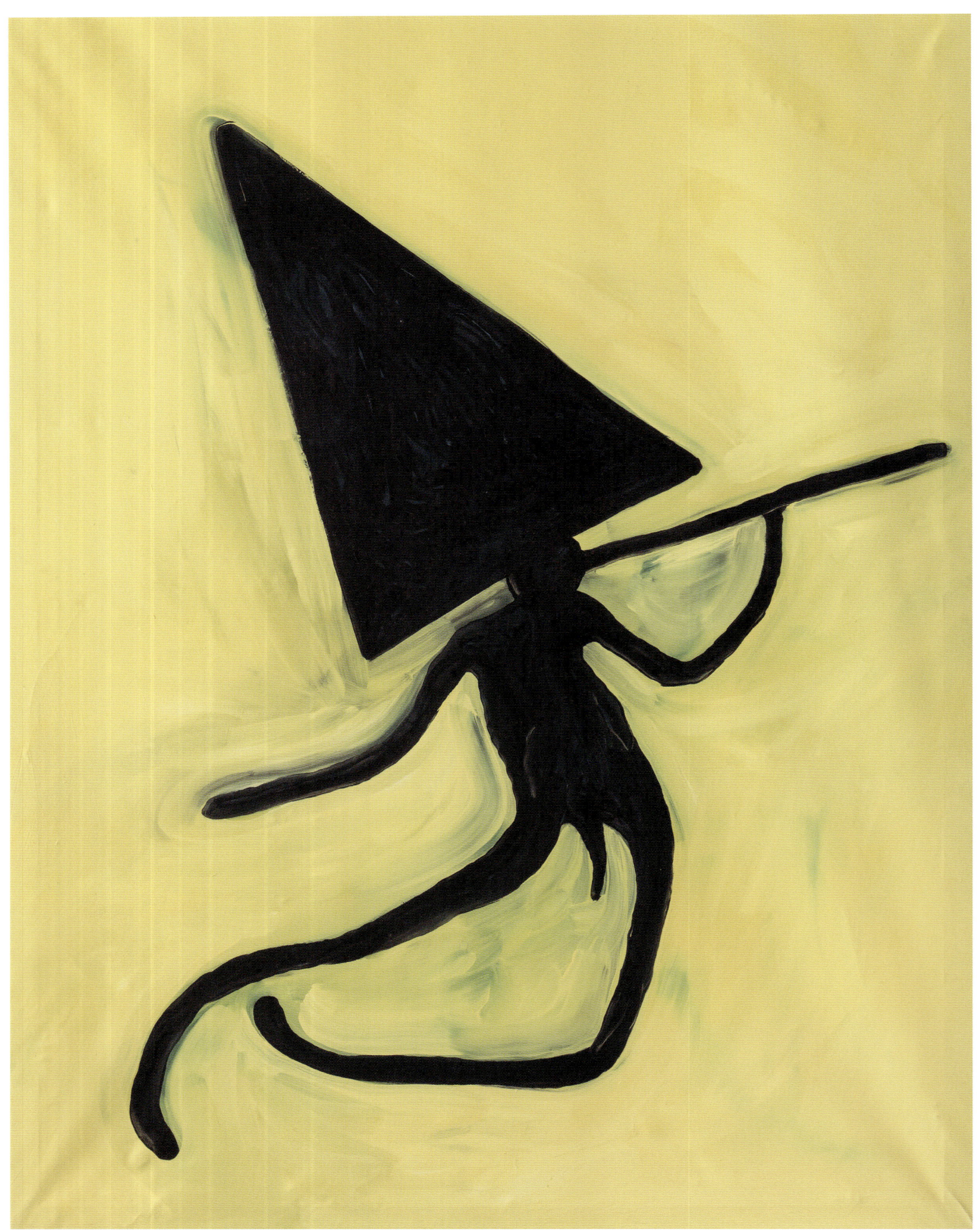

Misere des Herzens, 1984
acrylic on cotton, 225 x 160.5cm

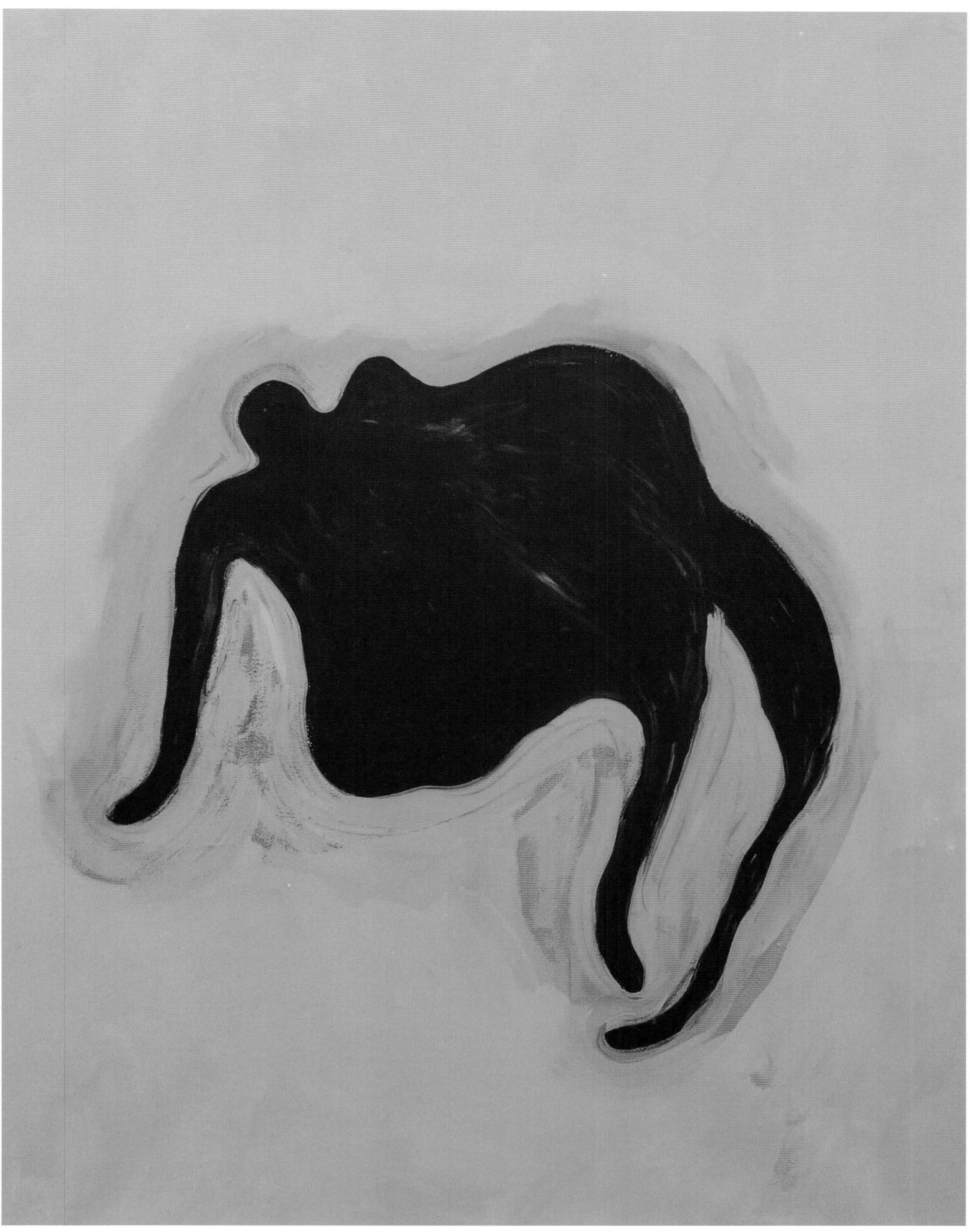

Untitled, 1984
acrylic on cotton, 225 x 160cm

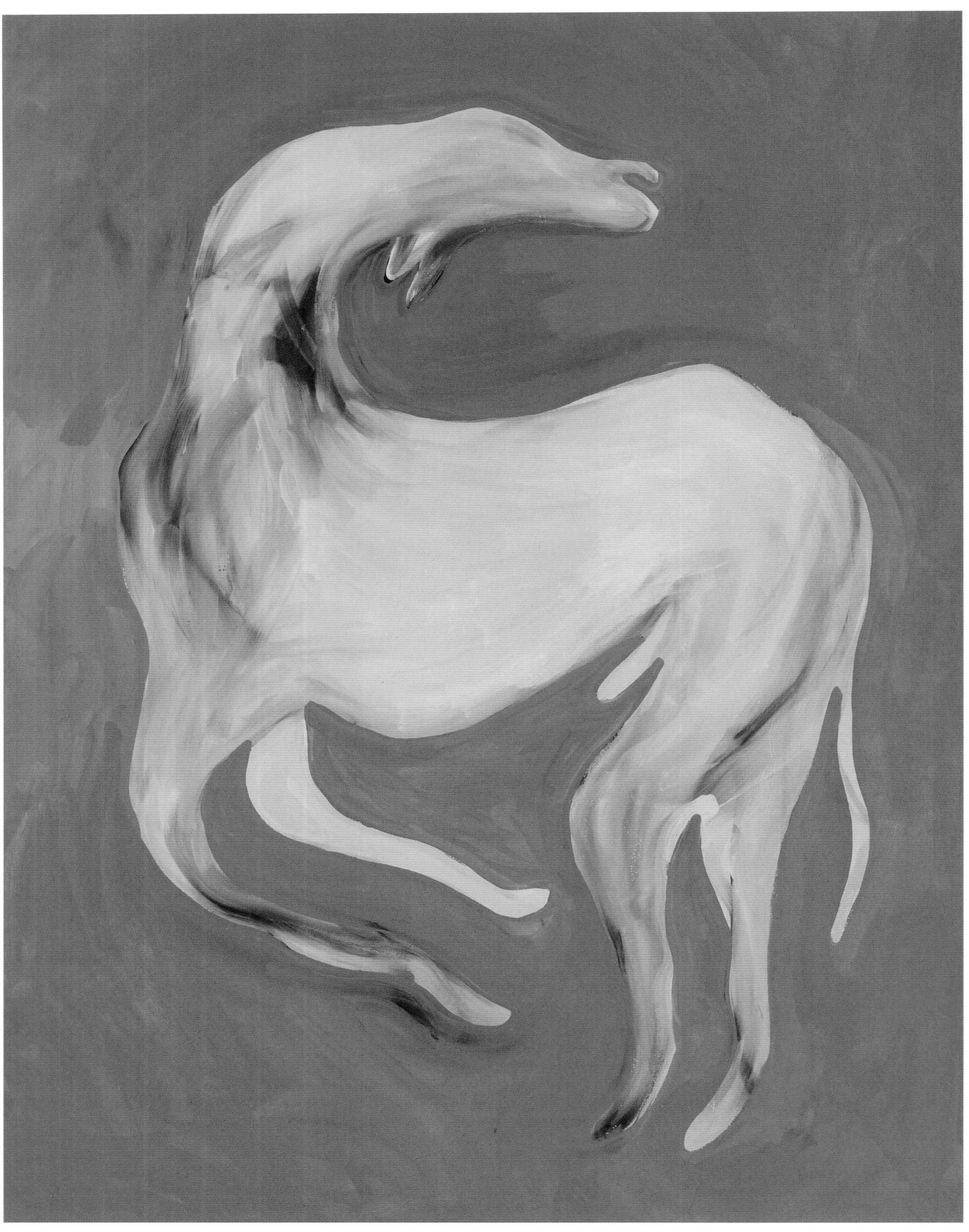

Misere des Herzens, 1984
acrylic on cotton, 225 x 160.5cm

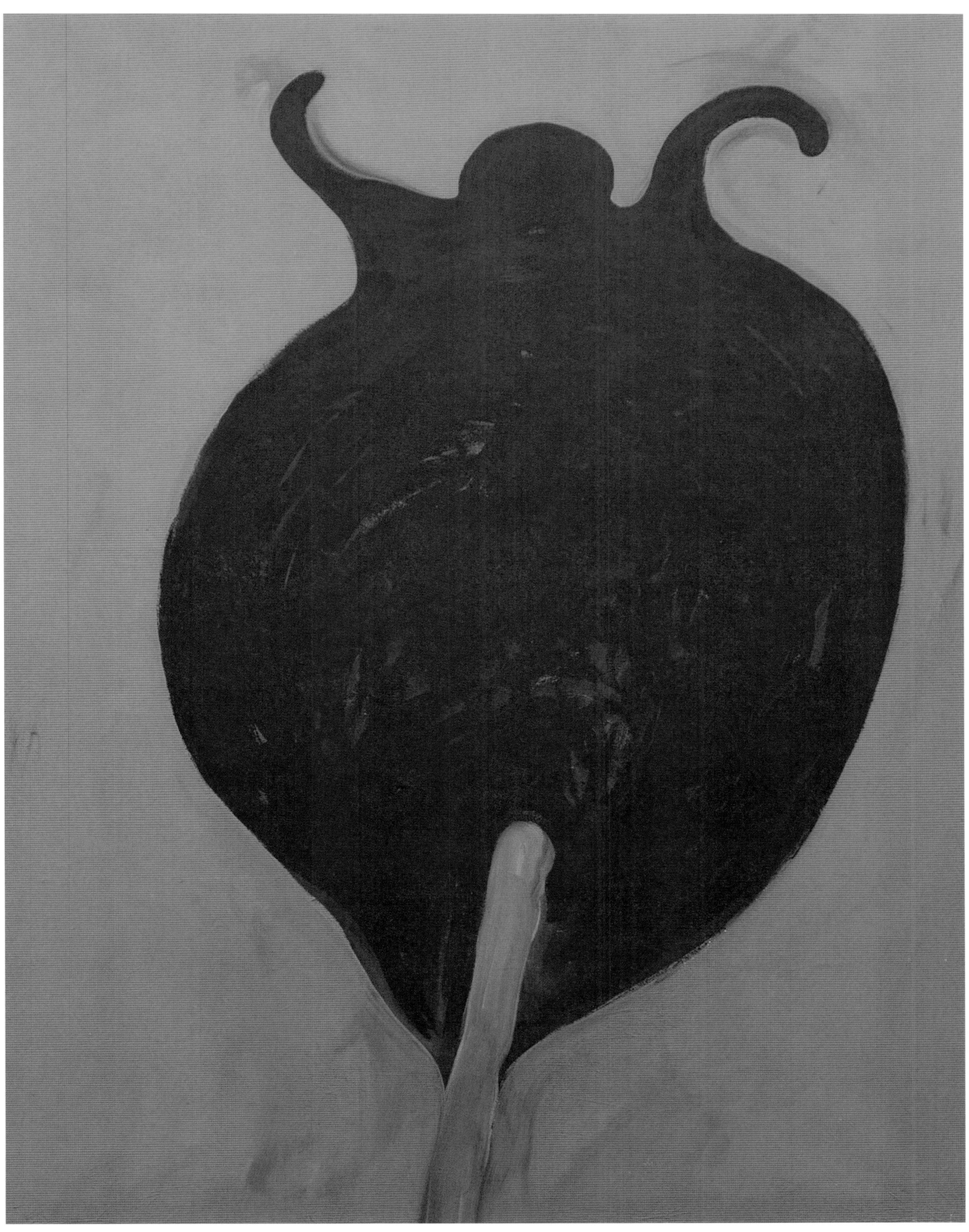

Misere des Herzens, 1984
acrylic on cotton, 225 x 160.5cm

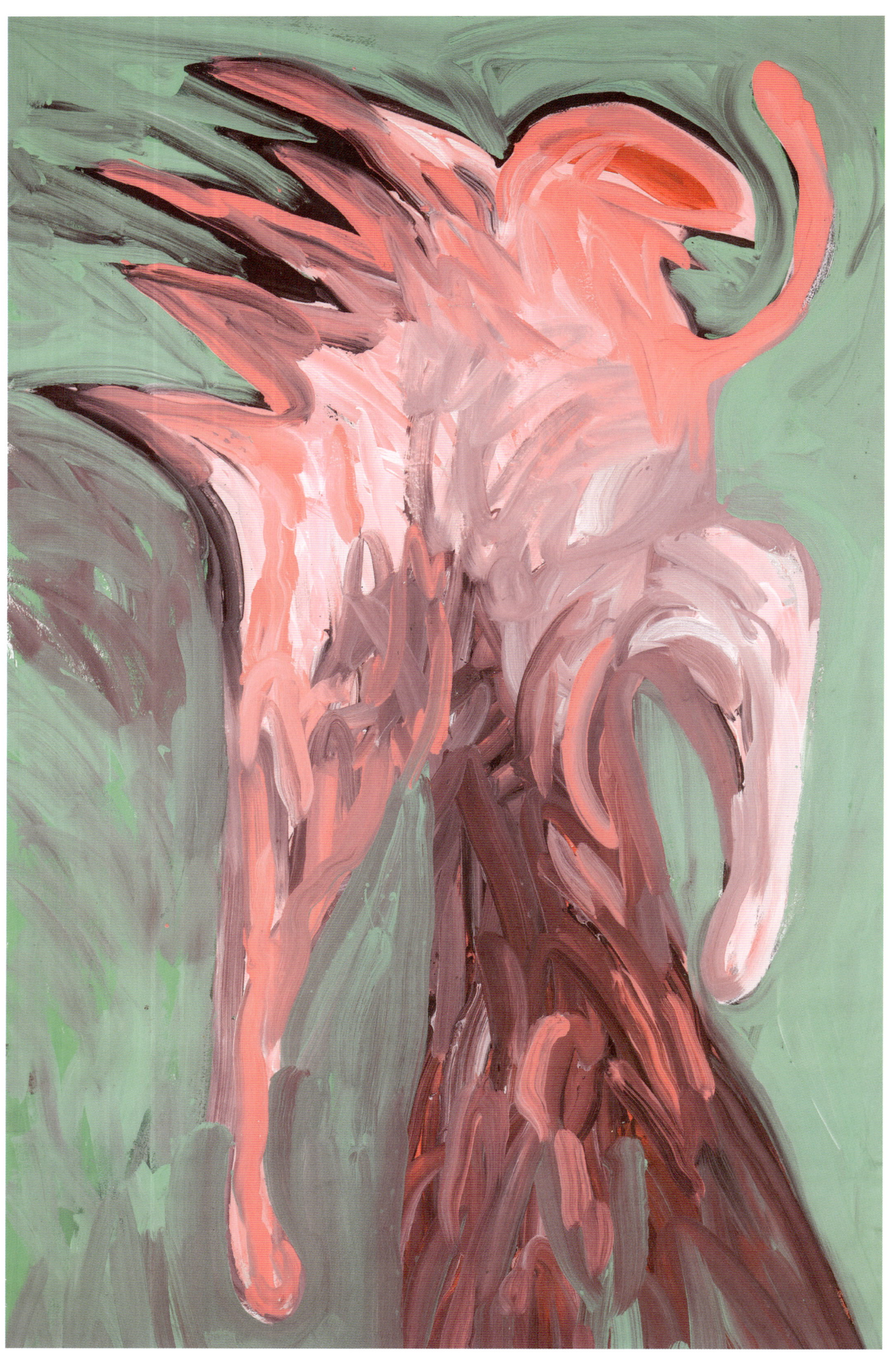

Untitled, n.d. (probably 1984)
acrylic on cotton, c. 279 x 171cm

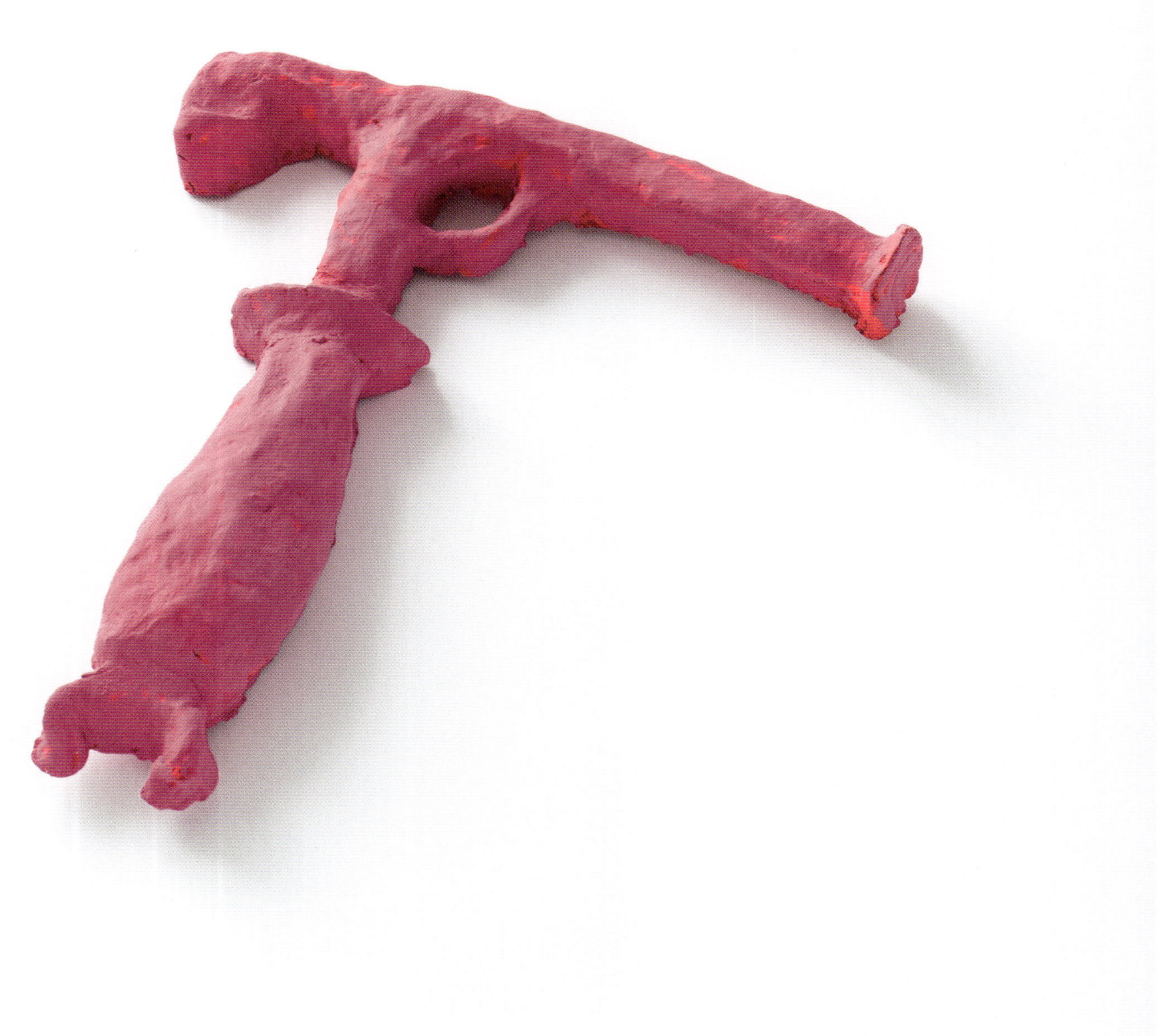

Bilder zur Lage, 1982
wooden mass, painted, 31 x 25 x 4cm

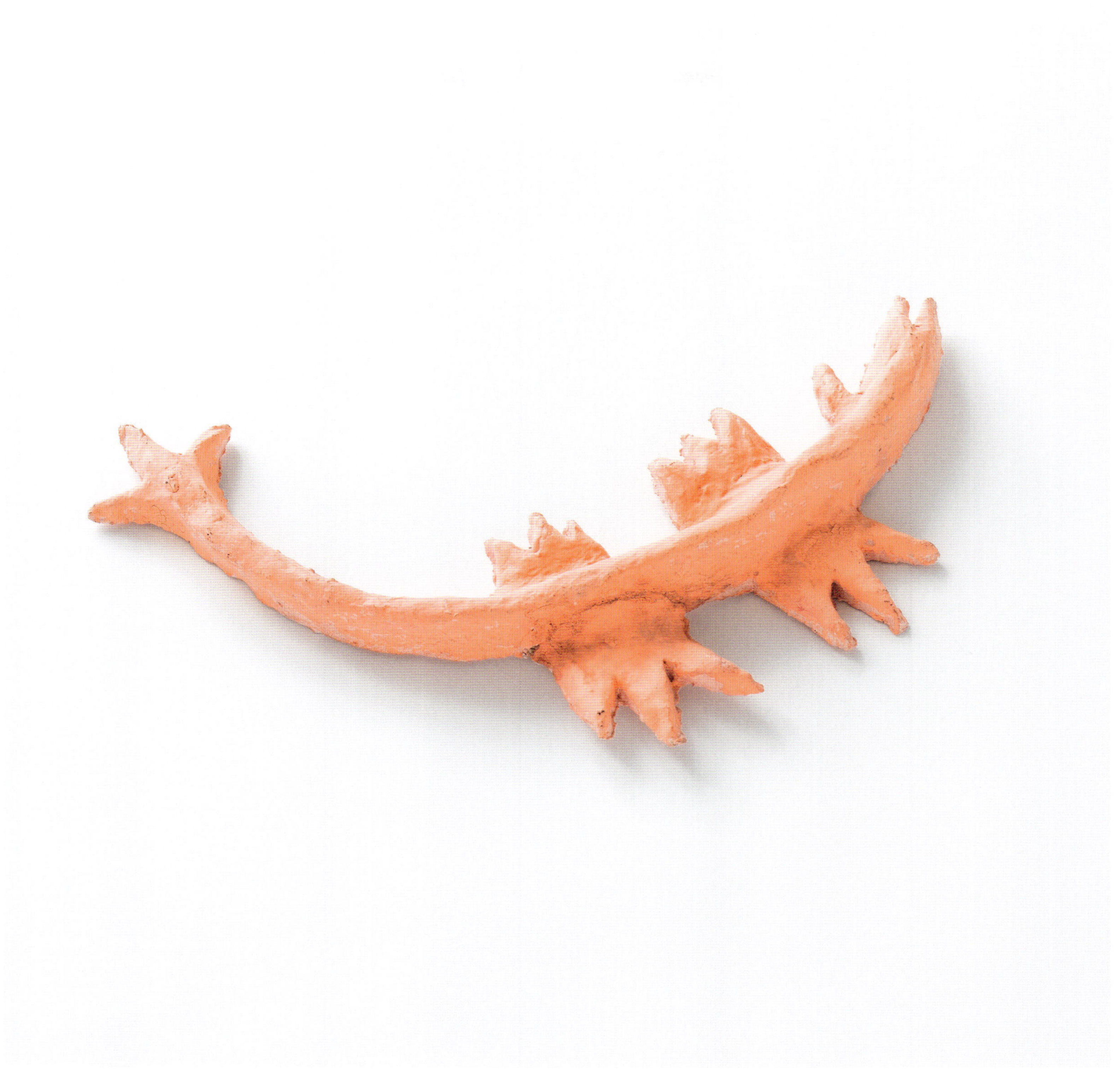

Bilder zur Lage, 1982
wooden mass, painted, 29 x 19 x 3cm

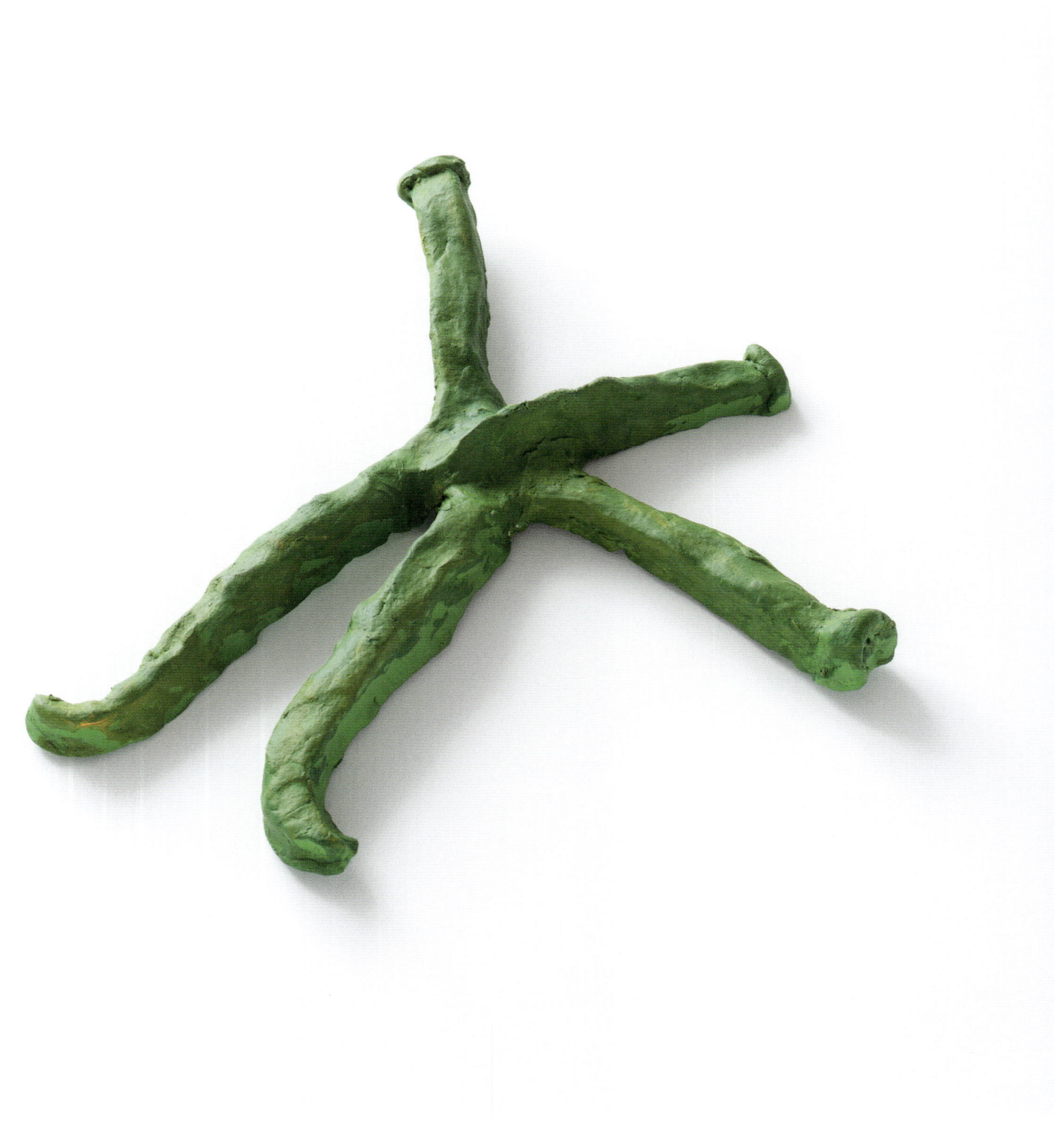

Bilder zur Lage, 1982
wooden mass, painted, c. 34 x 30 x 3cm

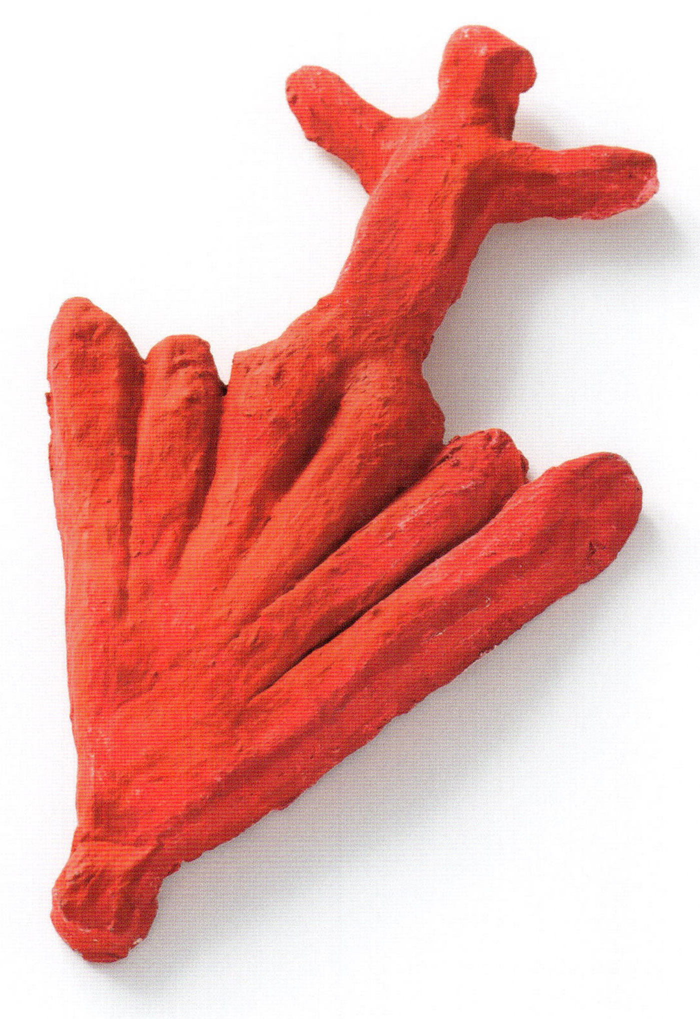

Bilder zur Lage, 1982
wooden mass, painted, 25 x 13 x 2cm

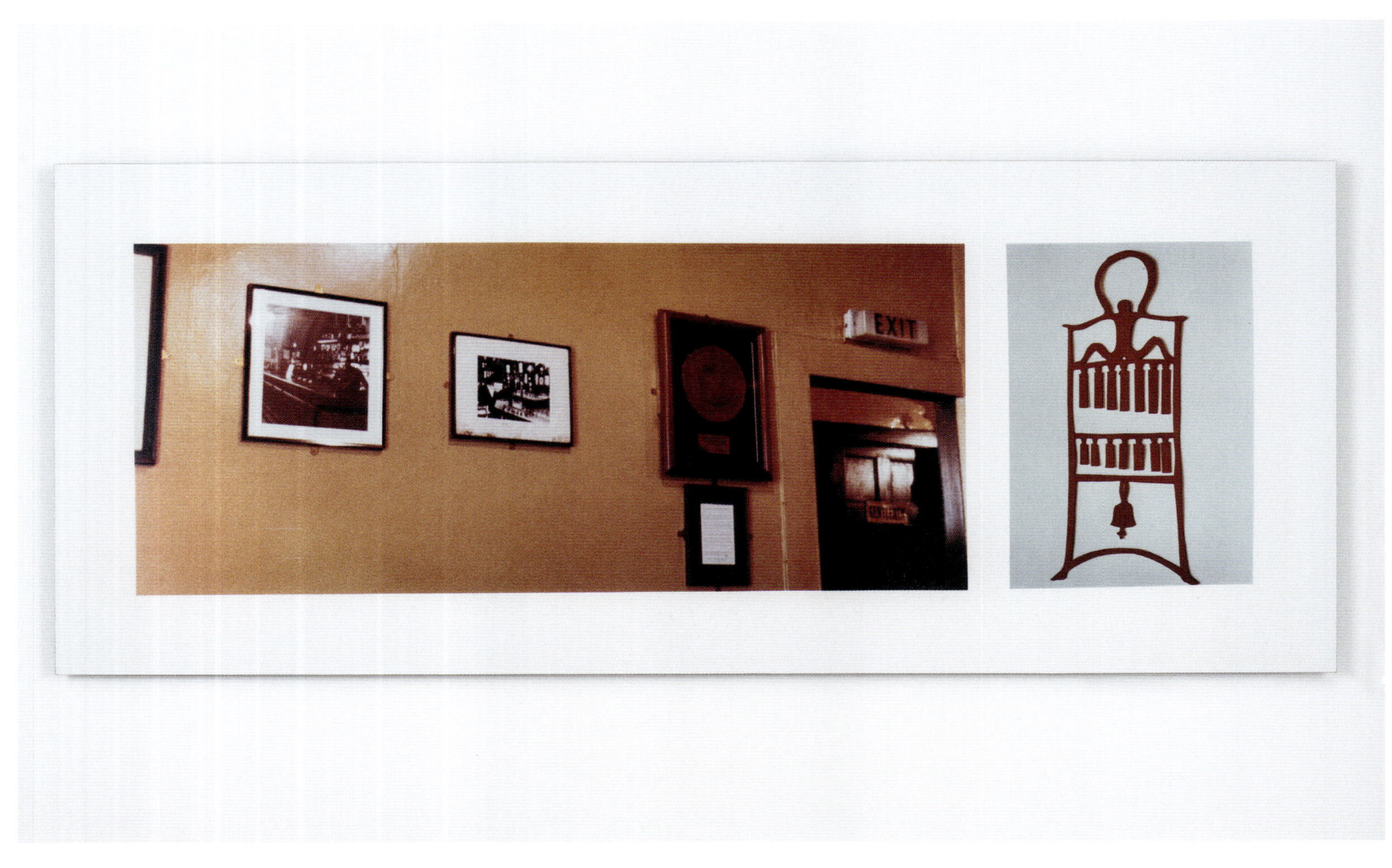

Untitled, n.d.
photograph on aluminium, 73 x 118cm

The left part of the work forms part of
Marianne Eigenheer's publication *The
Oxford Bar* published in Basel, 1999
(A little book about
„A PLACE FOR ART
A PLACE AS ART
A PLACE LIKE ART
ART AS A PLACE
ART LIKE A PLACE.")

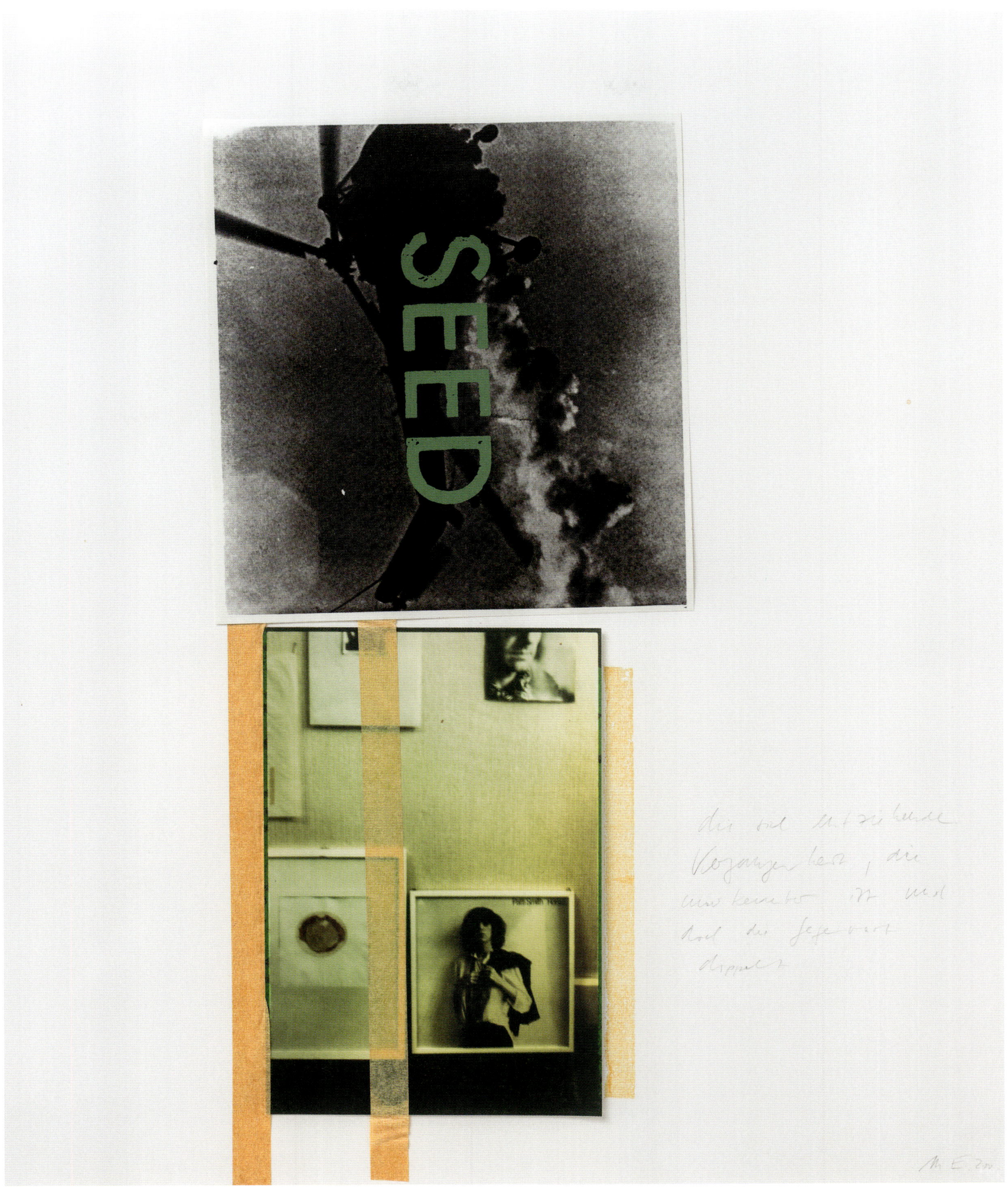

Untitled, c. early 2000s
photo collage and pencil on paper, 59.5 x 50cm

This Confidence That I Am Able to Take a Risk

By Max Dax and Jonathan Bragdon

Invited by Max Dax and Luci Lux, Marianne Eigenheer presented her mural *Deep Silence, Resounding*, 2016 at Santa Lucia Galerie der Gespräche in Berlin on the occasion of *situation 15* on 17 September 2016. The conversation with curator Max Dax and Marianne's longtime artist friend Jonathan Bragdon took place the day before her mural was officially unveiled.

Max Dax: Marianne, we whitened the walls in the gallery for you. Onto these white walls you then painted your mural in the front room. When you do such a wall painting, I assume, every brush stroke has to be in place. As a matter of fact, it would have been difficult to correct the lines and gestures once you've put them on the wall...

Marianne Eigenheer: The opportunity to do a mural in a gallery room is a great privilege. As a result, I have a huge respect and perhaps also sense something like fear when I stand in a white cube. However, the uncertainty of whether the idea I have for a mural can also be implemented in the room is outweighed by the joy of just doing it. The risk in Berlin was small, though. In the worst case I might have had to whiten everything again in order to tackle the mural in a second attempt. It would have become a race against time for sure. But luckily enough, everything fell into place right in the first attempt.

Jonathan Bragdon: Do you enjoy this risk of theoretically being able to fail?

ME: Yes, absolutely. But, to be honest: there is no real risk involved at all. Maybe the work would not have worked out. But would that have mattered? The people around us would continue to live on. And I will continue to live, too. So it's really only an *inner* risk. I have been making drawings for 50 years now, and I have always liked this process of free drawing. But it was a long time before I understood why I love this activity so much.

JB: Did you try to find out why you love drawing?

ME: Of course I asked myself this question more than once. Don't you sometimes ask yourself why you like having conversations or interview situations and then transfer them into text? Have you? On the one hand, there is the physical sensation I feel when I draw – especially when I am painting on a wall in a large space. But that's not all. It's also about a kind of non-predictability. Just as we both don't know where this conversation will lead us, I stood in front of the white walls of the gallery with an idea that was specific, but yet at the same time not formulated down to the last detail. I know that I have my line, just as every jazz musician or pianist hopefully has his or her own tone. I start at a certain point on the white wall, and I hope at that moment that a few hours or days later I will have delivered a coherent work. I titled the mural *Deep Silence, Resounding*. The idea that there might be an echo to a deep silence already inherits the concept of a dialogue. The title is actually pretty conceptual if you look at it closer.

MD: I find it amazing and interesting that you compare the act of drawing with that of conversation. I hear from this that in both cases it is a dialogue in which a work of art can emerge as a result. In your case, a dialogue between your line and the

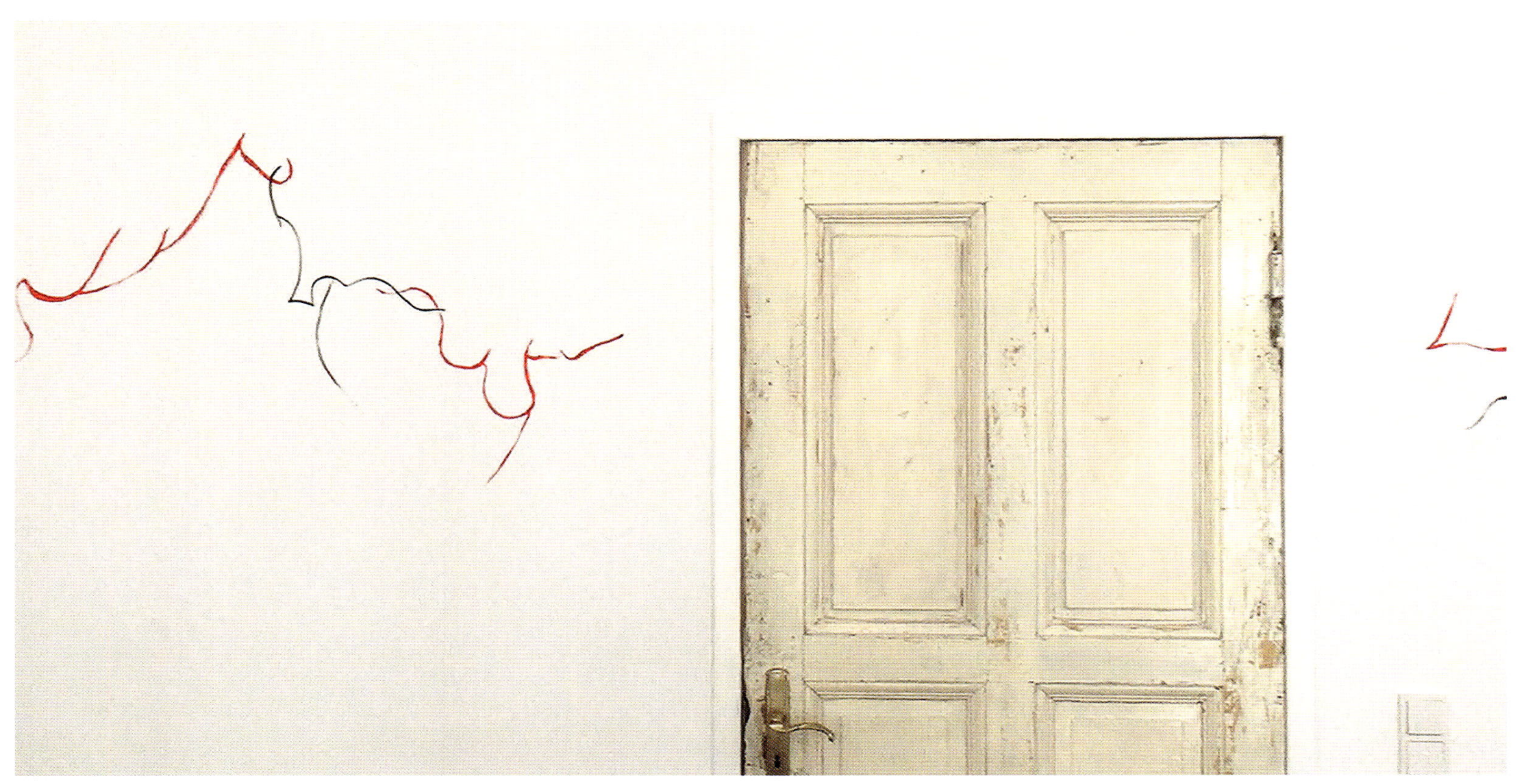

Deep Silence Resounding, 2016
mural at Santa Lucia Galerie, Berlin
Photograph by Luci Lux

white wall. I can very well imagine that there are analogies between drawing and conducting interviews. We feel we are moving on safe ground because we have already pursued our activity countless times. At the same time, every conversation, if it is conducted with the aspiration of being published, is in a way under pressure to succeed. Just as you as an artist might be under pressure to succeed when you are making an intervention in a room with a drawing.

ME: The whole situation reminds me of my childhood. I studied the piano as a child and often had to perform in front of an audience. These performances mostly consisted of compositions that I had previously learned by heart. I imagined, and I still remember it vividly, that I always knew how to begin, but I never did know for sure whether I would be able to finish a piece.

MD: And did you enjoy these moments of uncertainty?

ME: I remember studying the piano mainly as my mother's ambition for me to become a successful concert pianist. The fact that I went to the Lucerne School of Art and Design in 1964, where I wanted to learn drawing, had a lot to do with the fact that I no longer wanted my mother breathing down my neck, watching my fingers as I practised. Thirteen years of studying the piano, from the time I was five until I was 18, was enough. I didn't want to impersonate a proxy career for my mother. I wanted to do something of my own.

JB: That's an admirable stance. Especially when you take into consideration that, in 1964, times were much more conservative. Especially if you were a woman.

ME: You are hitting the nail on the head. Especially for women it was difficult to be respected if you dared to make your own decisions and followed your own direction. Bear in mind that there were professions, including careers in the art world, that women would not be allowed to study, at least in Switzerland.

MD: Today we know that things we learn in one discipline very often can have a significant influence on things we practise in another discipline. In this sense, were these 13 years of piano lessons won or lost?

ME: Of course I learned something from that time, even if I perhaps didn't want to or couldn't admit it to myself when I was a teenager. On the one hand, I might never have taken the initiative and escaped from my mother. On the other hand, I trained myself in self-discipline through 13 years of daily practising hours of results-oriented piano playing, which of course eventually also had an effect on my drawing practice.

MD: Only self-discipline?

ME: The self-discipline, but also this confidence that I am able to take a risk. To start something in an empty space can be a weight on your shoulders. It's like going through a secret door and having no idea where it will lead you. But that's also fun. And in concrete terms, I started here in the gallery with a stroke, a swing, a stroke width, a gesture, and that then showed me the way.

"To start something in an empty space can be a weight on your shoulders. It's like going through a secret door and having no idea where it will lead you"

JB: When you sit with a drawing for several days, you become your own audience and your own judge. Is this comparable to when you play in front of an audience as a musician?

ME: I have learned as a pianist that I have to block out the audience from the moment I play the first note. If I start thinking about the opinion of others, it doesn't work, or rather, the result will be different from when I work freely. Fading out the audience is again an act of discipline. It's like a meditation and I used this technique also when I started the *Deep Silence, Resounding* mural. But of course I'm delighted when I get a reaction afterwards, when people have ideally taken something from it for themselves and when they want to share this experience with me.

MD: Would you say that you work introspectively and then release a work into the world?

ME: Exactly. I am quite interested afterwards in what people see in a work, and how it speaks to them. When I look at a finished work, I don't necessarily know what exactly I've actually drawn there. It usually takes me two or three months to see and understand the connections between an idea and its execution. For this exhibition, I was tempted for a short while to extend the drawing from the interior space to the exterior wall as well, to extend *Deep Silence, Resounding* out into the public space, but then decided against it. Because in the end it makes no difference to me whether I have 100 running metres of wall or only ten available for a mural. Such a drawing simply follows its own path as soon as I have started it. It also has something to do with the sense of time. Young colleagues of mine are struggling with this terrible expression, "post contemporary". For them, space and time no longer move directly from A to B; instead, you are somewhere else. And then I notice, in a very old-fashioned way, that I simply enjoy the act of drawing from beginning to end, or, from A to B. After all, once I've started I can't return any more or change my plan.

JB: Is this fact that you can enjoy the act of drawing related to the fact that it is a physical activity?

ME: Yes, and this applies exactly in the sense that playing the piano depends on

"Each and every one of us carries within us things that we cannot see ourselves. And I have, so to speak, drawn what I cannot see in myself until it becomes visible"

the posture of the whole body. You don't play from your fingers. You become aware of this at the latest at the moment when your teacher tells you that you should play everything again, but this time with more feeling. Adding more feeling comes directly from the body, from the body tension, not from the fingers or the craft. In that sense, the piano training was a good preparation for everything I did afterwards – from the act of silently, introspectively drawing in my studio, to drawing performances in front of people. However, talking about all this, it does bring to mind that as a seven-year-old girl I developed an early desire to become a composer. I suffered so much from the fact that I was only ever allowed to play works by composers with wigs. Their busts, the plaster casts of Mozart and Beethoven, stood on my mother's piano with grim faces. I wanted to add my own compositions to their canon of wigs.

MD: Grim or reproachful?

ME: Grim and reproachful and, let's say it out loud: toxically masculine. I thought that if I composed music myself, it would definitely be interesting, certainly coming from a feminist perspective, and therefore no longer quite so masculine. My piano teacher was for it, but my mother was strictly against it. Perhaps because women weren't allowed to study composition back then. By changing gears and learning to draw, I did nothing else but compose in silence. In fact, I could "play" almost all my drawings, including the mural in the Santa Lucia Gallery. They are nothing other than scores.

MD: What would your mural sound like?

ME: That depends, of course, on the instrument used. And I would need some time meditating over the mural to decipher the composition and to translate it into music. But my lines can definitely be read as a musical score.

JB: When did you start doing murals in the first place, and did you experience this as an extension of drawing?

ME: It was in 1980, and rather by chance. It was the heyday of the Transavanguardia movement in Italy. I was part of the Aperto '80 exhibition in Venice, which focused on young new artists as part of the Venice Biennale. Aperto '80 was curated by

Achille Bonito Oliva and Harald Szeemann, whom I knew well back then, and I remember that I was one of only two women participating in a group otherwise entirely consisting of men. A few months later I took part in a group exhibition in Modena. This time, I was the only woman, and I had just given birth to my daughter. In Modena she was about four months old. Being her mother I had to take her with me at all times. The curator had invited me to show a drawing of mine that measured 20 metres. I had brought it with me as a roll, tucked under my arm. As I arrived a little late at the museum, the masters of creation had already occupied all the premium wall spaces. The curator then suggested that my drawing could also be hung over a movable wall. That hurt me deeply and made me very, very angry. But I was and still am a well-mannered person.

JB: How did that anger express itself?

ME: I thought, "Fuck him!" But I didn't say that aloud. Rather, I wanted to find a creative solution to the dilemma. I then got myself some wall paint, and I was allowed to stay with my baby overnight in the exhibition space to paint my first mural there on site in Modena – on two walls that were still uncovered. And that was great, in hindsight, because the work was extremely visible. It wasn't framed and it continued or reappeared on two walls. However, I was considered *the girl* who had slipped into this exhibition for some inexplicable reason, as if by mistake. I experienced a wall of silence. I simply didn't get any feedback even though my mural was super present in the exhibition. But for me it was an artistic breakthrough. Since then, whenever I could, I have done murals.

MD: Were your murals in Modena also abstract line drawings like today?

ME: No, back then I painted more figuratively. I had a grey and a dirty brown available as colours. And a little white. I had to come to terms with the colours available. But it was the first time that I didn't let them get me down. And at the same time it was a gamble at high stakes, because I assumed that I would never be able to realise my mural without a preliminary drawing, which I hadn't prepared. But to my surprise, it worked out perfectly nonetheless.

MD: Do you remember that night shift quite precisely?

ME: Extremely precisely. I started painting at 11pm at night, and every few minutes I looked into the corner where my little daughter was sleeping quietly on a blanket. It was a beautiful night. And that was the start of my free wall paintings. Sometimes you just have to take chances as they come.

MD: You just said that you got no feedback on your mural. How male was the art world in 1980 as compared to 1964?

ME: Extremely male dominated, still. It's hard to imagine it today. There were still hardly any women in the arts, and if there were, their qualifications were questioned. Just remember Yoko Ono. The narrative that she was the witch who had destroyed the Beatles dominated the narrative that she was a groundbreaking conceptual artist. And in my case, I have to correct myself: I actually did get feedback, also very positive, but

always with the restriction that the gallerists who liked it would "unfortunately" not be able to exhibit my "great" work because the gallery would only represent male artists as a matter of principle. You have to let that roll off your tongue. But that's how the art world was four decades ago. And not only in Italy.

JB: And how do you see the situation today? Is it fundamentally different?

ME: Yes, it is different, perhaps because curators and gallery owners have learned to somewhat conceal their rejection of female positions. It is no longer opportune to openly be a misogynist. And of course there are more female artists and curators and even museum directors than ever. But any look at any list of artists in a gallery in Berlin – or elsewhere – will reveal that they always represent far more male artists than female artists. How often have I experienced being rejected with the words that my art is "too feminine"? That a gallery would give me carte blanche for a mural and trust me – that happens only in absolutely exceptional cases.

MD: I actually had a vague idea of the direction your drawing might take – you had published sketches of the drawing on Facebook beforehand. Because you were allowing your followers to participate in the process I always had an overview. Regardless of that, I simply trusted you. Fun fact: a few years ago, Hans Ulrich Obrist practically urged me to get an account on Facebook, precisely so that I could follow the continuous work of artists in this way. And it was Hans Ulrich who introduced us to each other a year ago.

ME: Yes, Hans Ulrich is a dear friend and outspokenly empathetic, too. And he is right: via social media I can communicate very well as an artist what I am working on at the moment. I think that's great. Posting an image on Facebook theoretically makes you visible to the whole world. But the flip side of that, of course, is that artists today have to struggle a lot more than they used to because the beautifully backlit glass surfaces level everything and make everything seem superficially glamorous. Those who are not super famous still usually live precariously. I see this all the time. I don't know if it's good if artists can no longer devote themselves to art because otherwise they financially go down the drain.

JB: The oldest form of social media was probably the cave drawing. Is it a coincidence that your mural reminds me of a cave painting?

ME: It's not so long ago that people found out how these cave paintings really came into being. In fact, cave drawings became an obsession of mine. The German art historian Max Raphael was one of the first in America to write a great book about cave drawings, called *Die Hand an der Wand* (The hand on the wall).[1] His core thesis: the works of people who lived thousands and thousands of years ago were just as contemporary in their time as we are in art today. You anchor yourself in the present by drawing on walls.

MD: What continuity do you see in the past 50 years of your own artistic practice?

ME: It continues to go on and on. The only difference between now and the immediate past is that after 20 years in university, I no longer work in academia.

"In the act of drawing, I am myself. If I don't get to draw for a longer time, then something is missing"

From 1994 to 2013 I held successive teaching posts, most recently as Director at the ICE Institute for Curatorship and Education in Edinburgh and as a tutor at the Royal College of Art in London. Since leaving these teaching roles behind, I have made countless drawings. Though come to think of it, I also drew continuously during my academic years. I made many thousands of drawings over the course of those years. I found my line through constant practice. Through the drawings I found out what makes me tick. Each and every one of us carries within us things that we cannot see ourselves. And I have, so to speak, drawn what I cannot see in myself until it becomes visible. And that's why it's not surprising to me that I can complete a wall drawing in one day and it completely corresponds to my gesture and diction.

MD: What exactly is the invisible thing that defines us? Can you name it?

ME: I once had an interesting encounter in Edinburgh. A professor of computer technology specialising in artificial intelligence looked at my work and smiled. He said, "Do you know what you're actually doing? You're drawing your own DNA!" And so the repertoire or vocabulary of my strokes and gestures hasn't changed much over the years. Because these strokes belong to me.

MD: Physically or intellectually?

ME: Both, probably. Because my body movement is in the lines and in the drawings that are made up of these lines. But in the course of my life I have also worked a lot with photography, and I have also made sculptures. Especially with the triumph of Facebook and Instagram, I have also made my photos public. In the end, however, my drawings are nothing else than a media transfer: at first it was the ritualised daily five to six hours at the piano, then later the daily hours in which I drew. And in a way, the same thing happened: as a child, while I was practising my finger exercises, I always entered a different state of mind, as if in a kind of trance. Only afterwards did I realise that this trance-like state of mind was *myself*. As a child, of course, I could not yet articulate that. Through drawing, however, I also get into such states again and again. In the act of drawing, I am myself. If I don't get to draw for a longer time, then something is missing. Something is missing deep inside me. So everyone looks for their own ritual to stay alive. In the end, it's very simple.

1 Raphael, Max, *Die Hand an der Wand* (The hand on the wall), Zürich-Berlin: Diaphanes, 2013.

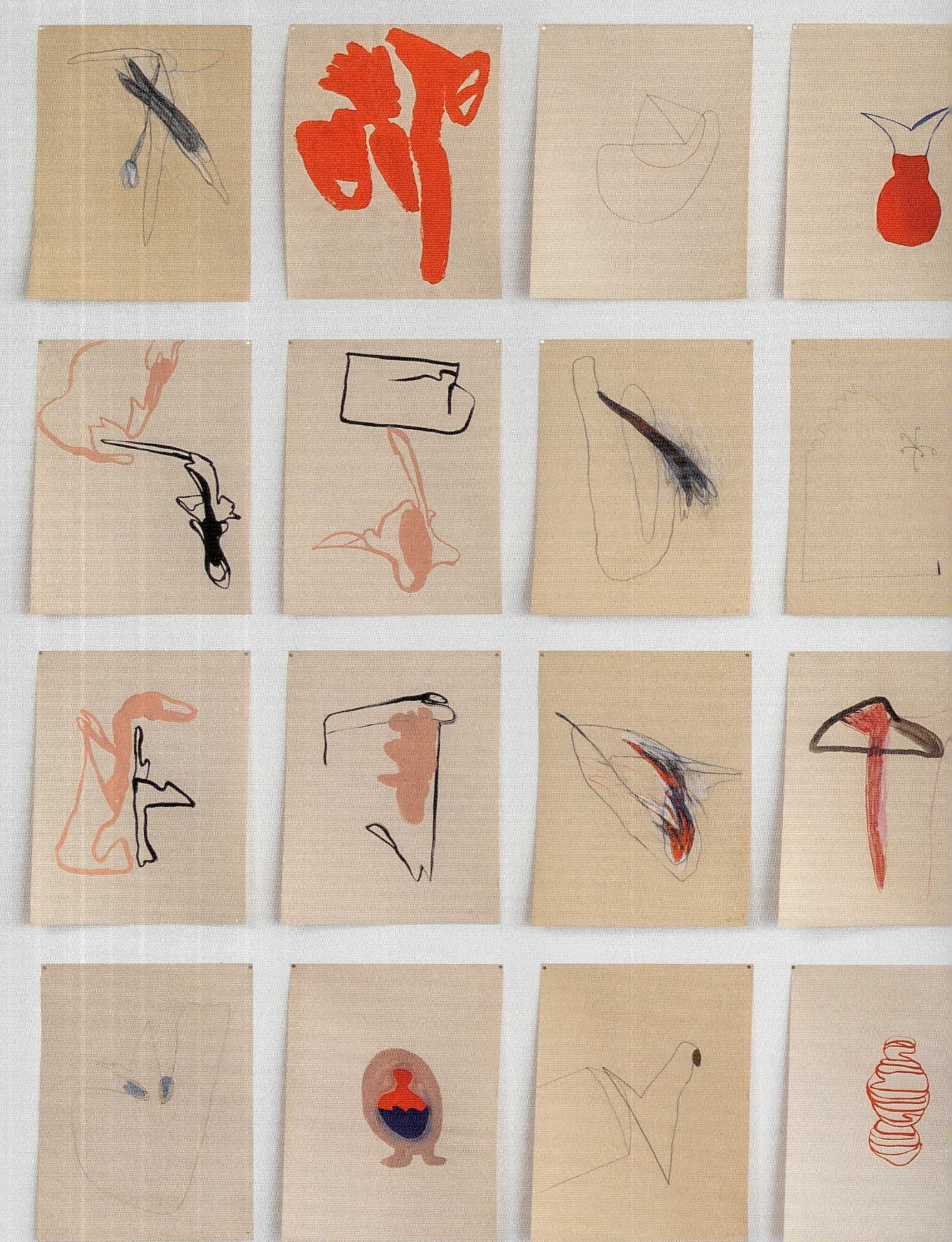

Untitled, 1978–82
mixed media on paper, each 40 x 30cm

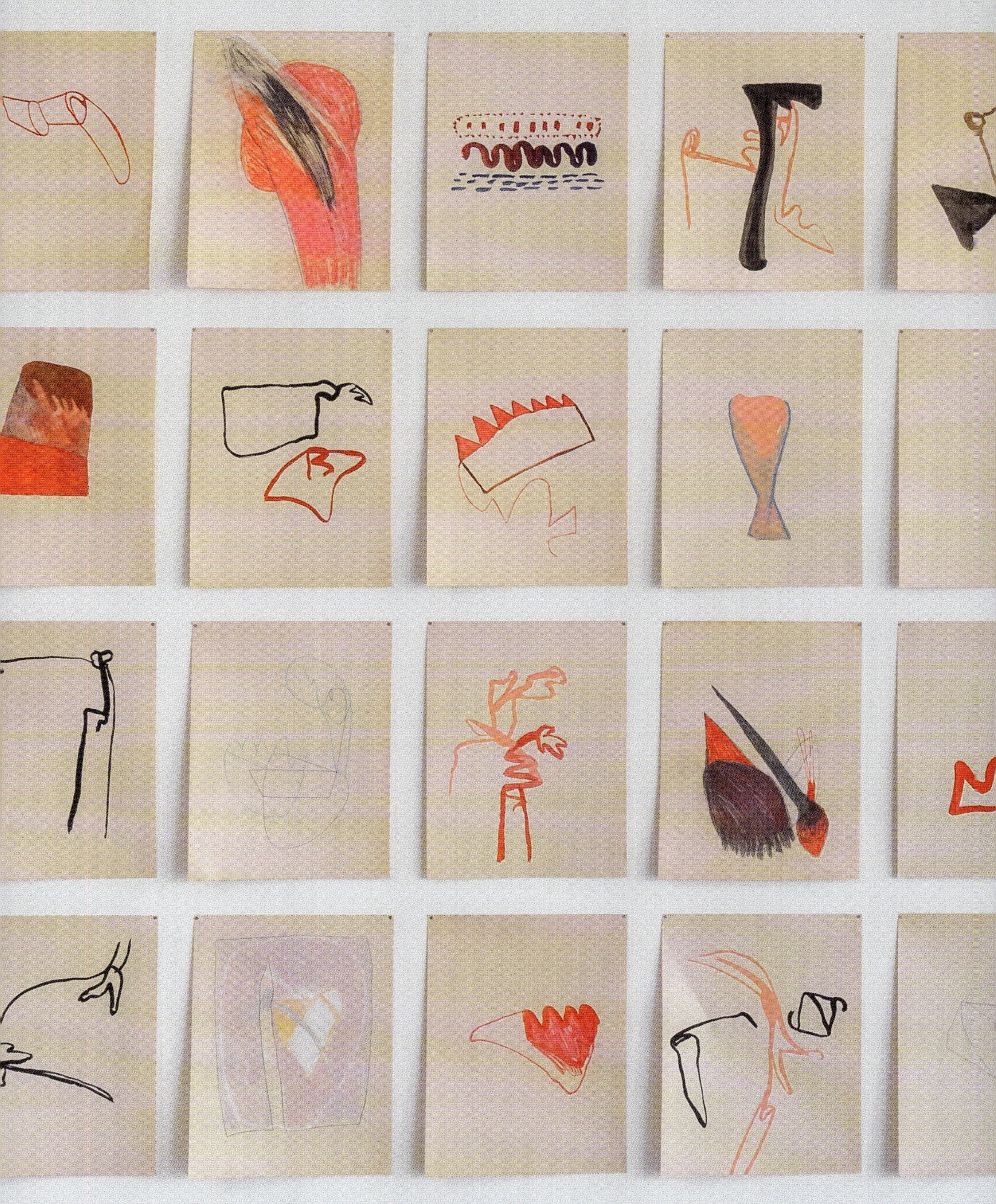

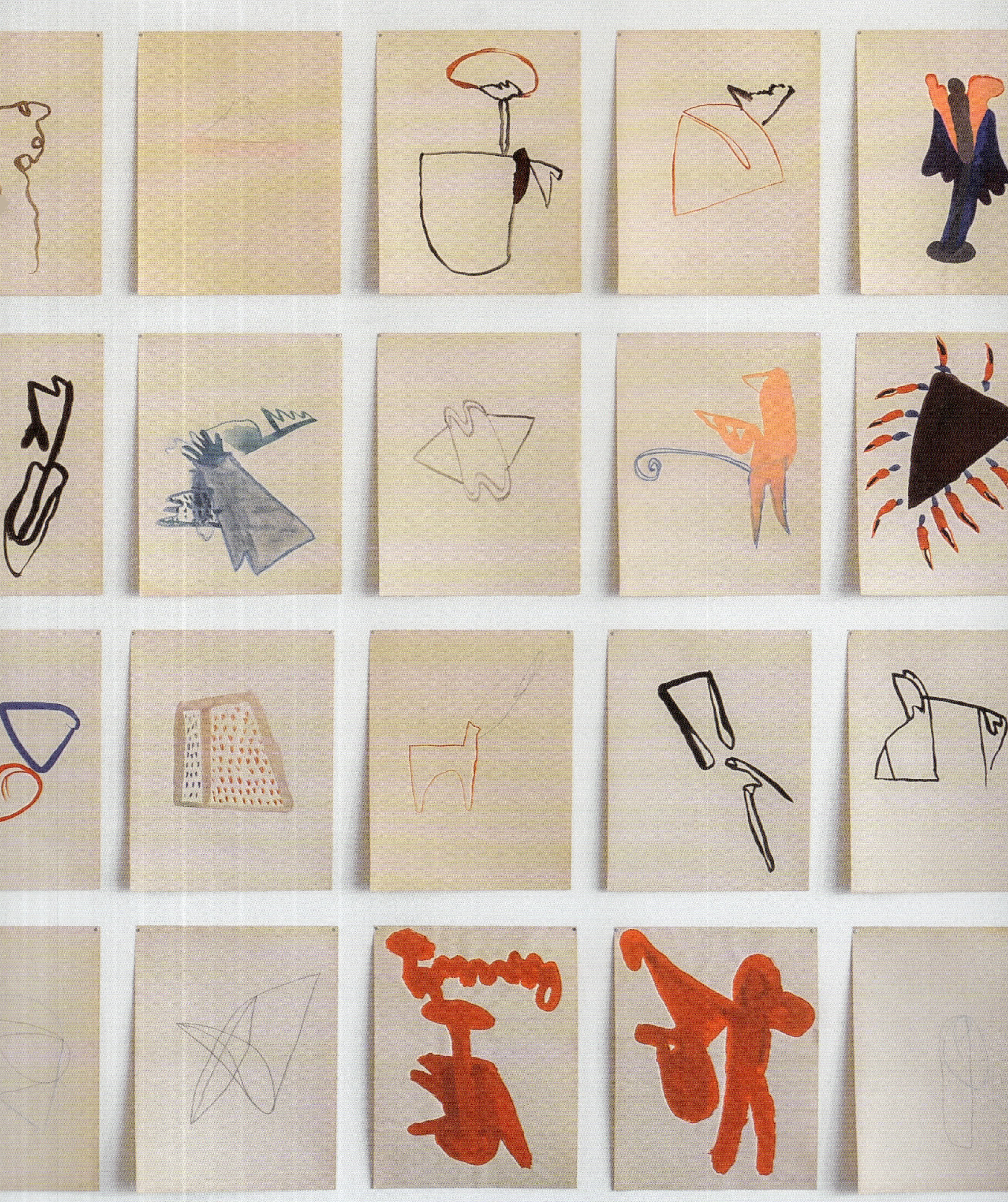

Untitled, 1978–82
mixed media on paper, each 40 x 30cm

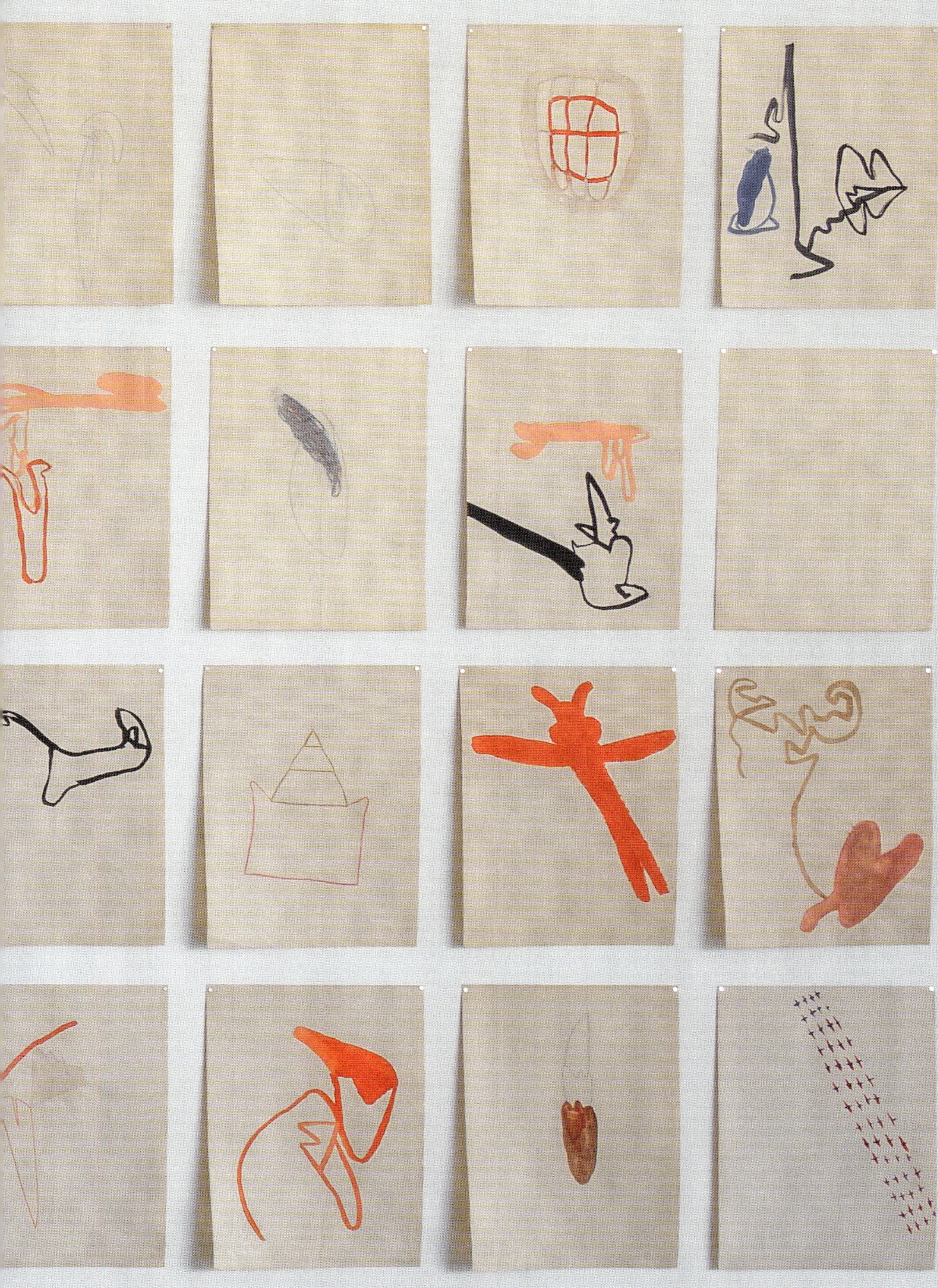

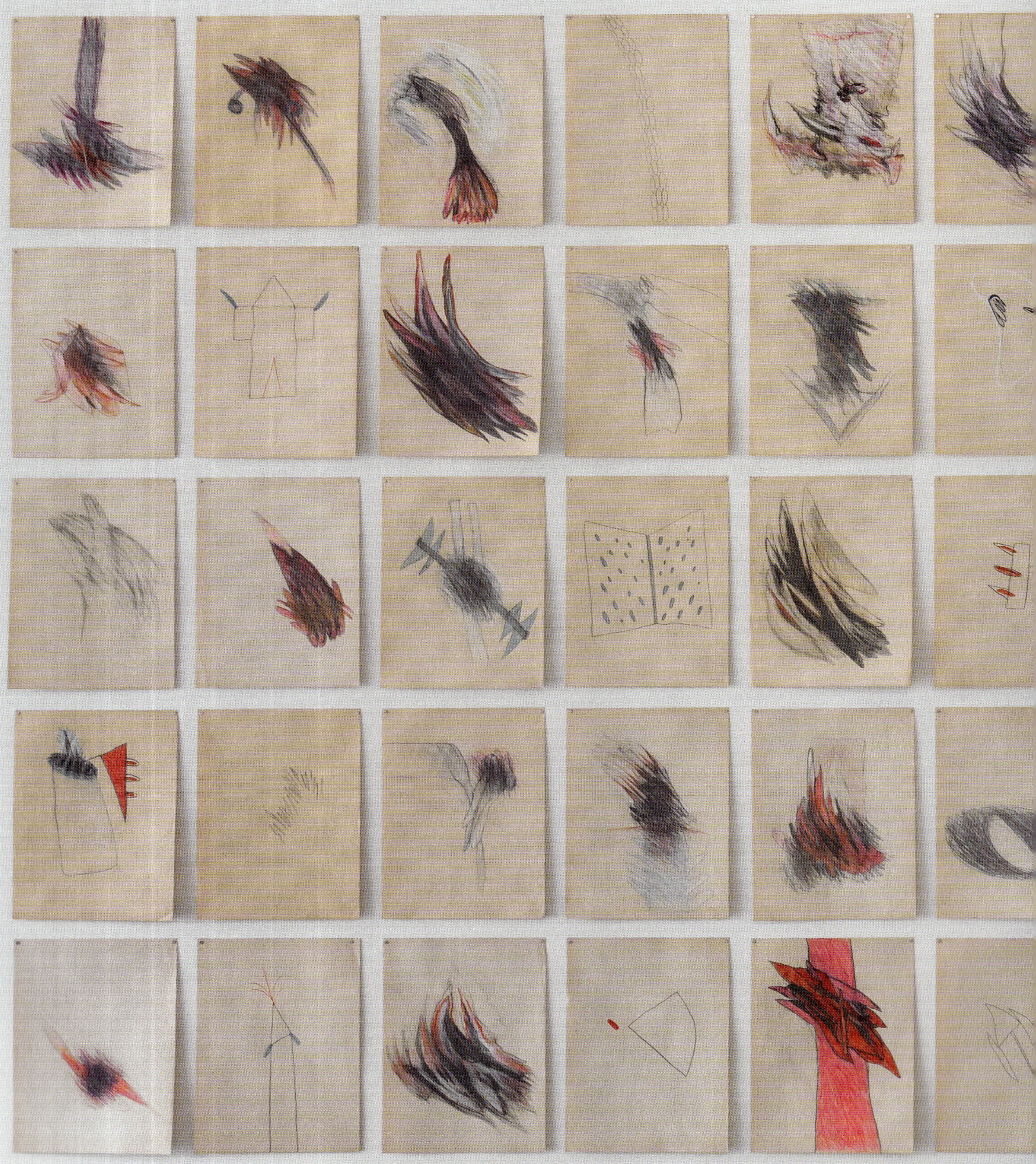

Untitled, 1977
mixed media on paper, each 32 x 24cm

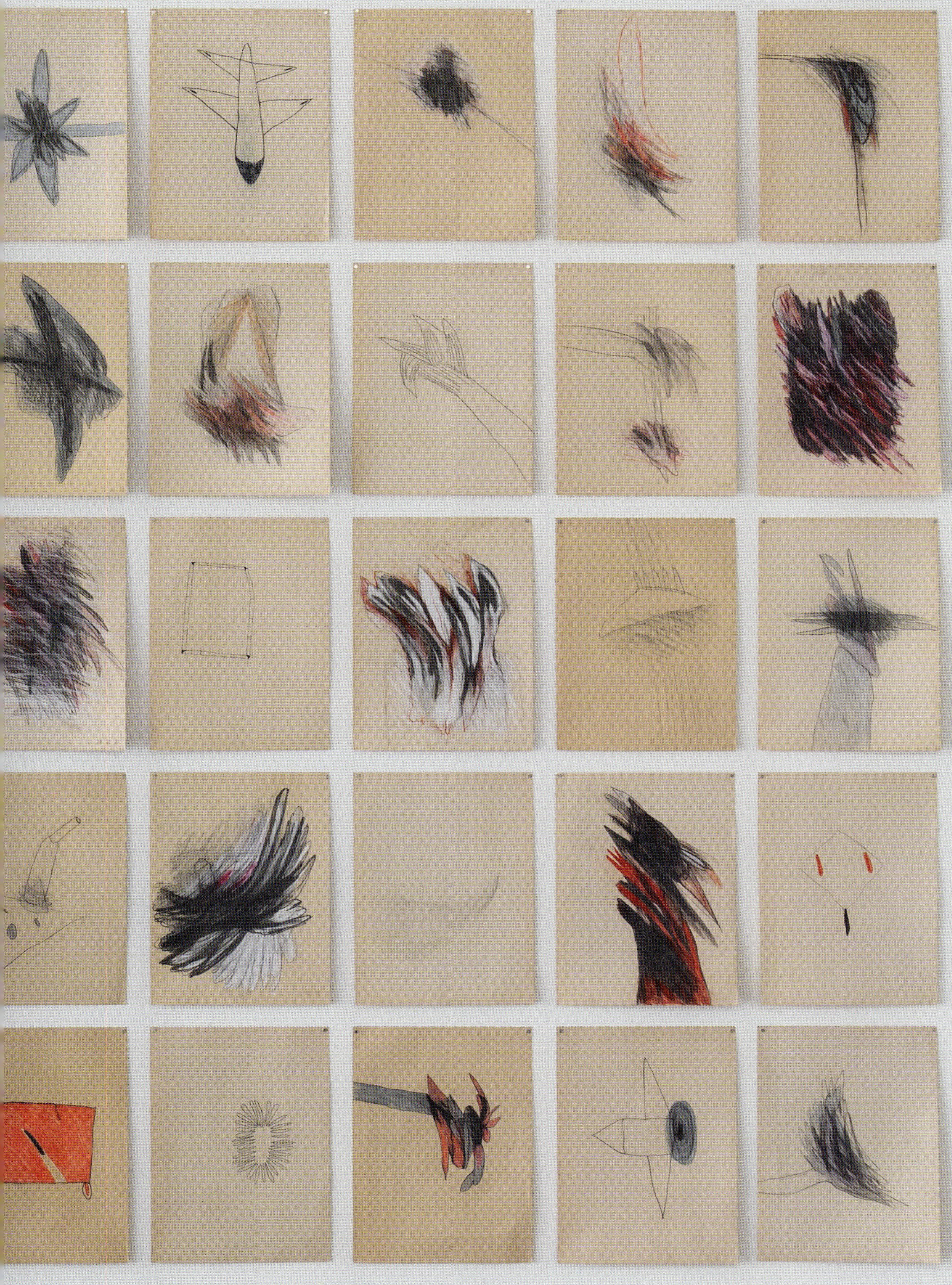

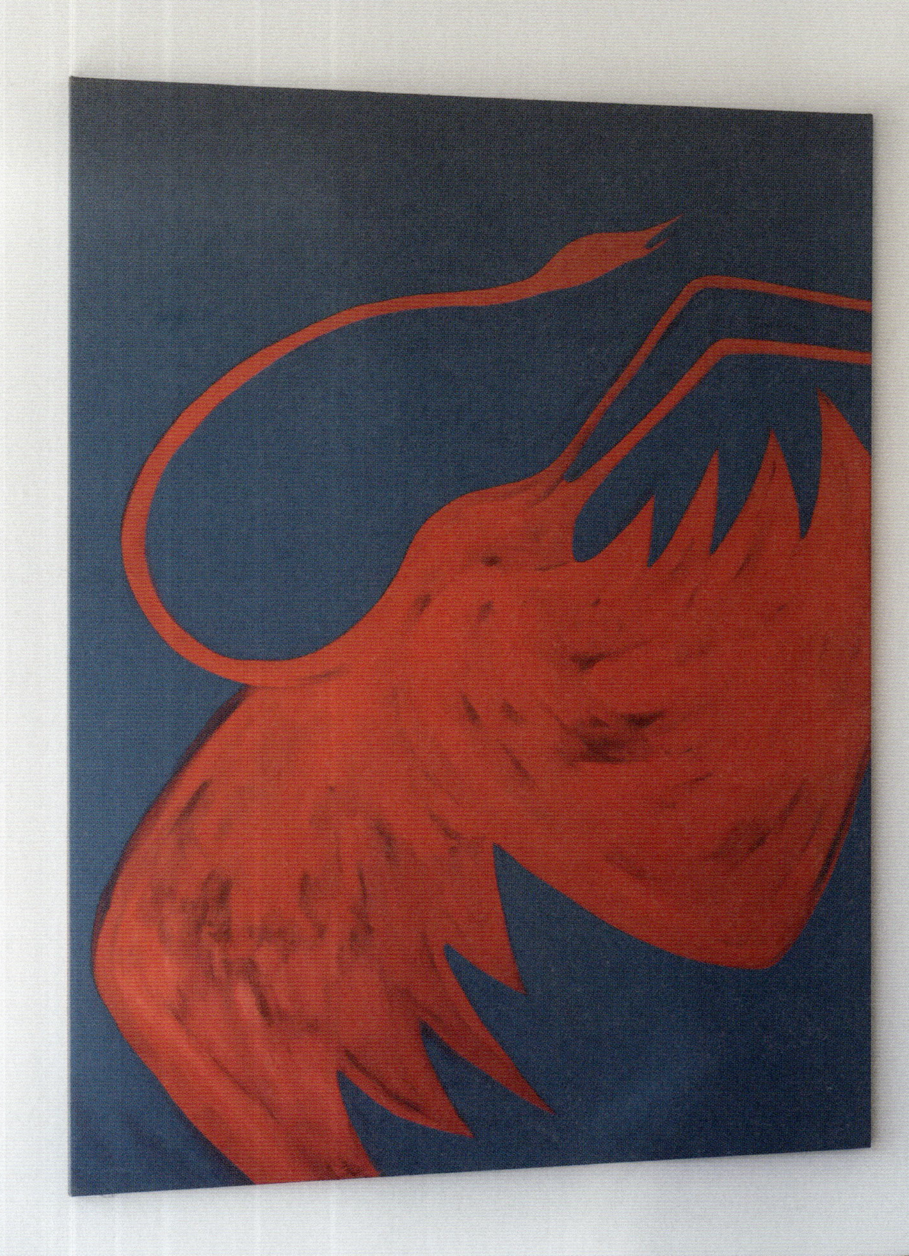

Exhibition view, 2019
von Bartha, Basel

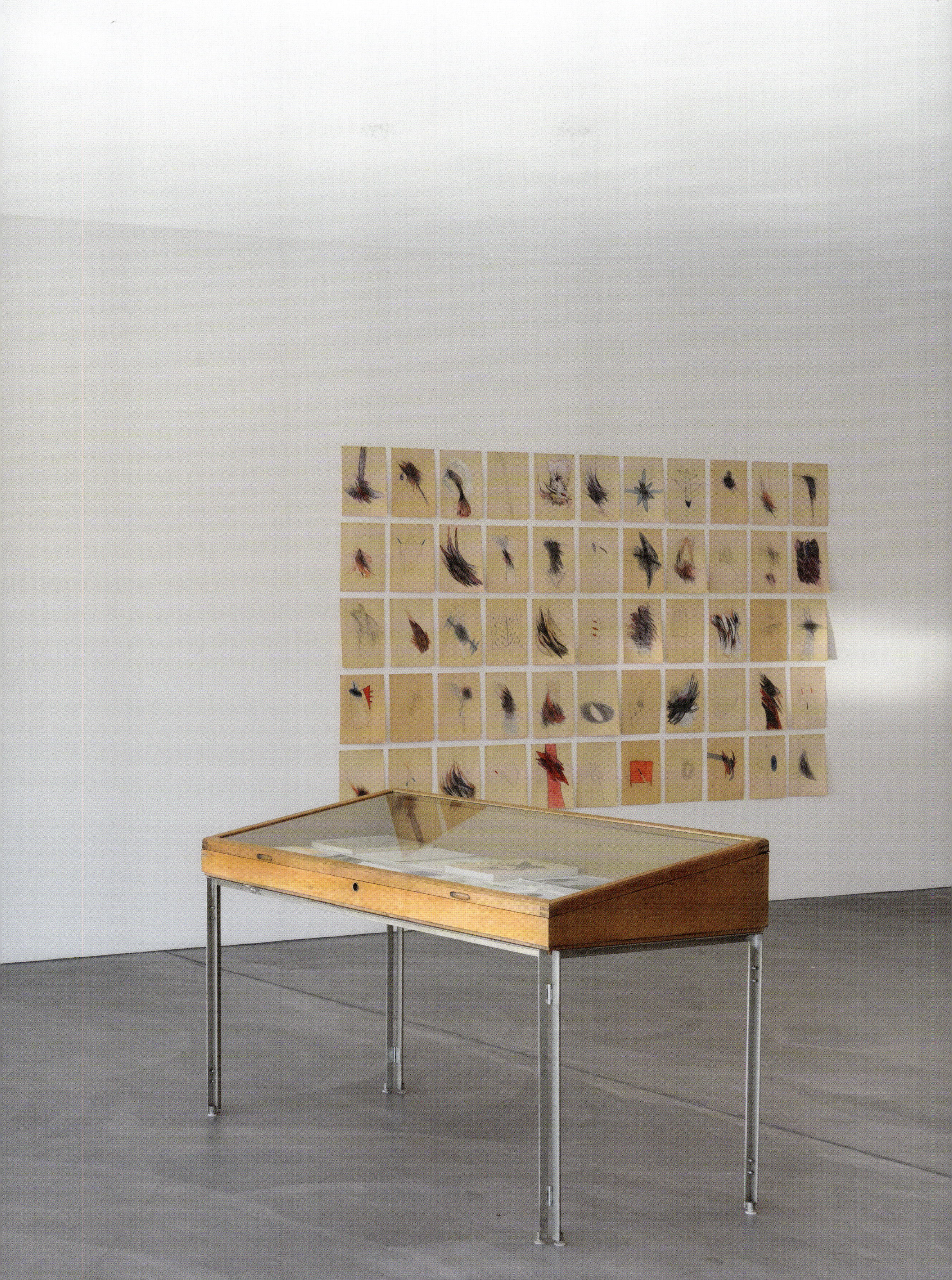

A Perpetual Becoming

By Matylda Krzykowski

"It should not be a mere one-off; it has to be intended indiscriminately, as we won't make any progress by simply proceeding in sequence"[1]

In November 2017, as Marianne was making a large wall drawing in the Museum Gegenwart Basel, she reflected on her own practice and her instinctive way of working as she underwent treatment for cancer. The aggressive chemotherapy drugs impacted her hands and feet; she didn't have as much feeling in her fingertips and sometimes the joints of her hand and fingers didn't cooperate as quickly as she would like. But she had wanted to learn new things all her life, and she kept learning here, too.

When Marianne draws, a picture she has never seen before emerges from the lines. These lines take on extensive and impressive dimensions; they are transformed into energies and confusions, realities and forms and beings, as is evident in her work for the Museum Gegenwart Basel. It was important for her to make this work directly on the wall – directly *in* the architecture of the institution. The work is a visible expression of a woman who, on the one hand, has the cheeky, unfiltered nature of a child and on the other hand wants to experience some self-efficacy, similar to a child that wants to draw on the wall. There was a personal certainty of being able to cope with the demands of producing this wall piece and at the same time being able to master the physical challenges she had come to face later in life. These resulting lines, colourful and strong, give honest value to her act of drawing. These lines reflect what Marianne felt.

[1] An excerpt from an email exchange between Marianne Eigenheer and Matylda Krzykowski in November 2017 while Eigenheer was preparing the installation for Museum Gegenwart Basel.

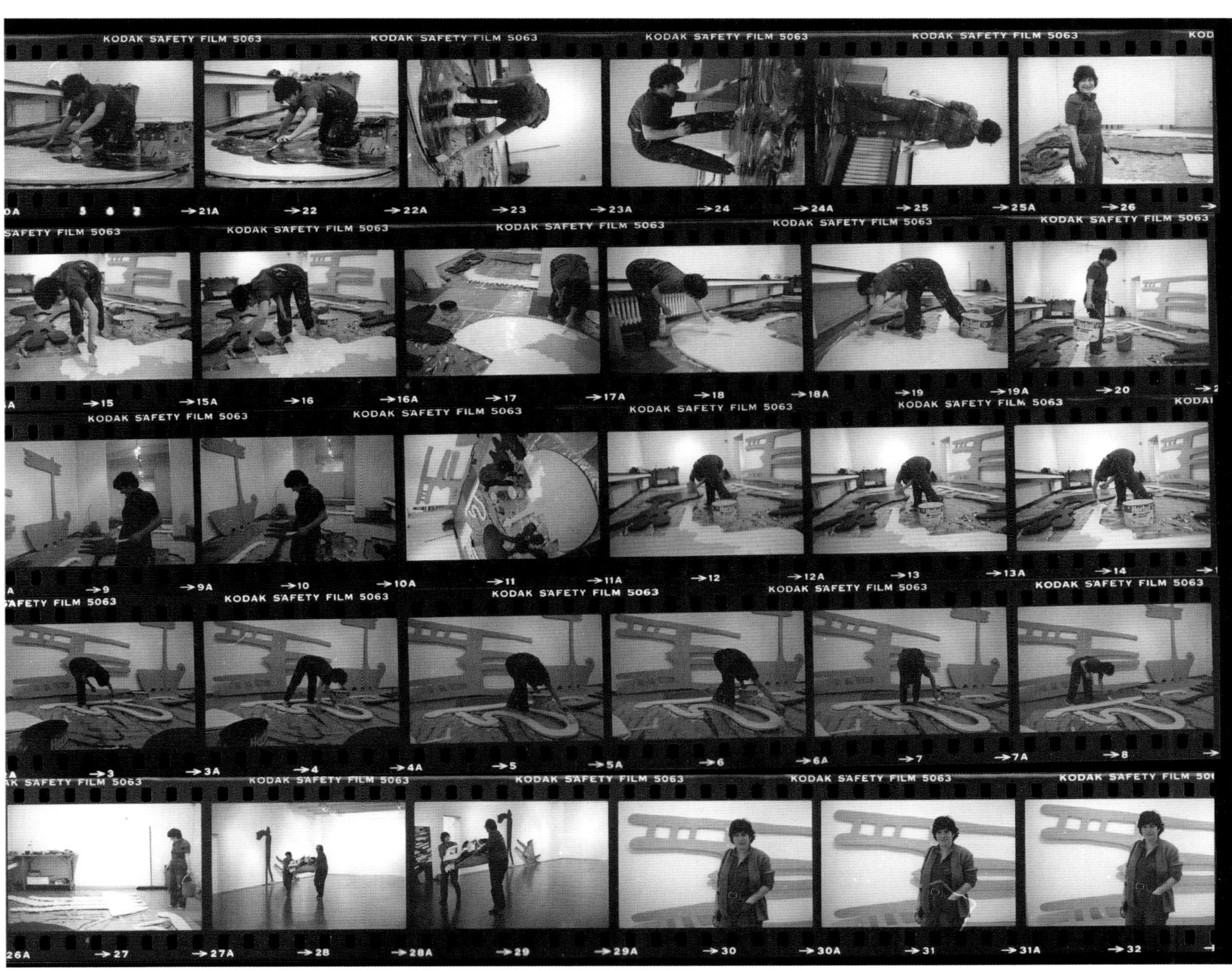

Marianne Eigenheer working
on sculptures, c. 1980s
Photograph on Kodak Safety Film 5063
Photographer unknown

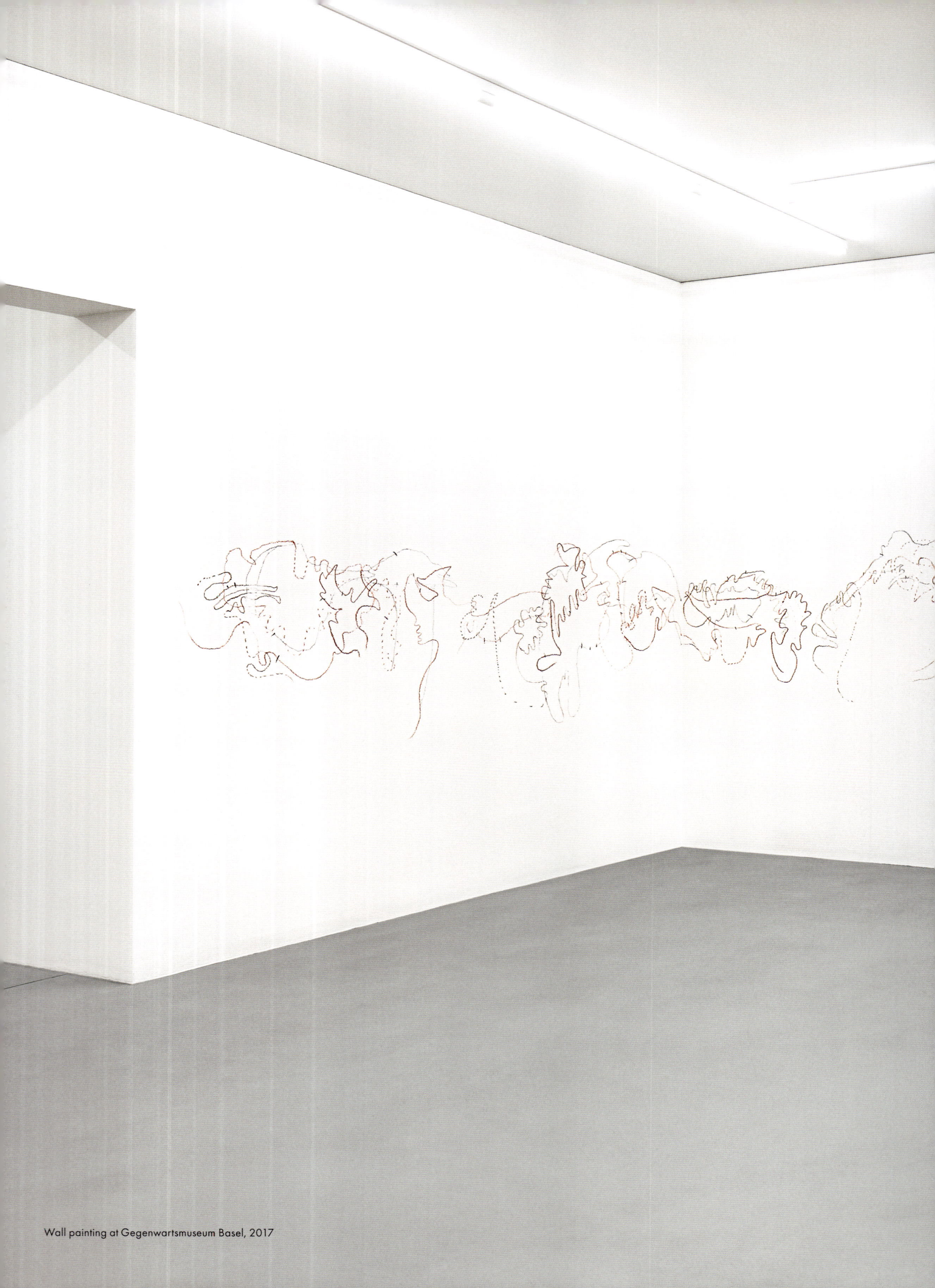

Wall painting at Gegenwartsmuseum Basel, 2017

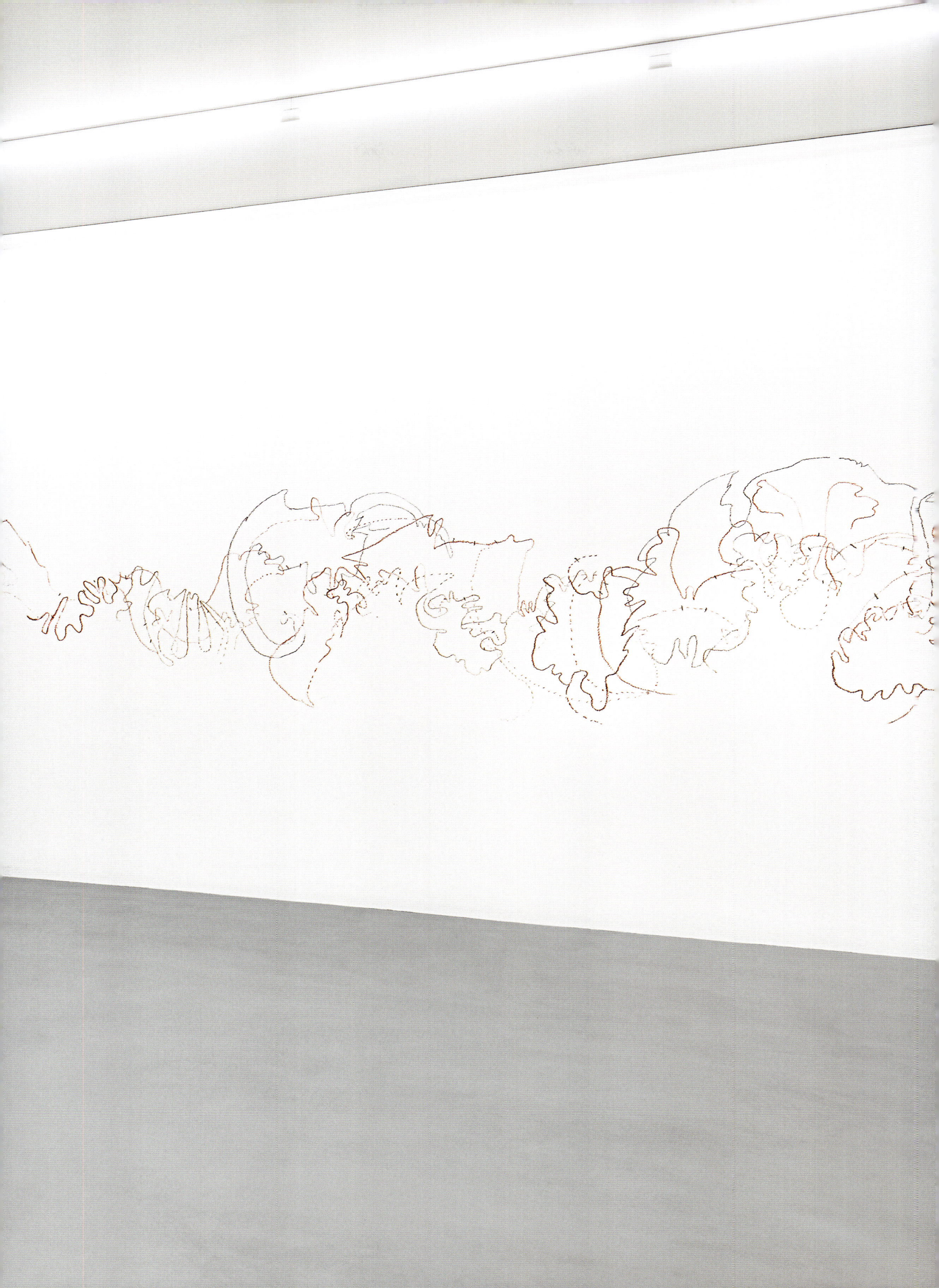

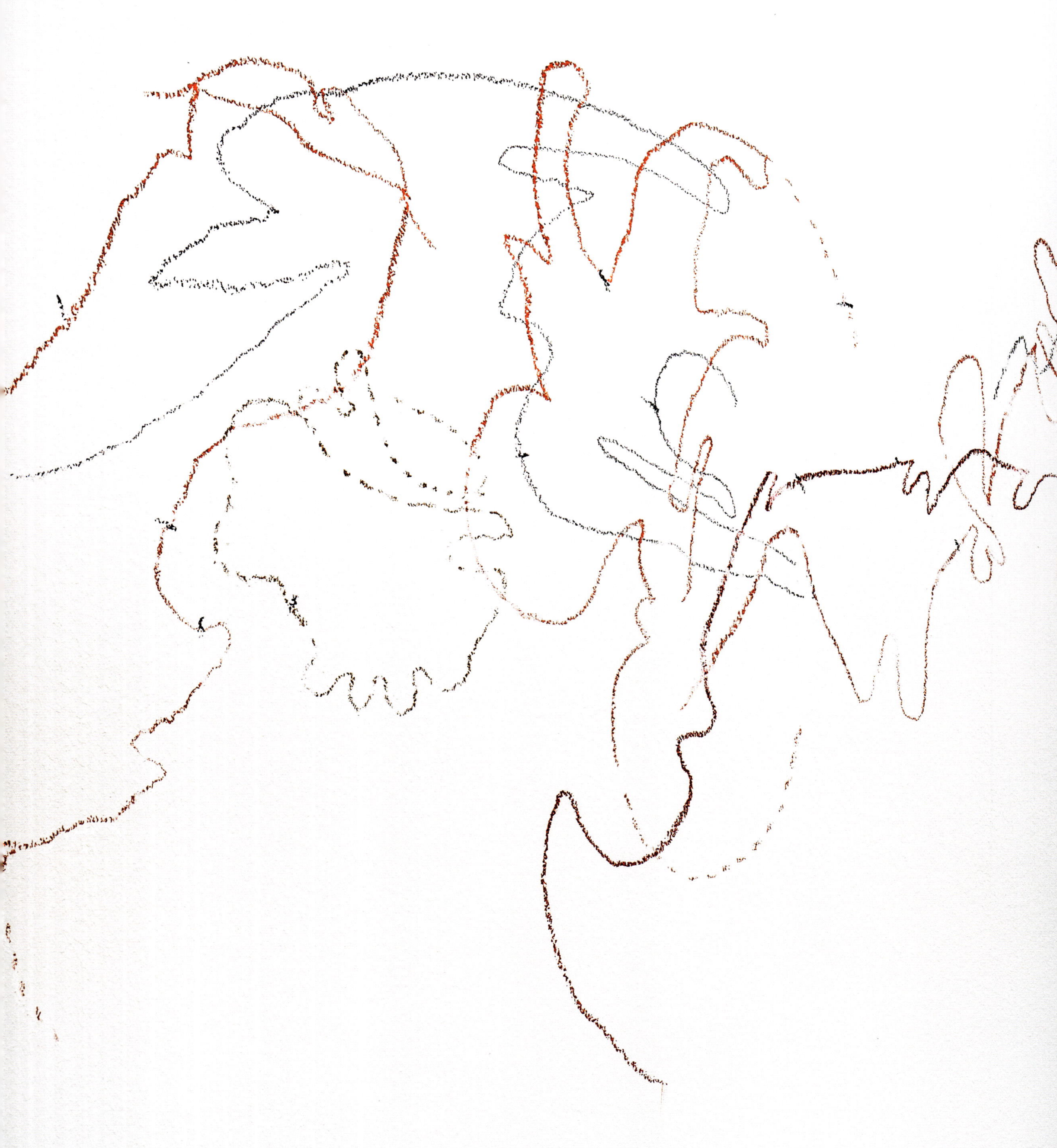

Wall painting at Gegenwartsmuseum Basel (detail), 2017

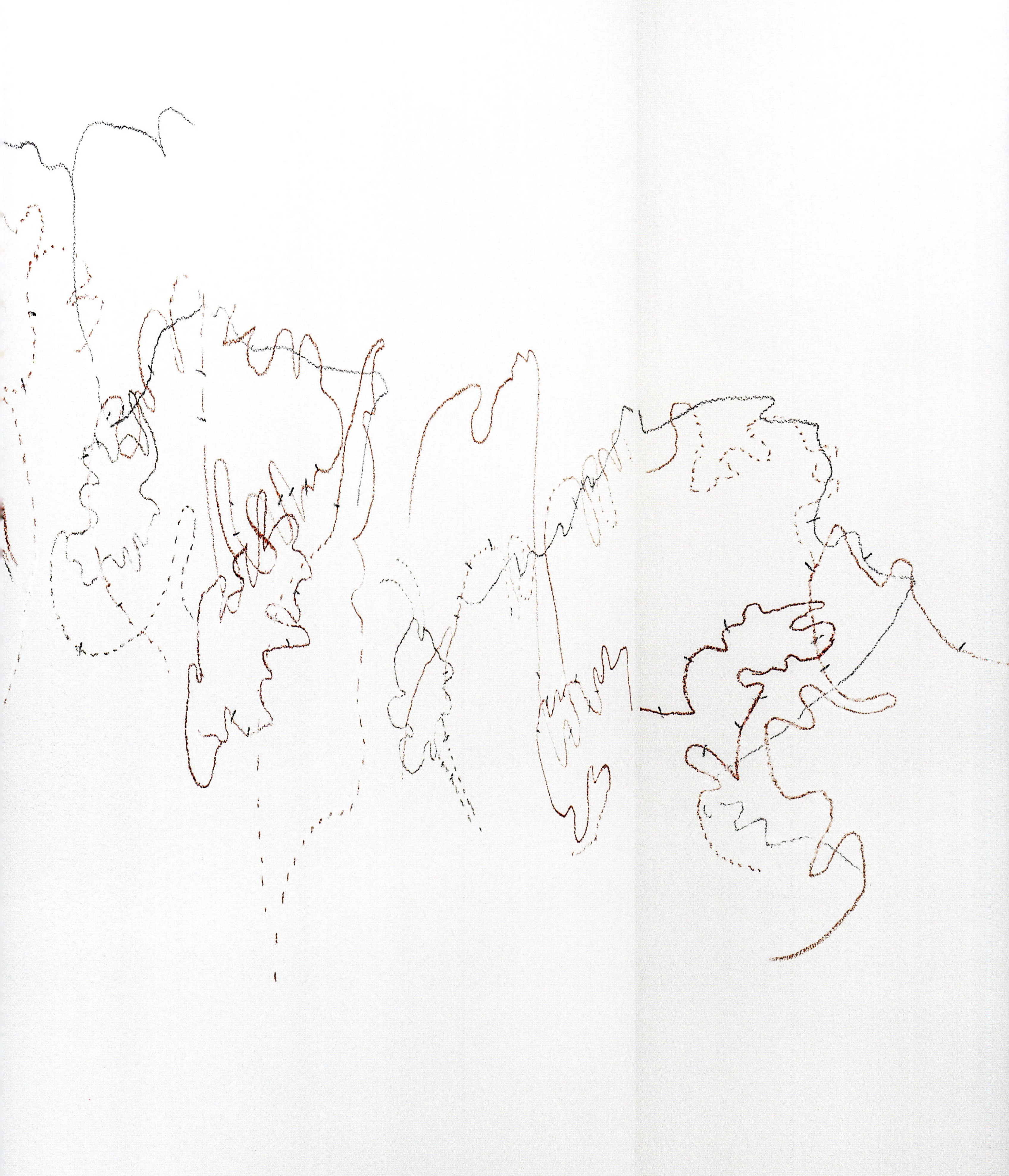

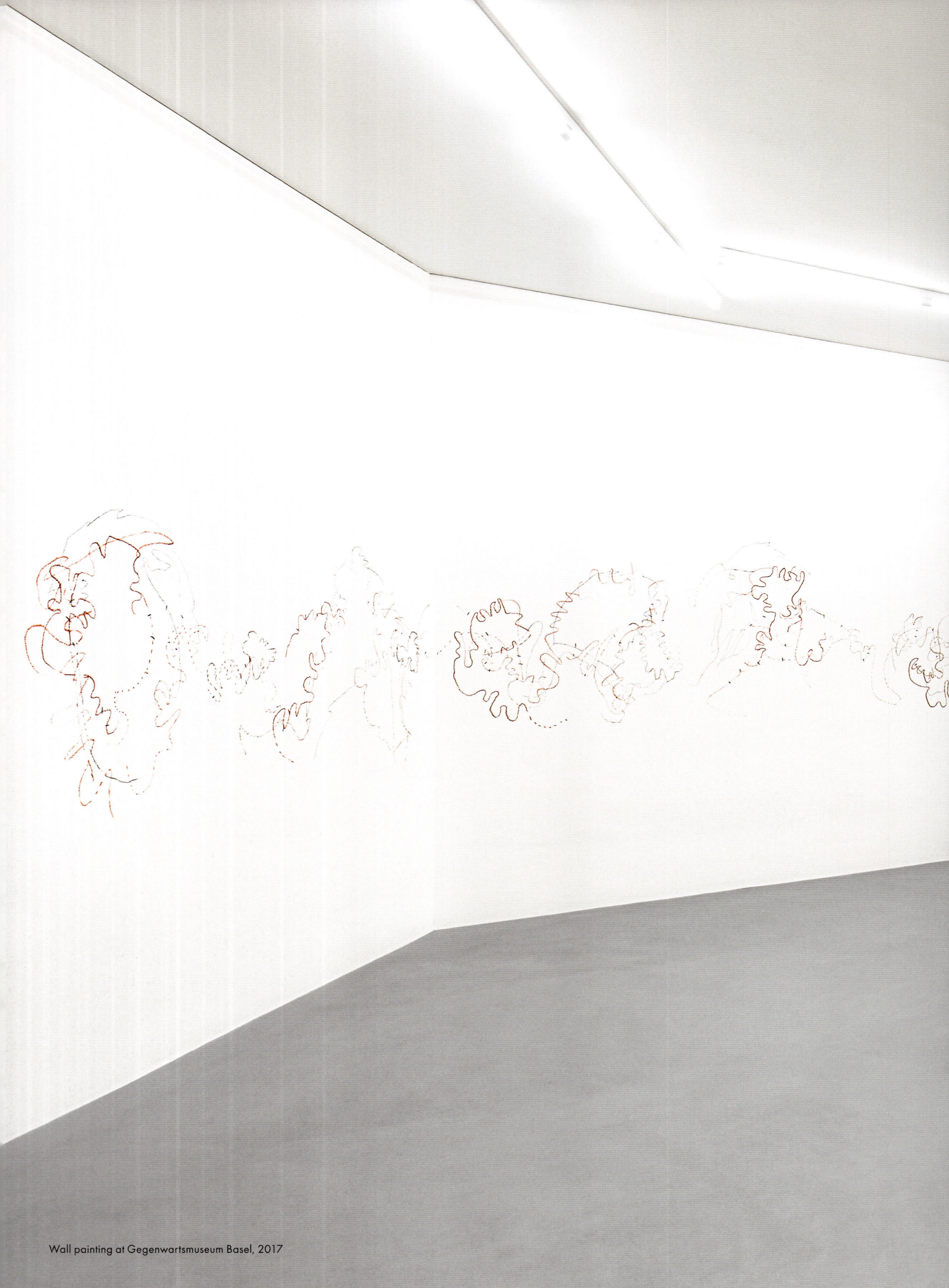

Wall painting at Gegenwartsmuseum Basel, 2017

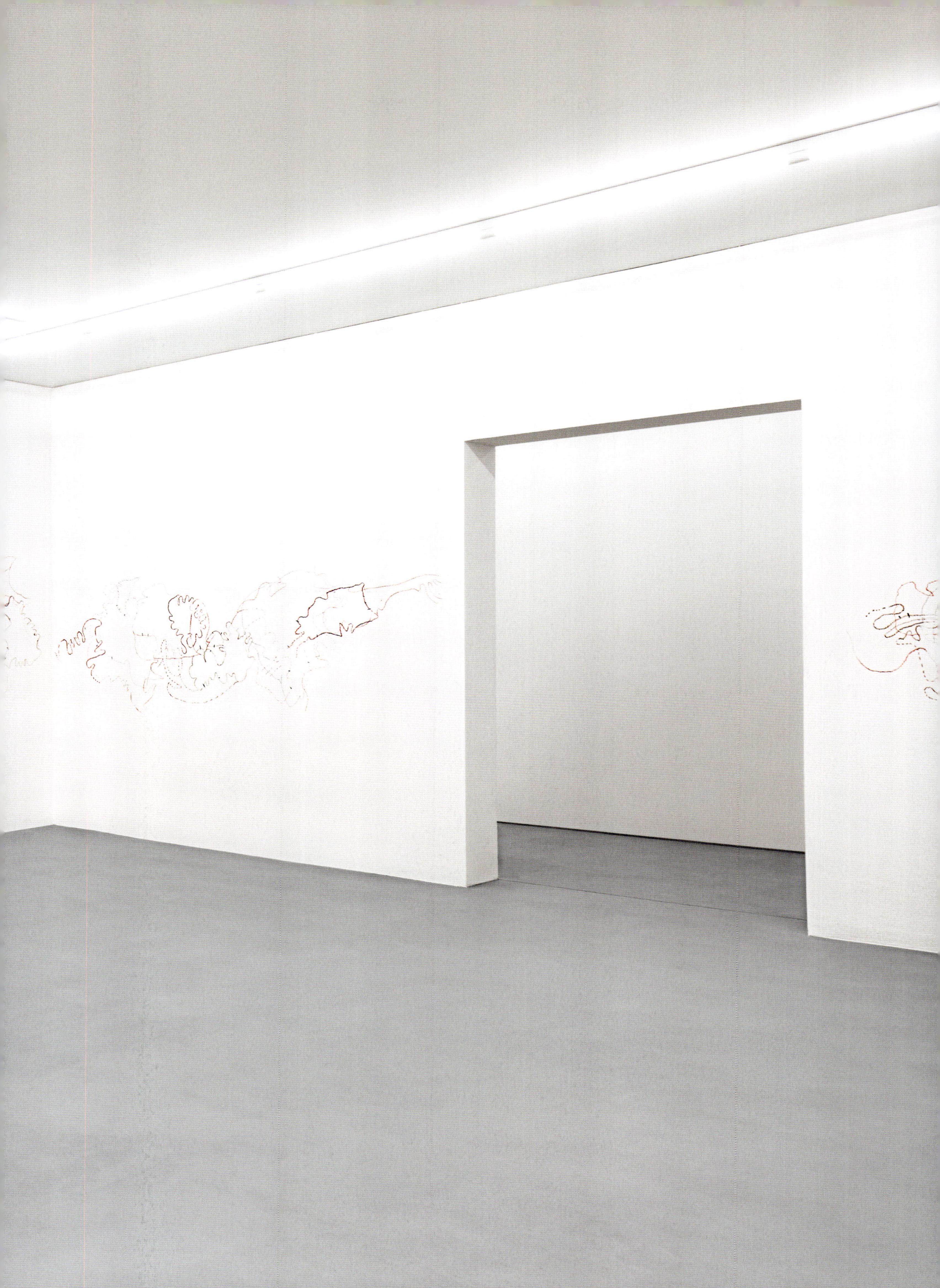

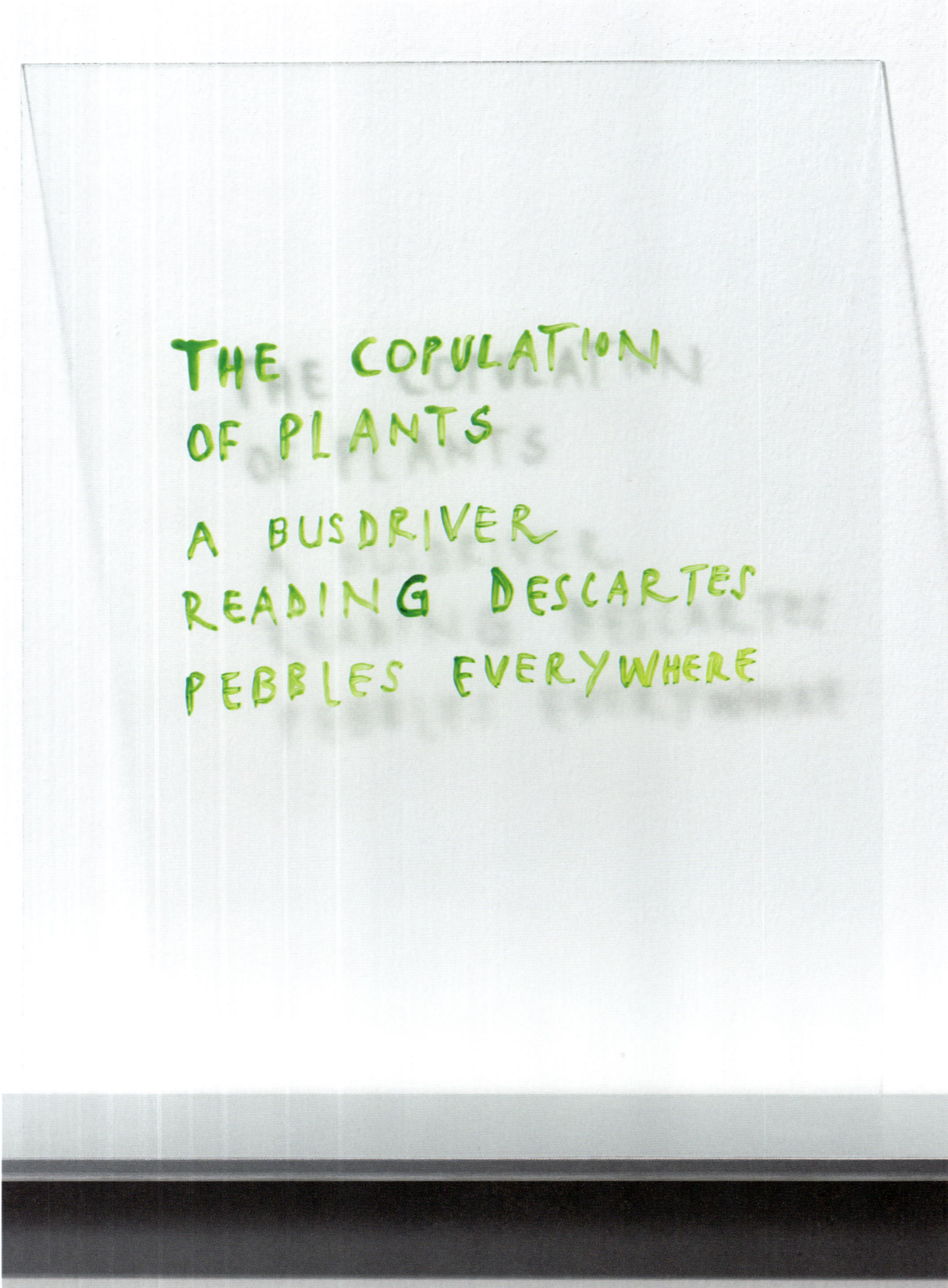

The copulation of plants A Busdriver reading Descartes Pebbles everywhere
From the series *Shingle Street,* 2004–2017
watercolour on glass, different formats

From the children's world of three colours figures move clearly into the pictures quietly of the Wall The Memories Rise I Dance with Antonin Artaud
From the series *Shingle Street*, 2004–2017
watercolour on glass, different formats

THE SONGS OF THE TOAD
AREN'T TO BE FOUND ANYMORE
BIRDS SUFFOCATE IN THE MUD
TREES SCREAM SILENTLY
WITH GREEN LEAVES
FLOCKS OF ANIMALS RUN INTO
DEATH
THE CLOUDS CONTINUE THEIR ROUTE

The songs of the toad aren't to be found anymore Birds suffocate in the mud trees scream silently with green leaves Flocks of animals run into death The clouds continue their route
From the series *Shingle Street*, 2004–2017
watercolour on glass, different formats

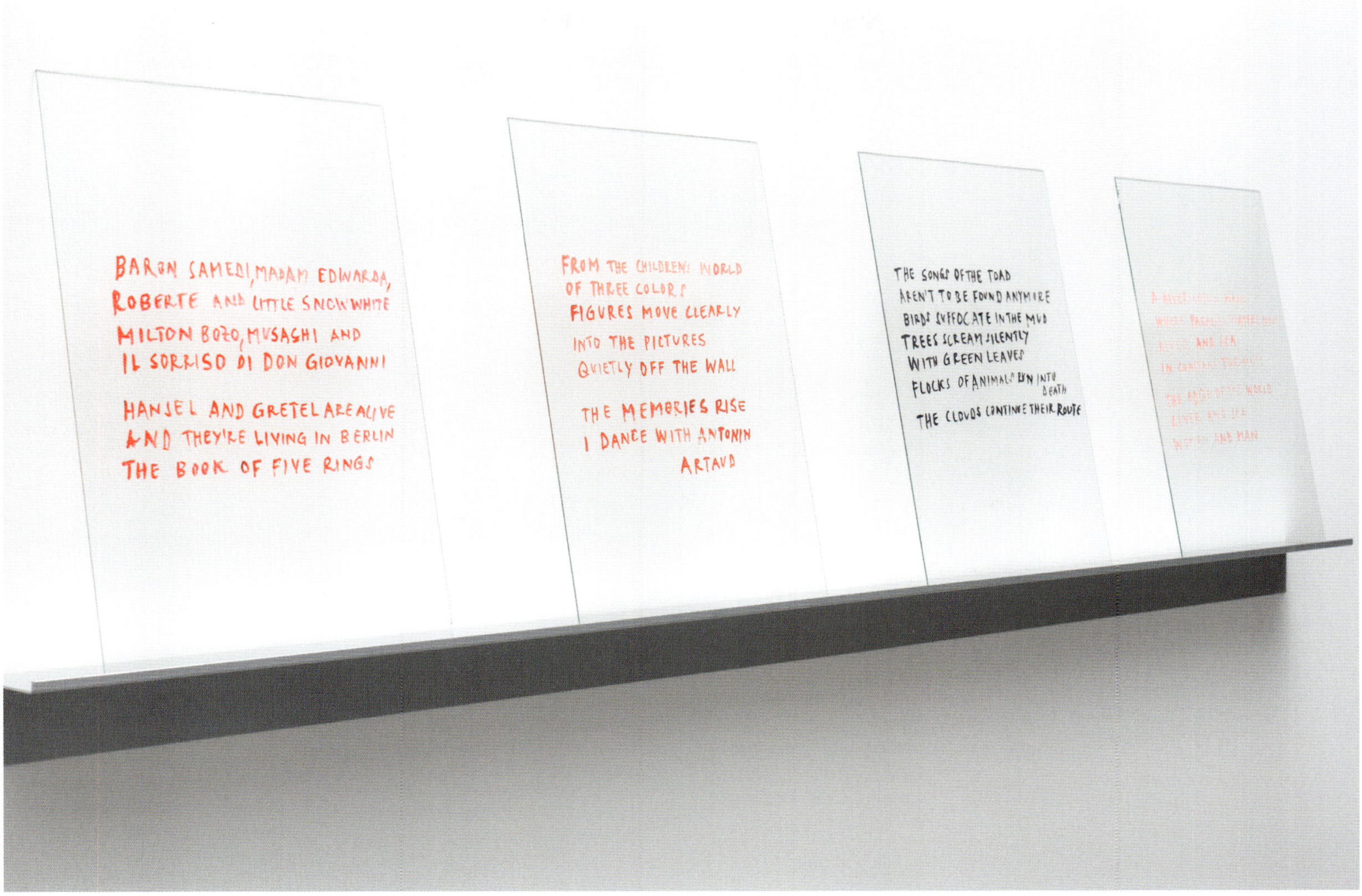

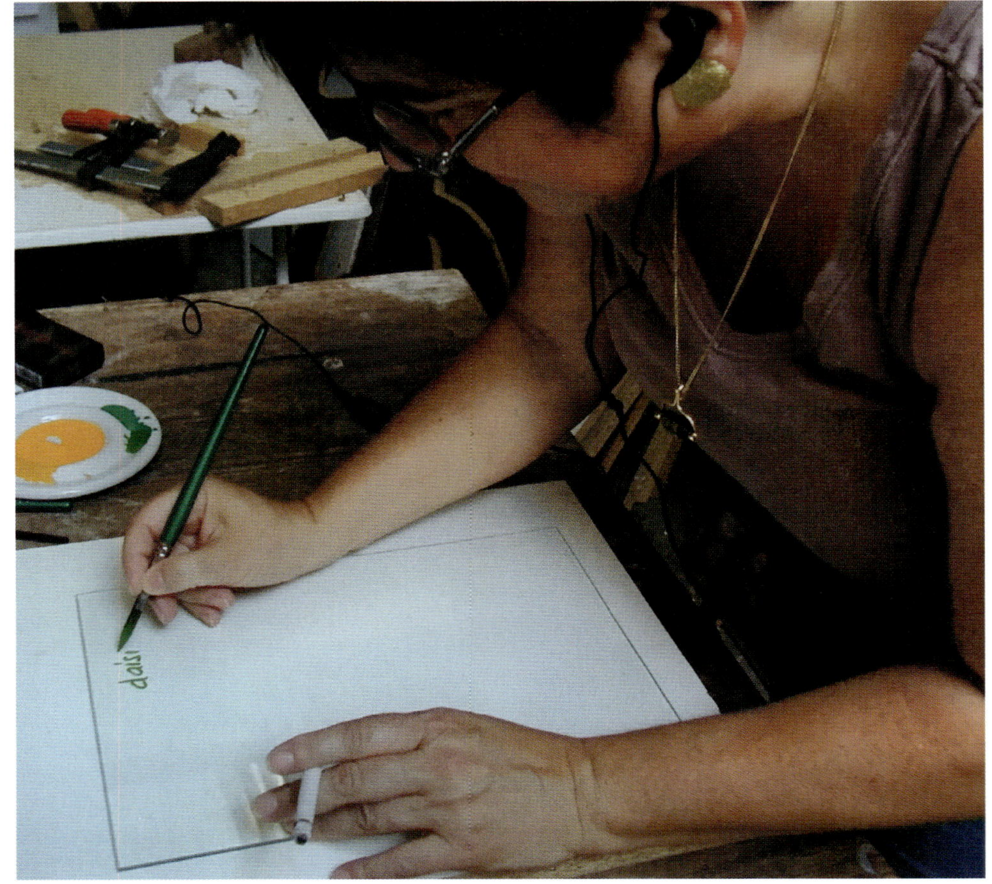

Above:
Various works from the series *Shingle Street*

Opposite:
Marianne Eigenheer in 2002,
creating one of the works from
the series *Shingle Street*
Unknown photographer

Remembering a Lighthouse and Why I Am a Tiny Part of the Milky Way

By Nadine Wietlisbach

There are, in every curatorial life – and I count this as one of the great privileges of working in the field – encounters that shape you, that cause you to doubt yourself and above all to reflect on your own ways of working. Marianne Eigenheer is one of those encounters for me. I am writing in the present tense because her influence continues and has indelibly impacted my curatorial biography.

We first got to know each other through a lively email exchange when a short message with recent work from Marianne landed in my inbox sometime in 2010. I knew the name (she had been a very active figure in the Lucerne art scene of the 1970s and '80s), but was convinced she lived abroad. We later met in Basel, where I was immediately captivated by her energy, intellectual acuity and sense of humour. Right away, it was clear that the Sälistrasse space occupied by sic! Raum für Kunst at the time was a perfect fit for her drawing and painting experiments. Best of all, Marianne was all in on the idea of doing an exhibition with us. It was she who showed me what trust can look like in a curatorial relationship, how it can grow and evolve in moments of disagreement and friction, while always working, agilely, toward the same goal. Trust is what makes experimentation possible. Unpredictable outcomes need space and time to play out.

All this is probably why the text I wrote for Marianne's 2012 exhibition at sic! Raum für Kunst, titled Les guédés dansent toujours, points to significant dynamism in the development process:

> "Upwards and outwards they break, bursting from their forms to hang across the surface. Mean and delicate, solemnly ironic-seeming, they take their place on the wall. Insistent as these signs appear, whatever proximity to the viewer they seek, there remains something perplexing, enigmatic about them. There is no right word to describe these paintings, as 'sign' clearly falls short. A sign presupposes that something is signified. This reference to a certain aspect of reality – an aspect that is abstracted to a sign and thus transposed to the realm of generality – does not suffice to describe Marianne Eigenheer's works …
> The dynamism of their arrangement on two opposing walls sets the space in motion, causes it to vibrate as though the images themselves had chosen precisely this room in which to temporarily manifest themselves. Contemplating Eigenheer's Les guédés dansent toujours, one can hardly help but view the signs as animated in their own right, as having assumed a life of their own. There is an immediacy to the way these works are made, they arise out of the moment and are hung on the wall as an all-encompassing expression of an instance, as a reflection of an inner state. In that respect, it seems only fitting to ascribe a secret identity to Eigenheer's pictorial signs; though in fact 'created' under the artist's skin, made somewhere between her foot, heart, belly and head, they are pure expression, autonomous phenomena."[1]

Marianne was an outstanding artist with a unique sense of poetry, form and colour. Leafing through her old publications, I am always surprised at how relevant and fresh her work seems. But moreover, and perhaps just as significantly, she was a lighthouse: an enduring beacon against wind and weather at a time when many

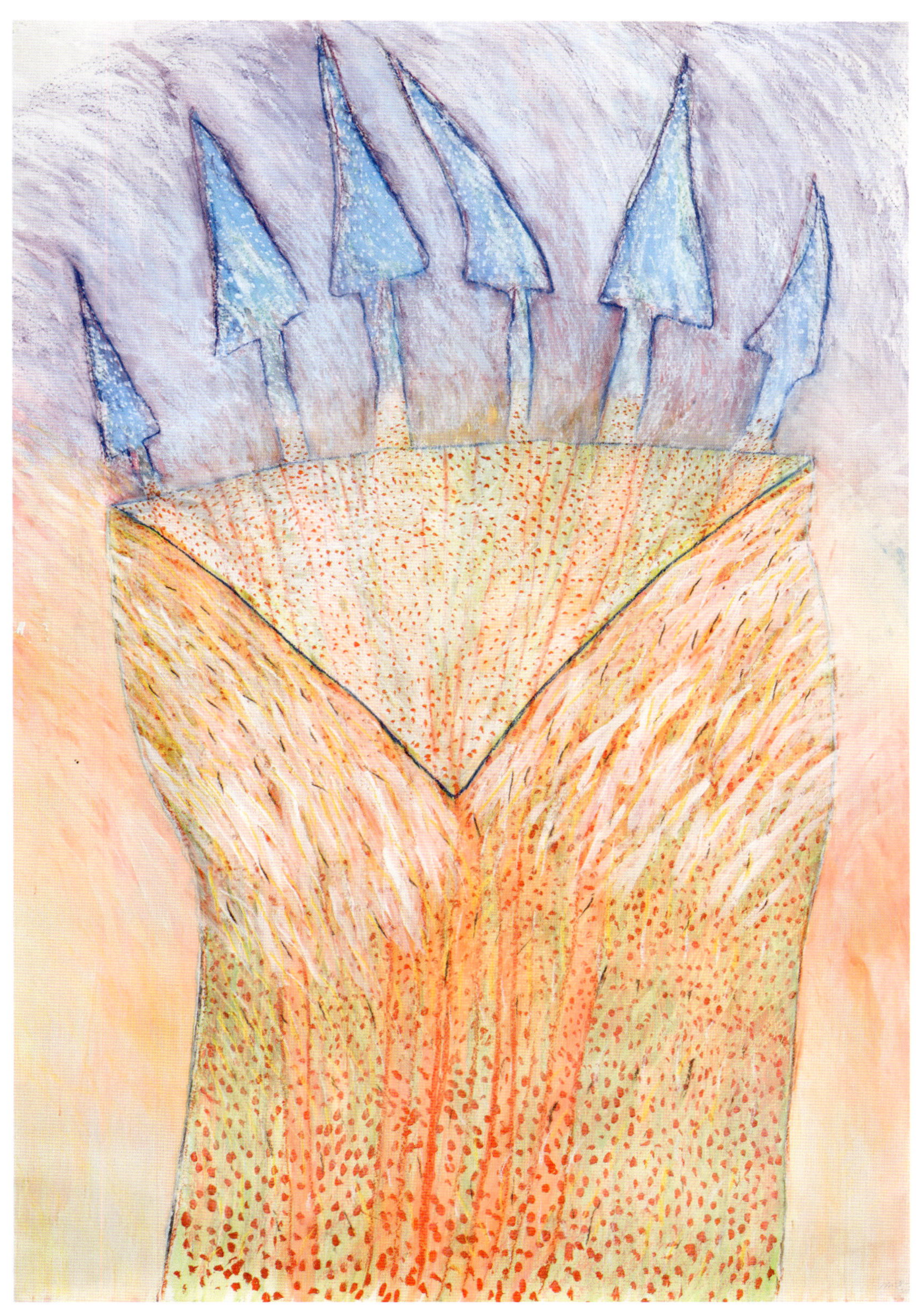

Lady Jane im Schnee, c. 1975
mixed media on paper, 215 x 150cm

female artists had to fight even harder for opportunities and possibilities than they still do today. She is a glaring example of how difficult the art world made it for women who chose to have a child in addition to their artistic practice; who occupied the charged area between care work and economic survival, between day-to-day life in the studio, exhibition presence and the greedy emphasis on performance that the art market camouflages so elegantly to the outside. Nonetheless, as a university lecturer, she helped a number of young artists early on in their career paths; she inspired and guided them. The tension she felt – as she encouraged students to strive for excellence where she herself was so often denied the opportunity – is evident in her reply to a question Hans Ulrich Obrist posed about her many years of teaching in a conversation printed in a small publication to accompany the exhibition. She said, "Whatever I do, I want to do well and to the best of my ability, even if I can't do what I might have wanted for myself."

We find broader consensus nowadays. There is more general agreement around the simple fact that female artists of her generation (and beyond) were indeed active and influential in their respective fields. It's just that they rarely enjoyed the same visibility and recognition as their male counterparts. Even now, Marianne is front of mind whenever someone feels compelled to explain that female artists are simply less active, or that there just aren't that many exciting ones around. Sometimes angrily and with recurring bouts of pity, I wonder how, after so many years, these people have still not yet learned to see what is right in front of them.[2]

As for Marianne's message to young artists as a lecturer, these are words I continue to live by today, and I am happy to pass them on. She said, "See as much as you can, go out as much as possible and come to view yourself as part of a whole. Looking up at a starry sky, think, 'I am a tiny part of the Milky Way, but I am, and I am also something'."[3]

[1] Wietlisbach, Nadine, "Les guédés dansent toujours" [The Guédés Always Dance], Lucerne: sic! Raum für Kunst, 2012.

[2] Obrist, Hans Ulrich, "Marianne Eigenheer im Gespräch mit Hans Ulrich Obrist" [Marianne Eigenheer in conversation with Hans Ulrich Obrist], Lack/Lack [Lucerne], no 3, January 2012.

[3] Obrist, "Marianne Eigenheer im Gespräch mit Hans Ulrich Obrist".

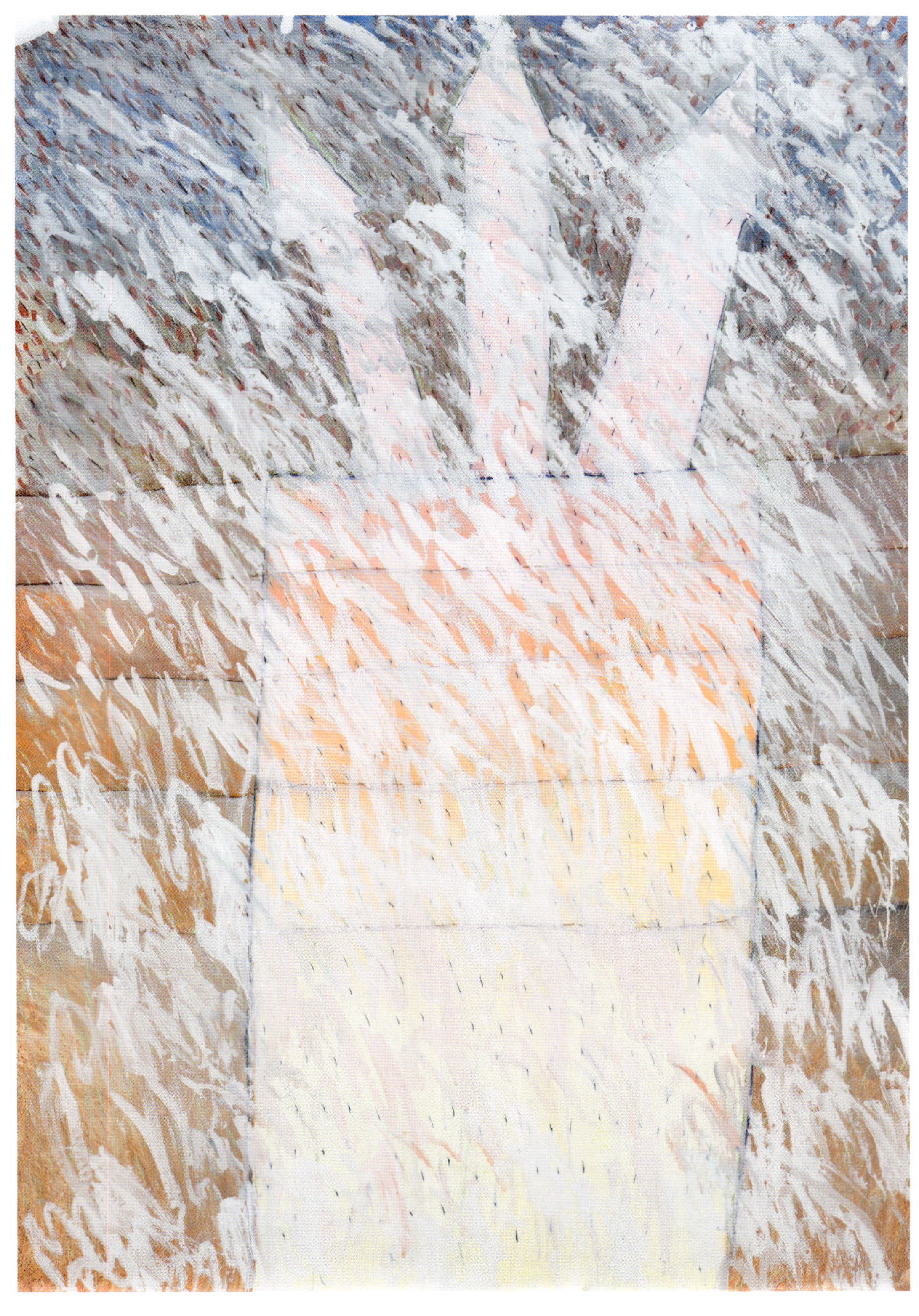

Untitled, n.d. (c. 1970s)
mixed media on paper, 215 x 150cm

Rosa Dame, 1974
mixed media on paper, 225 x 150cm

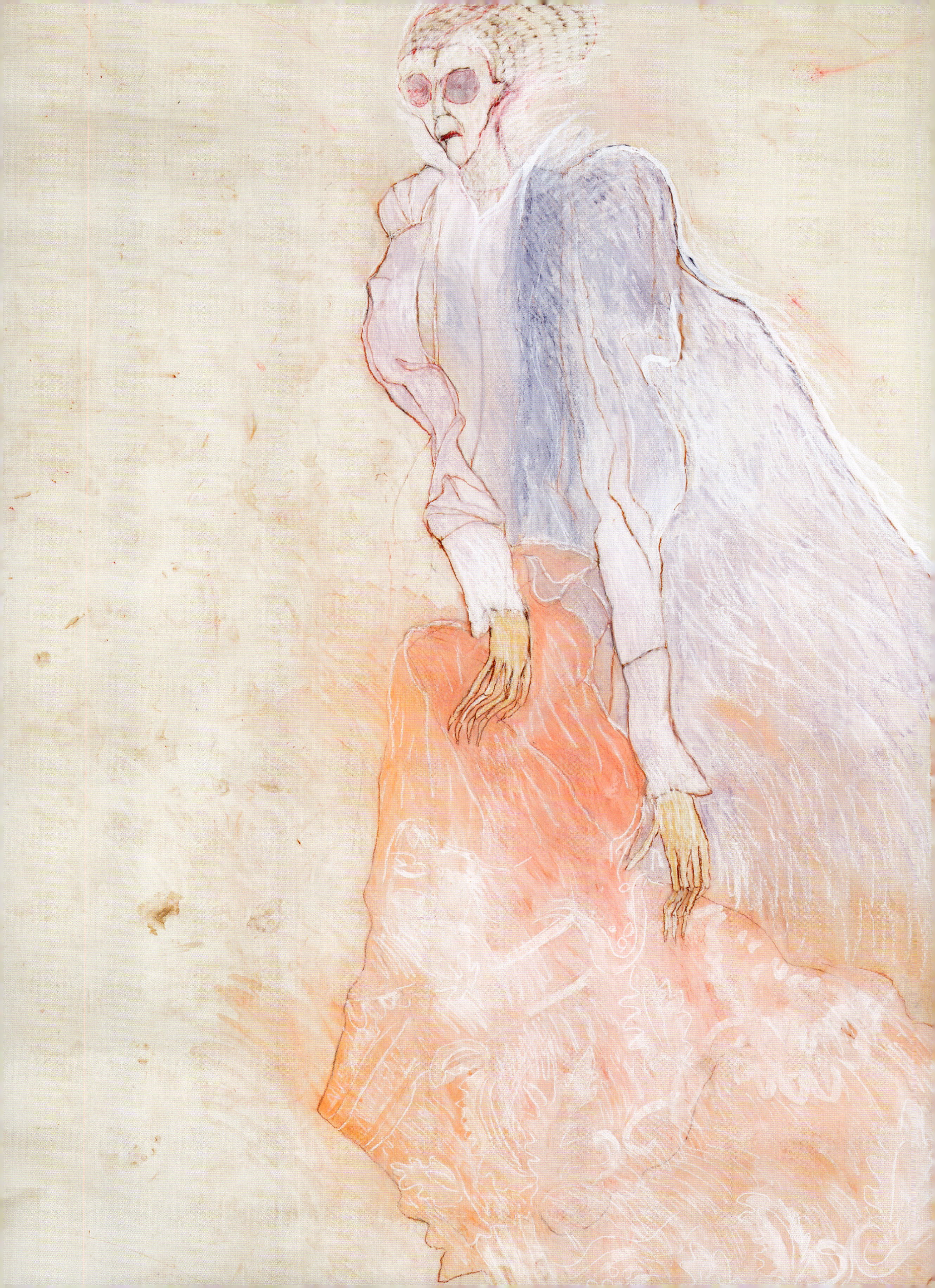

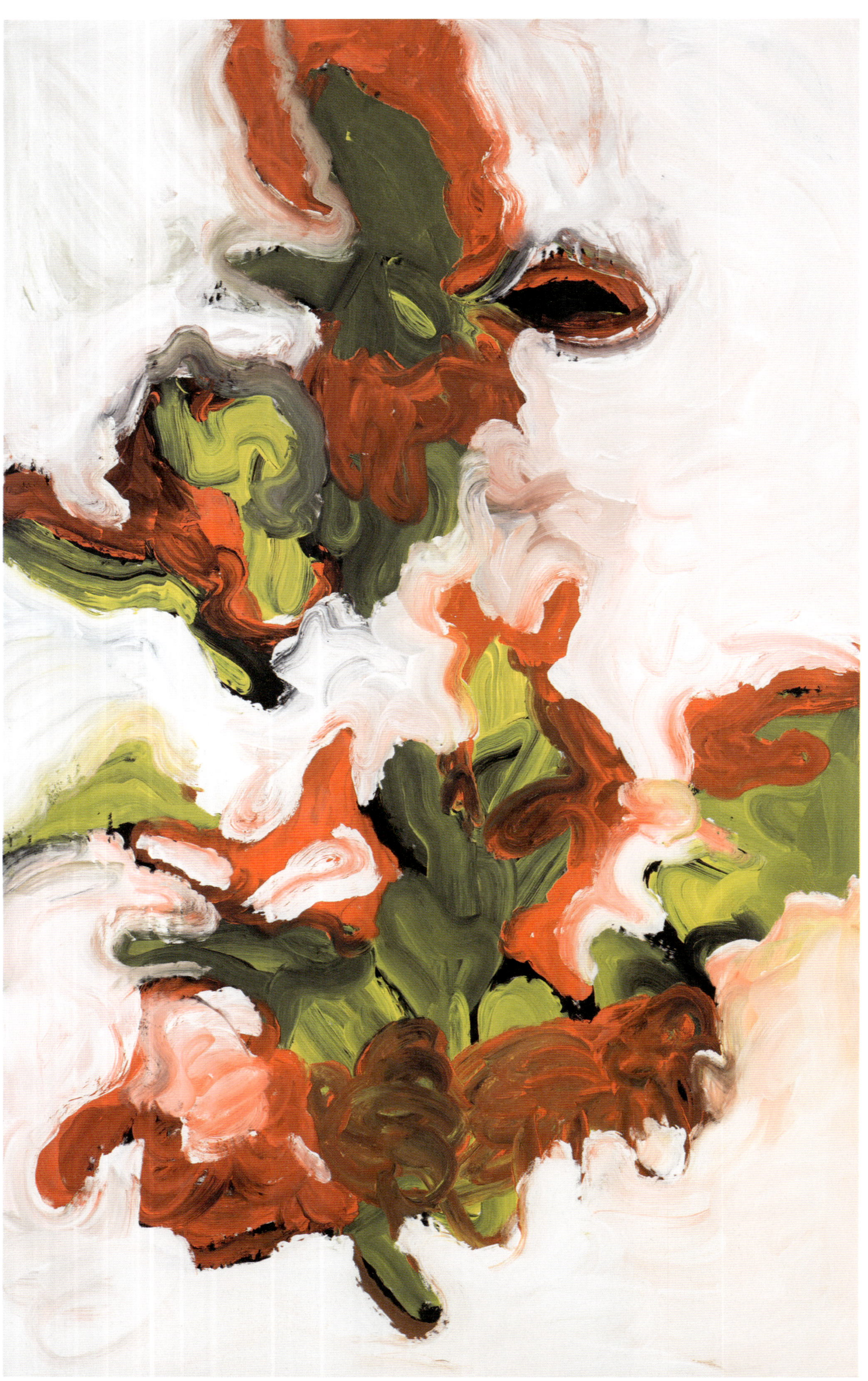

What is behind that curtain?
n.d. (probably 1984)
acrylic on canvas
c. 241 x 148cm

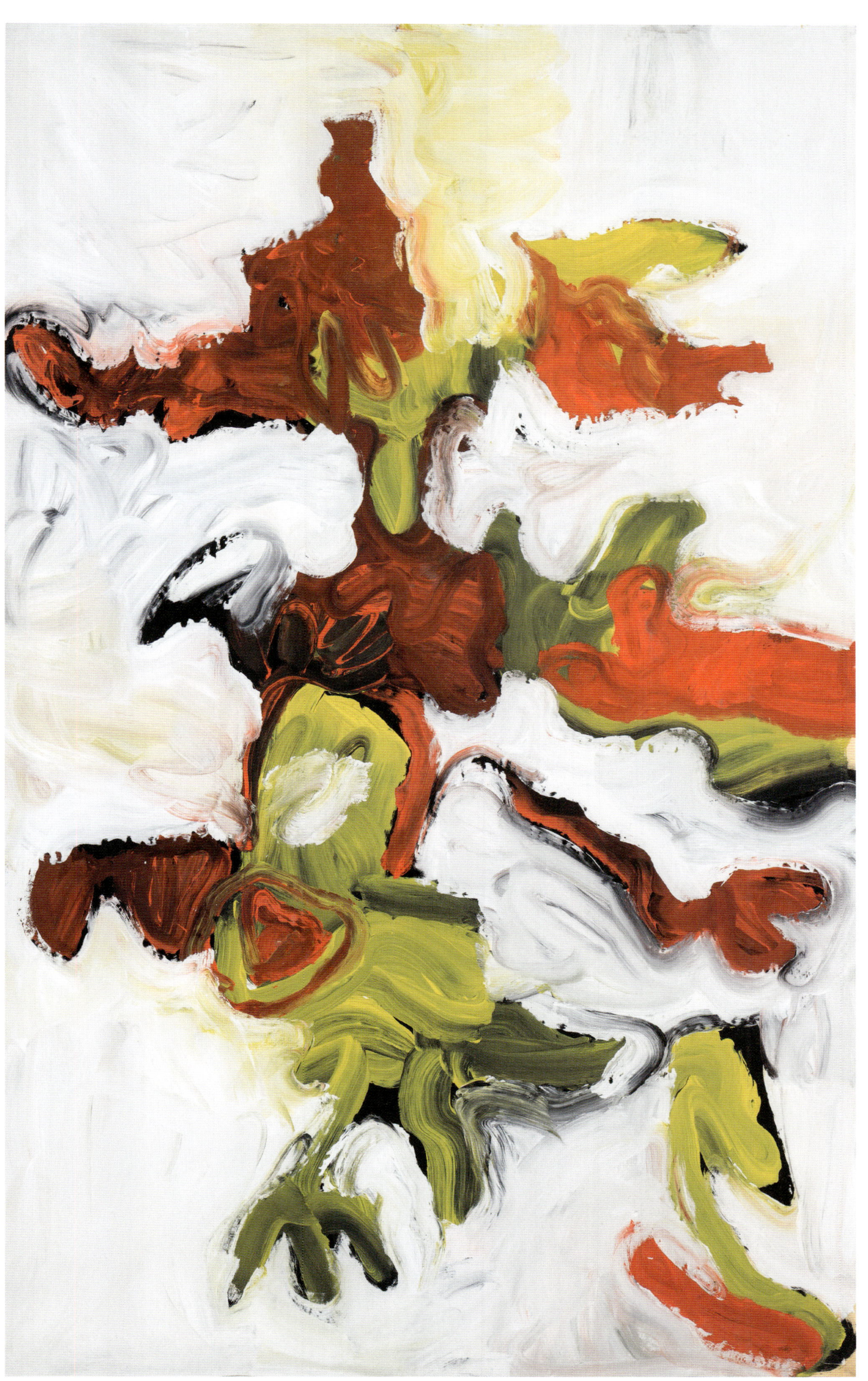

What is behind that curtain?
n.d. (probably 1984)
acrylic on canvas
c. 245.5 x 150cm

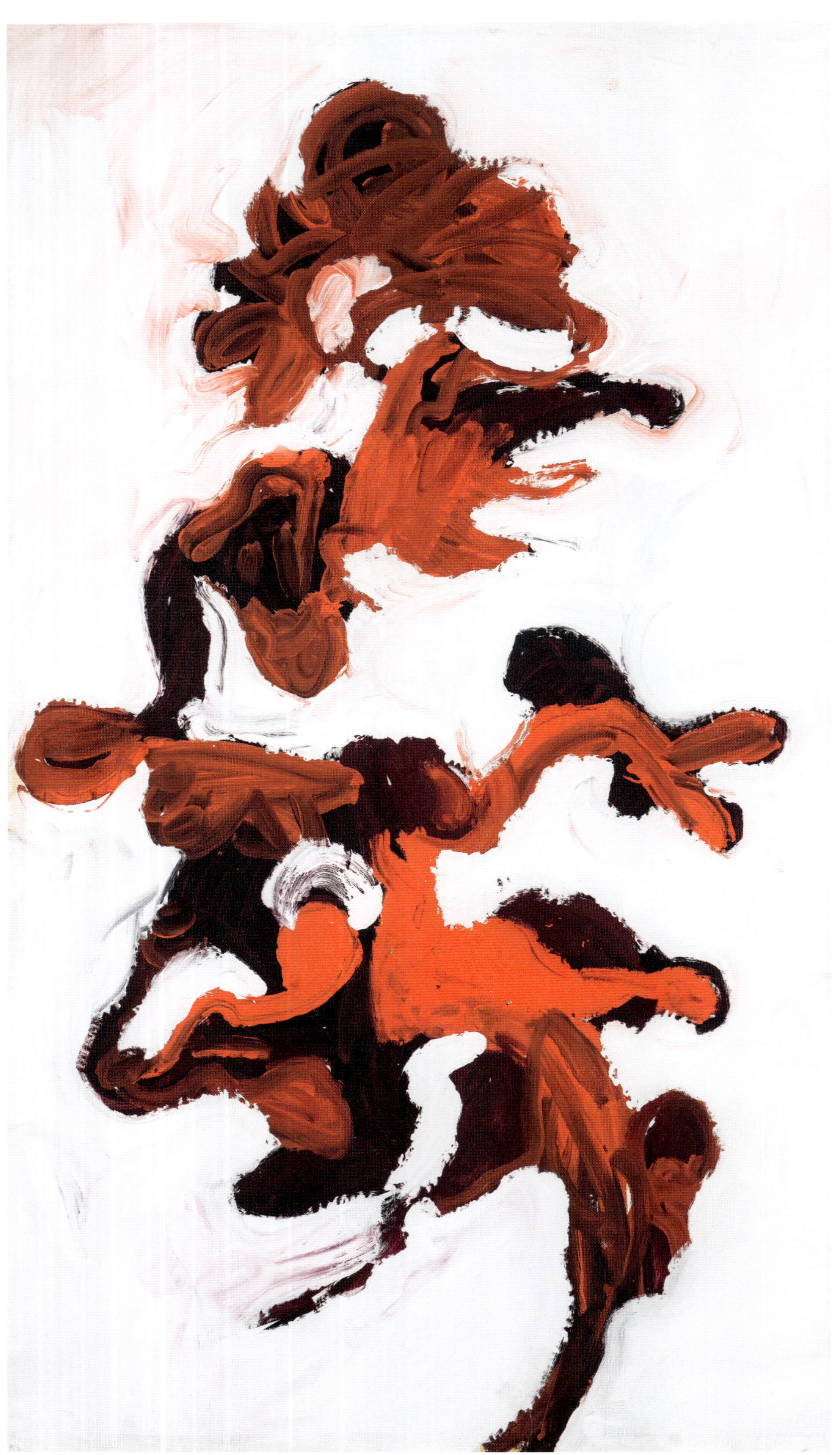

What is behind that curtain?
n.d. (probably 1984)
acrylic on canvas
c. 243 x 148cm

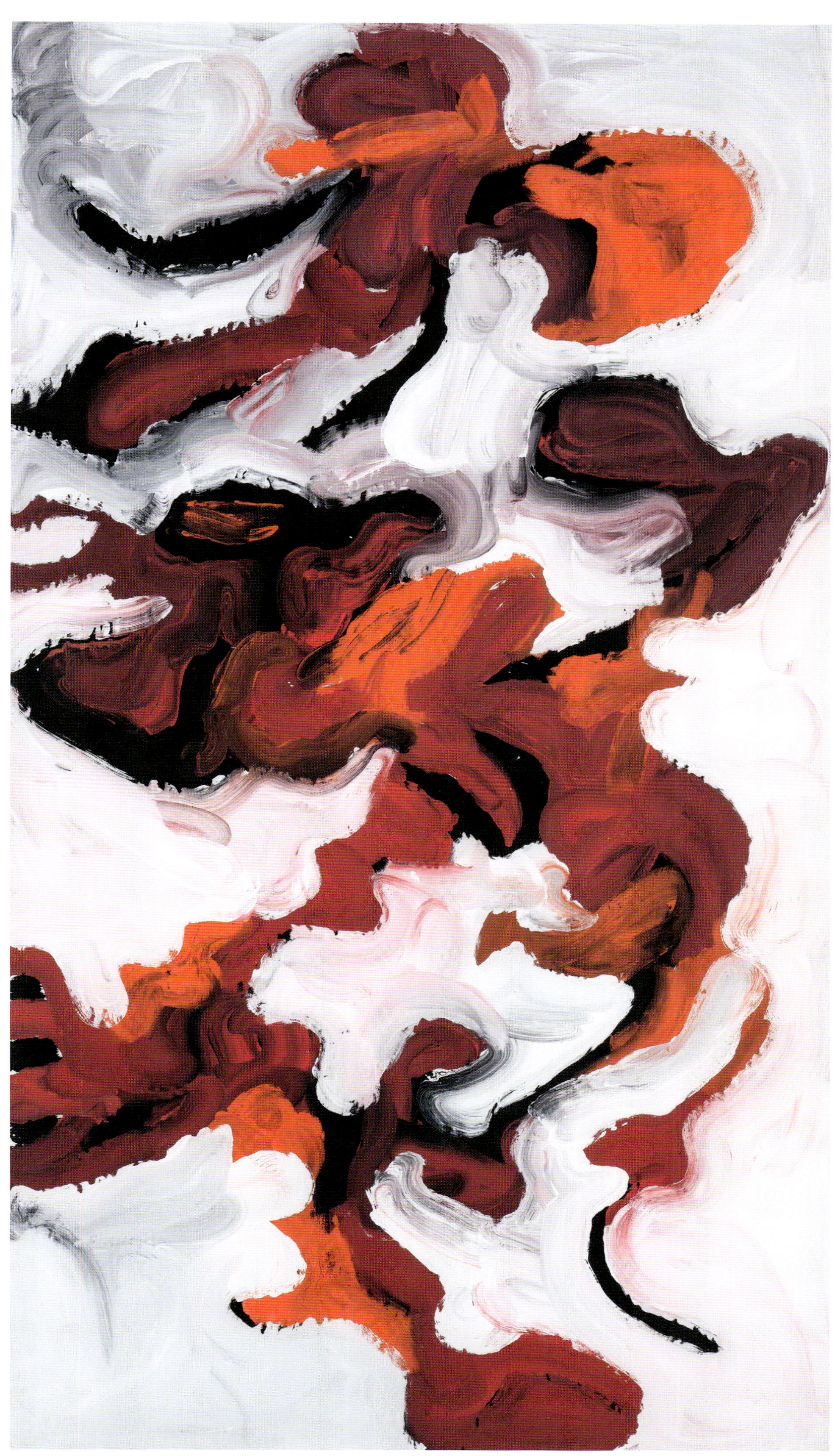

What is behind that curtain?
n.d. (probably 1984)
acrylic on canvas
c. 274 x 148 cm

DAS LÄCHELN DES DON GIOVANNI ODER WARUM ICH AUCH LIEBER NICHT DIE NACHTIGALL DES JAPANISCHEN KAISERS SEIN MÖCHTE[1]

BY MARIANNE EIGENHEER

Sehen Sie, so einfach ist das gar nicht, Ihnen zu erklären, was es denn mit diesen einfachen blauen, roten und goldenen Linien auf sich hat, mit Don Giovanni und so. Sie fragen mich auch immer wieder, warum um Himmelswillen ich denn in letzter Zeil beinahe obsessiv nur auf Papier arbeite, da ich doch auch ebensogut mit Bronze oder Leinwand umgehen könne – und hinter vorgehaltener Hand haben Sie mir auch verraten, dass es doch gerade heute, in postmoderner Zeit, sehr unklug sei, so unprätentios zu arbeiten – jawohl, das weiss ich ja alles, und vielleicht auch noch ein bisschen mehr, als Sie sich es vorstellen können, aber sehen Sie, warum ich trotzdem bei meinem „armen" Material bleibe und damit vielleicht verpasse, in lhre Sammlung von handfesten wertbeständigen Meisterwerken zu kommen ... kennen Sie übrigens das Andersensche Märchen von der chinesischen Nachtigall?

Vor einigen Jahren glaubte ich, für mich einen Weg gefunden zu haben, mein Leben, meine Erfahrungen wirklich in meine Arbeit einzubinden, um in einer eigenen visuellen Sprache sprechen zu können, d.h. um mit anderen Menschen einen Dialog aufzunehmen. (Es war die Zeit, wo viele Frauen dasselbe versuchten und davon berichteten und wo für die Berichte auch Interesse und Platz vorhanden war.) Ich hatte für mich das Bild der tanzenden griechischen Königstochter Ariadne vor Augen, die keine Heldenfiguren mehr braucht, keinen heiligen Lukas mehr, der sie malt, da sie das nun selber tun will und kann.[2] Ich stellte mir vor, dass es mir gelingen konnte, das singende Vokabular der Frauen zu finden, das Vokabular, das helfen konnte, die starren, begrifflichen, bereits zu bekannten Bilderdefinitionen in lebendige sprechende Gegenwartsbilder für heutige Menschen zu verwandeln. Ich fühlte mich zum ersten Mal frei, wie ein Vogel, und ich war glücklich darüber. Auch andere Menschen schienen mich nun zu verstehen, waren interessiert, was ich machte, ich konnte die entstehenden Arbeiten auch zeigen.

Doch irgendwas stimmte einfach nicht ... Es ging mir wie dem Vogel im Märchen, der sich unendlich freut, an den Hof des Kaisers zu kommen, weil er glaubt, dass dies das Höchste sei. „... Ja die Nachtigall machte wahrlich ihr Glück. Sie sollte nun bei Hofe bleiben, ihr eigenes Bauer und ihre Freiheit haben, zweimal des Tages und einmal des Nachts herausspazieren. Sie bekam dann zwölf Diener mit, welche ihr alle ein Seidenband um das Bein geschlungen hatten ünd sie gut festhielten. Es war durchaus kein Vergnügen bei einem solchen Ausfluge ..."[3]

In den nächsten Jahren lernte auch ich dieses Hofleben immer besser kennen, und es waren nicht nur die goldenen Seidenbänder, die einschnitten. Ich lernte, dass es vor allem das Singen war, das

DON GIOVANNI'S SMILE, OR WHY I ALSO PREFER NOT TO BE THE JAPANESE EMPEROR'S NIGHTINGALE[1]

You see, it is not so easy to explain to you what these simple blue, red and gold lines have to do with Don Giovanni and all that. Over and over, too, you ask me why (for Christ's sake) I have recently worked exclusively and almost obsessively on paper – since I could, after all, just as well handle bronze or canvas. And behind closed doors you have also shared with me that it is very ill-advised to work so unpretentiously, especially these days, in our postmodern age. Yes, yes, I know all that, and perhaps even a little more than you can imagine. But look, as to why I still stick with my "poor" material and in doing so possibly miss out on appearing in your collection of tangible masterpieces of lasting value... Well, anyway, do you know Hans Christian Andersen's fairy tale about the Chinese nightingale?

A few years ago I believed that I had found a way of truly integrating my life and my experiences into my work, of being able to speak my own visual language – in other words, of starting up a dialogue with other people. (It was the time when many women were trying the same thing and telling others about it, and there was interest and space for their narratives.) I had for myself a mental image of the dancing Greek princess Ariadne, who no longer needs any hero figures, no longer needs Luke the Evangelist to paint her, because now she wants, and is able, to do it herself.[2] I imagined that I could succeed in finding the singing vocabulary of women – the vocabulary that could help transform rigid, abstract, over-familiar definitions of images into living, speaking pictures of the present, for the people of today. For the first time I felt free as a bird – and happy to be so. Other people, too, seemed to understand me; they were interested in what I was doing. I could even display the resulting works.

Yet something simply wasn't right... I was like the bird in the fairy tale, who takes endless joy in coming to the

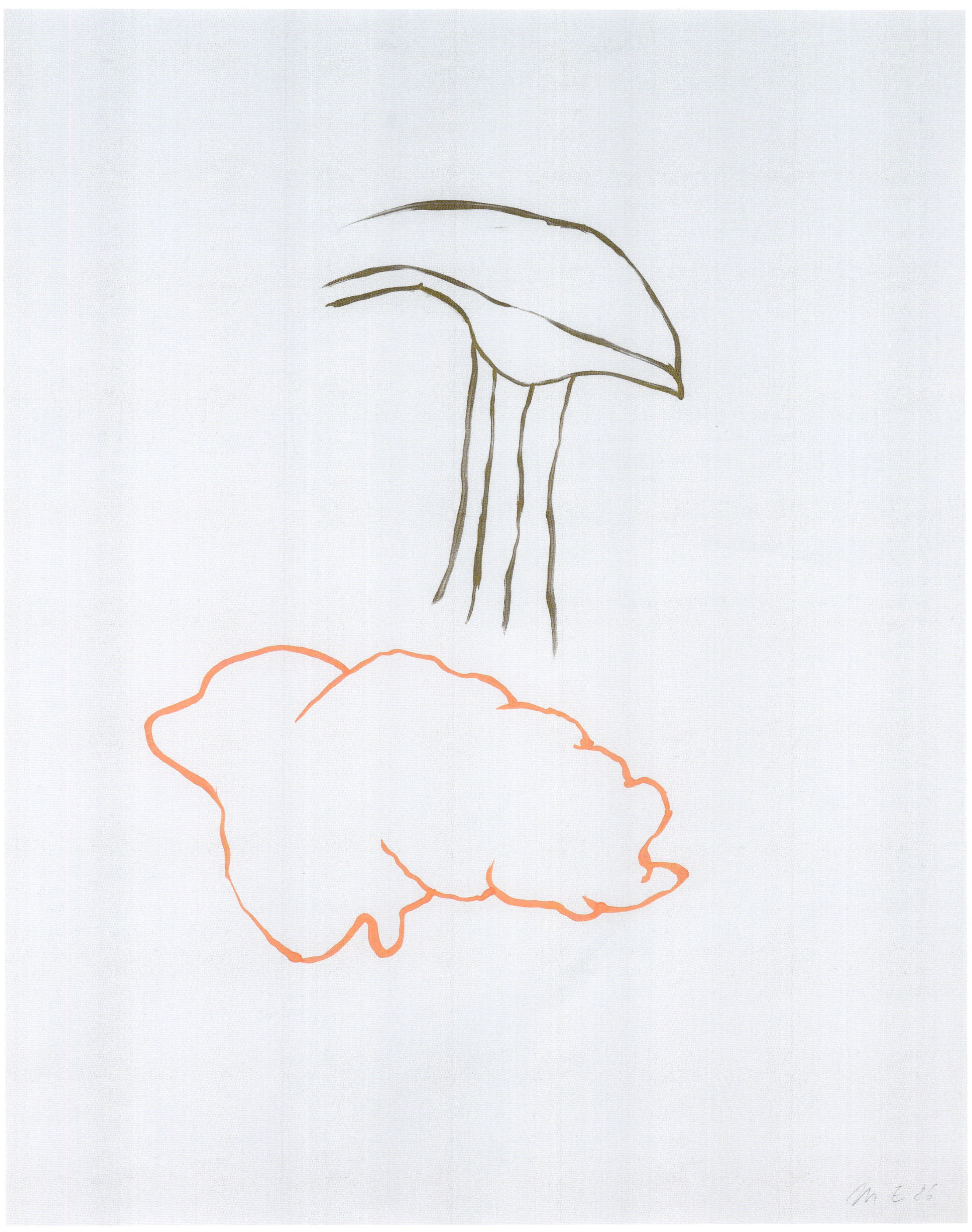

Untitled, 1986
mixed media on paper, 100 x 74cm

The formal language of this work is based on Marianne's 1986 series *Il sorriso di Don Giovanni*.

"Are you now better able to understand why, while working, it's all the same to me – rather, it must be a matter of irrelevance to me – whether my works do or do not end up in your collection of masterpieces?"

„Können Sie sich nun besser vorstellen, warum es mir eigentlich während des Arbeitens egal ist, gleichgültig sein muss, ob meine Arbeiten nun in Ihrer Sammlung von Meisterwerken landen oder nicht?"

eigentlich gar nicht so gerne gehört wurde, man stelle sich bei Hofe doch etwas ziemlich anderes vor. „Es war eine künstliche Nachtigall, die der lebendigen gleichen sollte, aber überall mit Diamanten, Rubinen und Saphiren besetzt war. Sobald man den Kunstvogel aufzog, konnte er eines der Stücke singen, die der wirkliche Vogel sang; und dann bewegte sich der Schwanz auf und nieder und glänzte von Silber und Gold. Um den Hals hing ein kleines Band, darauf stand geschrieben ‚Die Nachtigall des Kaisers von Japan ist arm gegen die des Kaisers von China'. ‚Das ist herrlich', sagten alle, und die beiden Vögel mussten nun zusammen singen, aber es wollte nicht richtig gehen, denn die wirkliche Nachtigall sang auf ihre eigene Weise und der Kunstvogel ging auf Walzen. Nun sollte der Kunstvogel allein singen. Er machte ebenso sein Glück wie der wirkliche, und dann war er ja viel niedlicher anzusehen, er glitzerte wie Armbänder und Brustnadeln. Dreiunddreissigmal sang er ein und dasselbe Stück und war doch nicht müde."[4]

Unterdessen flog die echte Nachtigall unbemerkt aus dem Fenster zurück in den Wald, dies störte nur den Kaiser ein bisschen, doch der Hofstaat war zufrieden, denn sie hörten nun zum vierunddreissigsten Mal dasselbe Stück. Sie konnten es doch noch nicht ganz auswendig, denn es war gar so schwer. Und vor allem, das Beste, man konnte den Kunstvogel öffnen, die Walzen herausnehmen und erklären. Der Spielmeister, der dies konnte, wurde der wichtigste Mann bei Hof.

Ich weiss nicht, ob Sie mich wirklich verstanden haben, was auch mich bewog, wieder in den Wald zurückzufliegen. Ich selbst war mir damals nicht klar darüber, es war ein noch unbestimmtes Unbehagen, das Tag und Nacht da war, was mich am Atmen, am Leben hinderte. Die Jahre waren lang, bis ich dahinter kam, warum ich auch im Wald, weit weg vom Hof, immer noch die goldenen Seidenbänder um die Knöchel geschlungen hatte; den ganzen aalglatten Hofstaat trug ich in mir selbst herum! Es waren also nicht nur diese Personen und Umstände, die nicht wollten, dass ich singen durfte, ich musste diese bei mir selbst suchen gehen. Theoretisch war mir das alles bald einmal ganz klar, aber begreifen Sie, das bringt beinahe gar nichts. Und das Allerschlimmste war, zu entdecken, dass ich gar nicht wirklich singen konnte, dass andere Menschen ernsthaft glaubten, mich singen zu hören, doch ich wusste es nun besser. So waren die letzten Jahre sehr schwierig und die Bilder, die trotzdem entstanden, oft traurig oder auch, wie Sie es zu nennen beliebten, ohne offensichtliche Energie. Nur merkwürdig fand ich dann doch, dass dabei Bilder waren, die Ihnen die Haut aufritzen konnten, vor deren Lebendigkeit Sie beinahe davonlaufen mussten? Wie auch immer, ich hatte mir einzugestehen, dass ich in bestem Glauben auf mich selbst reingefallen war und nochmals an den Anfang zurück musste. Das war verdammt mühsam. Rundherum wandelte sich nun auch noch die Zeit. Postmoderne war angesagt, auch für die Frauen. Es schien besser zu gehen, wenn man nicht genau hinschaute, welchen Preis der Anpassung dafür die Künstlerinnen bereit waren zu zahlen. Auch mir ging es eigentlich sehr gut, und ich hatte mich wohl auch einschläfern lassen, wenn mich mein eigener Weg nicht zu ungehinderter Ehrlichkeit mir selbst gegenüber gezwungen hätte. Ich liess mich auch nicht damit beruhigen, dass nun Frauen sogar hin und wieder in kunstwissenschaftlichen Texten auftauchten. Haben Sie das alles einmal daraufhin wirklich durchgelesen? Was da Wesentliches ausgesagt wird? Doch das ist wieder eine andere Geschichte für sich, und ich will mich auf diejenige von Don Giovanni beschränken. Ich will Sie nicht langweilen und erzählen, wie ich nun dazu gekommen bin, mich mit dieser Figur zu beschäftigen. Es war auf jeden Fall ein langer und steiniger Weg, an das Geheimnis, das in dieser Geschichte enthalten ist, heranzukommen. Ein Geheimnis lässt

emperor's court, because he thinks this the highest honour. "Certainly, the nightingale was a success. She was to stay at court now, had her own cage and her own freedom. She could go out for walks twice a day and once a night. With her would go twelve attendants, each of whom held tight to a silk ribbon fastened to the bird's leg. There was no pleasure at all to be taken in such excursions..."[3]

Over the following years I too got to know this courtly lifestyle better and better, and it was not just the golden silk ribbons that cut into me. I learned that, above all, it was the singing that people did not actually like to hear so much; one imagined something quite different at court. "Then an artificial nightingale arrived, which resembled the living one but was studded all over with diamonds, rubies and sapphires. As soon as you wound up the fake bird, it could sing one of the pieces which the real bird sang, and then its tail moved up and down, glittering silver and gold. Around its neck there hung a small ribbon, on which was written 'the nightingale of the Emperor of Japan is a poor one compared to the Emperor of China's'. Everyone said that this was splendid, and that the two birds had to sing together. But it didn't work properly, since the real nightingale sang in its own way and the fake bird ran on mechanical drums. Now the fake bird had to sing alone. It had just as much success as the real one and was certainly much prettier to look at; it sparkled, like bracelets and brooches do. It sang the same tune 33 times and still was not tired."[4]

Meanwhile the real nightingale flew out of the window, unnoticed, and back to the forest. This bothered the emperor somewhat, but the court were content with hearing the same tune for the 34th time (they did not quite know it by heart yet, because it was so difficult). And the best of all was that you could open up the fake bird, take out the mechanical drums and explain their workings. The music master who could do this became the most important man at court.

I don't know whether you have properly understood me — what motivated me, too, to fly back to the forest. It was not clear in my own mind at the time; it was an indeterminate unease, present day and night, and which stopped me from breathing, from living. It was several years until I figured out why I still had the golden silk ribbons around my ankles — in the forest as well, far away from court. I was carrying the whole slippery retinue around inside me! It wasn't just these people and situations that didn't want me to sing; I had to go looking for that impulse in myself. In theory that was all quite clear to me at once, but you must understand that this barely did any good. And the very worst of it was the discovery that I really was not able to sing; that other people genuinely believed they heard me singing, but that I now knew better.

So the last few years were very difficult and the pictures that came into being, despite everything, were often sad or else — as you loved to put it — without palpable

sich nicht erklären, doch wenn Sie sich Mozarts Musik anhören, ist es da: Vor allem kommt es auf die Szene an, in der der steinerne Kontur zu Besuch kommt und Don Giovanni, nachdem er dem Gast die Hand gegeben hat, in die Hölle fährt, doch musikalisch wird gleichzeitig eine andere Geschichte erzählt! Diese Geschichte nun ist für diejenigen wichtig, die auf der Suche sind nach einer lebendigen Sprache, welcher Ausdrucksmittel sich diese auch immer bedient. Mir selbst wurde vieles klar: Ich hatte mir vorgestellt, dass ich viele der Mechanismen kennen würde, die mich daran hinderten, wirklich als freie Künstlerin arbeiten zu können, doch dachte ich vor allem daran, den Körper, die Gefühle, die sozialen Beziehungen zu befreien. Ich fragte mich nie, ob ich denn meinen Geist, den Verstand und den Intellekt wirklich zur Verfügung hatte, da ich dies alles dauernd benutzen konnte. So müssen Sie sich mein Entsetzen vorstellen, als ich in diesen Räumen, die ich als die meinen empfunden hatte, nun eine ganze Schar von steinernen Gästen vorfand, eben einen ganzen grauen Hofstaat, wie Denkmäler standen sie herum. Es waren zu Stein gewordene Ideen, Vorstellungen, die von vielerlei Autoritäten hier abgestellt worden waren, und ich konnte nichts anderes tun, als zu ihnen hinaufzuschauen. Vieles war da, das ich selbst als richtig empfand, doch merkte ich, dass diese Steinfiguren mit beeinflussten, auch wenn ich wusste, dass es nicht so war. Ich konnte nicht selbst entscheiden, weder im Guten noch im Bösen, die Angst vor den steinernen Gästen war zu gross. Don Giovannis Geschichte erzählte mir nun, dass es eine Zeit gibt, wo diese steinernen Figuren noch lebendig sind, das Recht haben, dir Eindruck zu machen, dass aber der Punkt kommt, wo du lernen musst, nicht gegen sie zu kämpfen sondern sie als Gleichgestellte zu verabschieden, und das ist sehr schwer. Ich glaube, das ist einer der unheimlichen Augenblicke des Lebens, wenn du vor deinem steinernen Gast stehst und er dir die Hand anbietet, und du weisst, damit kannst du zur Hölle fahren, oder vielleicht auch nicht, denn das ist die Geschichte Don Giovannis, dass er in dem Augenblick, wo er die Hand des Vaters ergreift im vollen Bewusstsein, was alles geschehen kann, er eben nicht in die Hölle der ewigen Jugendlichkeit fällt, sondern als erwachsener endlicher Mensch dasteht. Was das denn nun wieder mit Kunst zu tun habe, wollen Sie wissen. Ich glaube, sehr viel. Denn erst jetzt, wo ich weiss, wie ich auftauchende Direktiven, Vorstellungen die mir aufgesetzt erscheinen, hinterfragen kann, ohne mich dann immer danach richten zu müssen, habe ich einen eigentlichen Freiraum für meine eigene Arbeit, denn Sie können sich nicht vorstellen, wie stark auch in der „freien" Kunst, solche inneren und äusseren Direktiven sind. Denken Sie z.B. nur einmal an so einfache Sachen wie Zentralperspektive, an Gegenständlichkeit, an Inhalte, an das, was ein Bild ausmacht oder nicht, lauter steinerne Gäste im Haus ... von den eigenen Vorstellungen gar nicht zu reden. Erst heute, mit meinen einfachen Linien, die ich mir nicht mehr zuerst „absegnen" lassen muss, kann ich nun ohne Widerspruch das tun, was ich schon lange tun wollte, ich versuche ganz einfach, Dinge wie Körpergefühle, Sehnsüchte, Bewegungen, Beziehungsmuster, alles Dinge, die eigentlich kaum in Worte zu fassen sind, visuell in Erscheinung treten zu lassen, also all das, was mich ganz direkt jeden Tag berührt, bedroht, beschäftigt, und das nicht direkt über ganz konkrete Begriffe läuft, da es viel zu vielfaltig ist, alles Lebendige nämlich. Damit komme ich auch endlich zum Singen, da ist auch nie nur ein Ton befestigt, da schwingen viele mit, die alle zusammen die Bewegungen der Melodien begleiten. Was ich vorher machen konnte, war wie eine gute Illustration davon, wie das Nach-Singen einer Melodie, die man bereits gerade gehört hat. Es wird mir natürlich auch beim millionsten Versuch nicht gelingen, an alles, was ich ausdrücken

energy. Yet I then found it strange that there were pictures which could cut open your skin, pictures from whose vibrancy you almost had to run away... Anyway, I had to admit that I had fooled myself in good faith and once again had to go back to the start. That was damn tedious. All around the times were changing now too: post-modernism was the order of the day, even for women. It seemed to get better, if you didn't look too closely at what the price of conformity was, and that women artists were prepared to pay. Things went very well even for me in fact, and I probably would have let myself be lulled to sleep if my own path had not forced me into unrestricted honesty with myself. I also did not let myself be pacified by the fact that now women could turn up every so often in books on art history. Have you ever once read through all these properly in this light? What is said there of any importance? But that is once more another story for you, and I want to restrict myself to the one about Don Giovanni.

I do not want to bore you and recount how I came to occupy myself with this character. In any case, it was a long and stony path to arrive at the mystery that is contained within this story. A mystery defies explanation, but when you listen to Mozart's music, it's there. It appears primarily in the scene in which the Stone Guest comes to visit and Don Giovanni, after he has given this guest his hand to shake, goes down to hell — and yet at the same time the music tells a different story! Now this story is important for those on the search for a living language, independently of which it might use the means of expression. Many things became clear to me. I had imagined that I would know lots of the mechanisms that stopped me from being able to work as a truly free artist, and yet I thought above all about freeing my body, my feelings and my social relations. I never asked myself if my spirit, my mind and my intellect were really at my command since I was able to use them all continuously.

So you must imagine my horror, as I now came upon a whole crowd of Stone Guests in these rooms that I had thought of as mine — a whole grey court, even, standing around like memorials. They were ideas and concepts turned to stone — concepts which had been suppressed by authorities of various kinds — and I could do nothing other than look up at them. There was much there that I perceived as right, yet I noticed that these stone figures exerted an influence, even though I knew that this was not the case. I could not make up my mind, neither for good nor evil; the fear of the Stone Guests was too great. The story of Don Giovanni tells me that there is a time when these stone figures are still living and have the right to make an impression on me, but that there is a point coming where I must learn not to fight against them but rather to part with them as equals, and that is very hard. I believe that it is one of the uncanny moments of life when you stand before your Stone Guest, and he offers you his hand — and you know that as a result you can go to hell, but then again perhaps not. Because that is the story of Don Giovanni: in that moment, when he grasps the father-statue's hand in full

möchte, heranzukommen, aber da jede Minute des Lebens wieder so voll an neuen Eindrücken ist, geht mir die Lust nie aus, mit meinen einfachen Linien alldem nachzuspüren. Und dass immer eine goldene Linie dabei ist, hat den Grund, dass Gold als Material und nicht nur als Farbe kontrastiert, und damit habe ich noch etwas dabei, was das Leben ausmacht, es gibt keine genaue Antwort auf eine genaue Frage, es gibt nur die Annäherung daran, das Ähnliche ist nicht das gleiche. Können Sie sich nun besser vorstellen, warum es mir eigentlich während des Arbeitens egal ist, gleichgültig sein muss, ob meine Arbeiten nun in Ihrer Sammlung von Meisterwerken landen oder nicht?

Tokio, Anfang Oktober 1987 [5]

awareness of everything that can happen, it is precisely not that he falls into the hell of eternal youthfulness so much as that he stands there as a fully grown, finite human being.

You want to know what that has got to do with art. A great deal, I think. Because only now – now that I know how to scrutinise emerging directives and ideas that seem to me insincere, without then having to conform to them – only now do I have proper breathing space for my own work. Because you cannot imagine how powerful such internal and external directives are, even in "free art". For example, think just for a moment of such simple things as central perspective, representationalism, content; of that which constitutes a painting or not, nothing but Stone Guests in the house, not to mention one's own imaginings. Only now, with my basic lines that I no longer need to get initially "approved", can I do what I have long wanted to do without any objections. Very simply, I try to allow things to manifest themselves visually, things like physical sensations, longings, movements, patterns of relationships; all things that can barely be captured in words, all things that quite directly affect me, threaten me, occupy me, every day and that do not directly function on wholly concrete terms, because they are much too multi-faceted. That is to say: everything living.

In doing this I finally get down to the singing, which never has just the one tone affixed to it, but many, all of which resonate and accompany the movements of the melodies together. What I was able to do previously was like a good illustration of it, like singing along to a melody that you have just heard. Even on the millionth try, I naturally don't succeed in equalling everything that I could express, but since each minute of life is full of new impressions afresh, the passion in me for tracking them all down with my simple lines never runs out. And the reason for there always being a gold line involved is that gold contrasts not just as a colour but also as a material. For this reason something else is present too, something that constitutes life – there is no exact answer to an exact question, only the approximation of one, for similar does not mean the same. Are you now better able to understand why, while working, it's all the same to me – rather, it must be a matter of irrelevance to me – whether my works do or do not end up in your collection of masterpieces?

Tokyo, early October, 1987 [5]

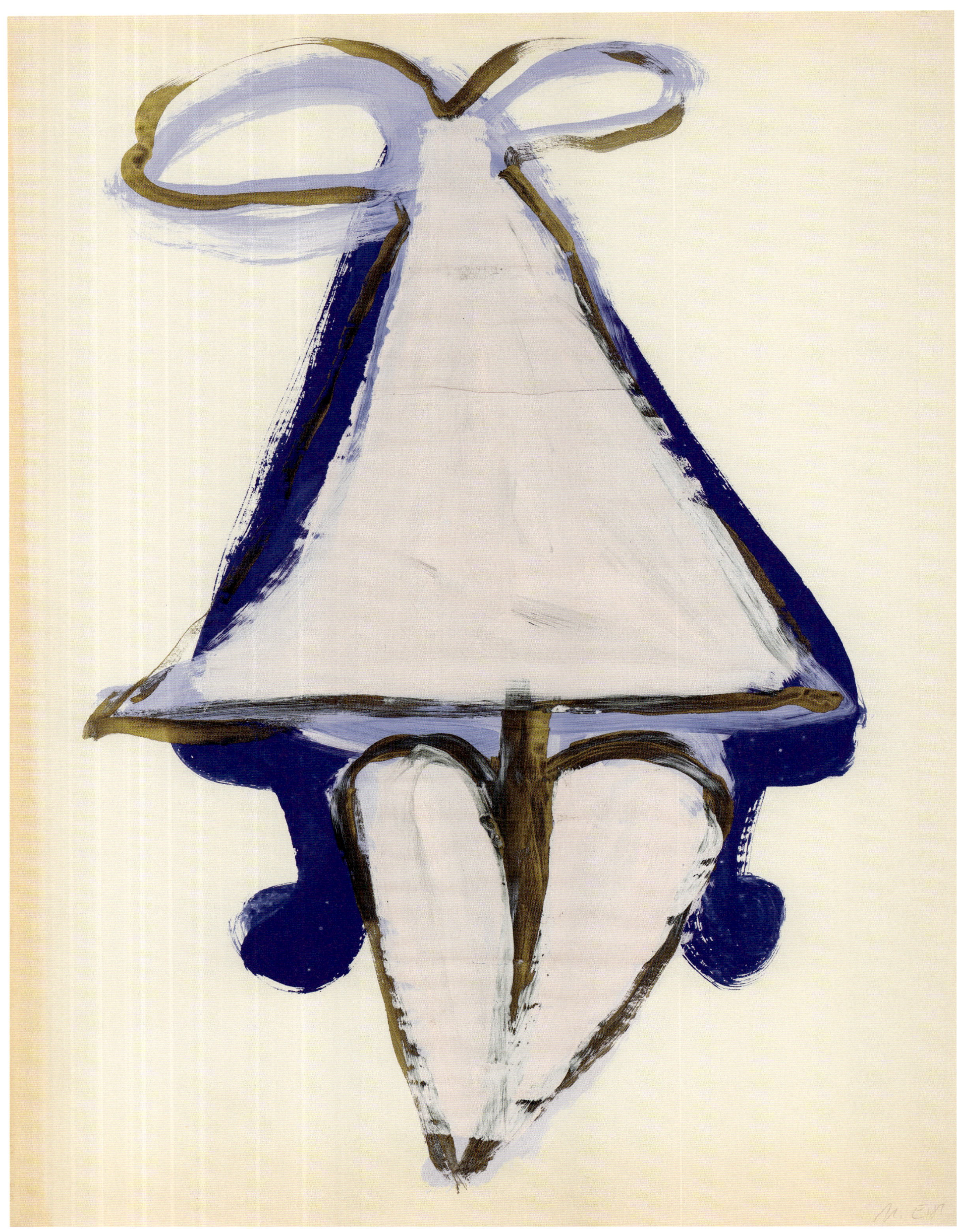

Untitled, n.d. (probably 1970s–80s)
mixed media on paper, 80 x 60cm

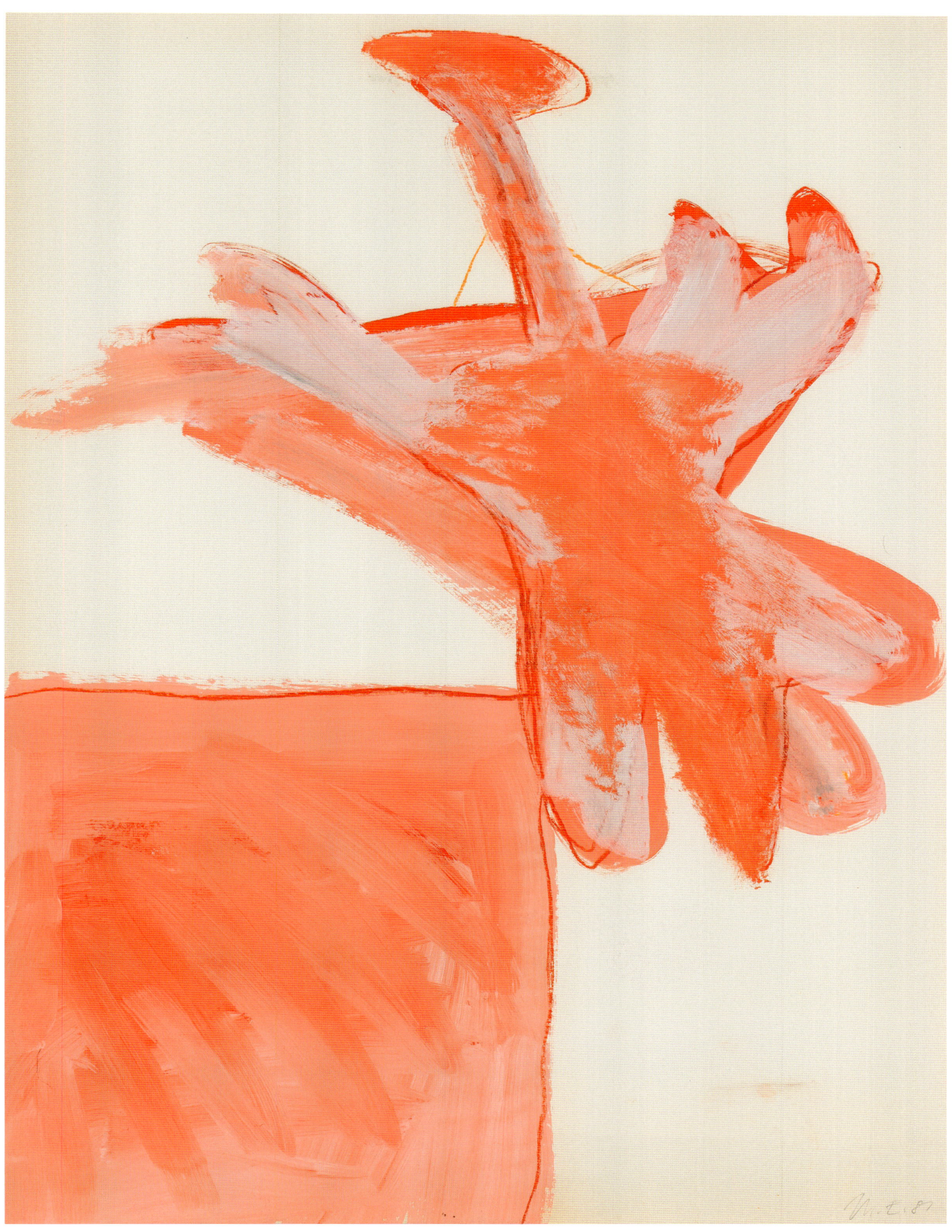

Untitled, 1981
mixed media on paper, 80 x 60cm

Lithography from the portfolio Marianne
Eigenheer, Rose Ausländer, 1991, 50 x 35cm

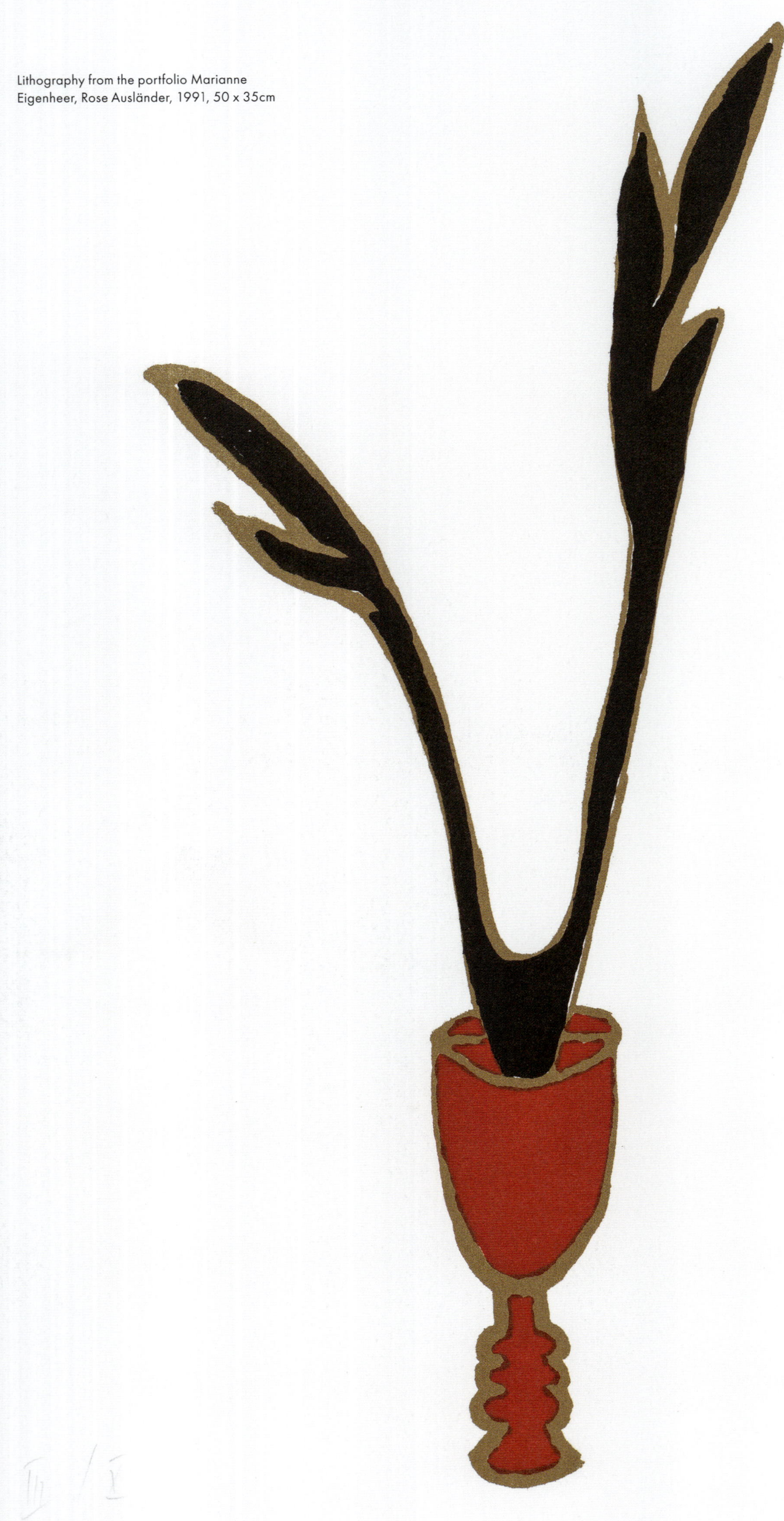

Untitled, 1991
mixed media on paper, 109.5 x 75cm

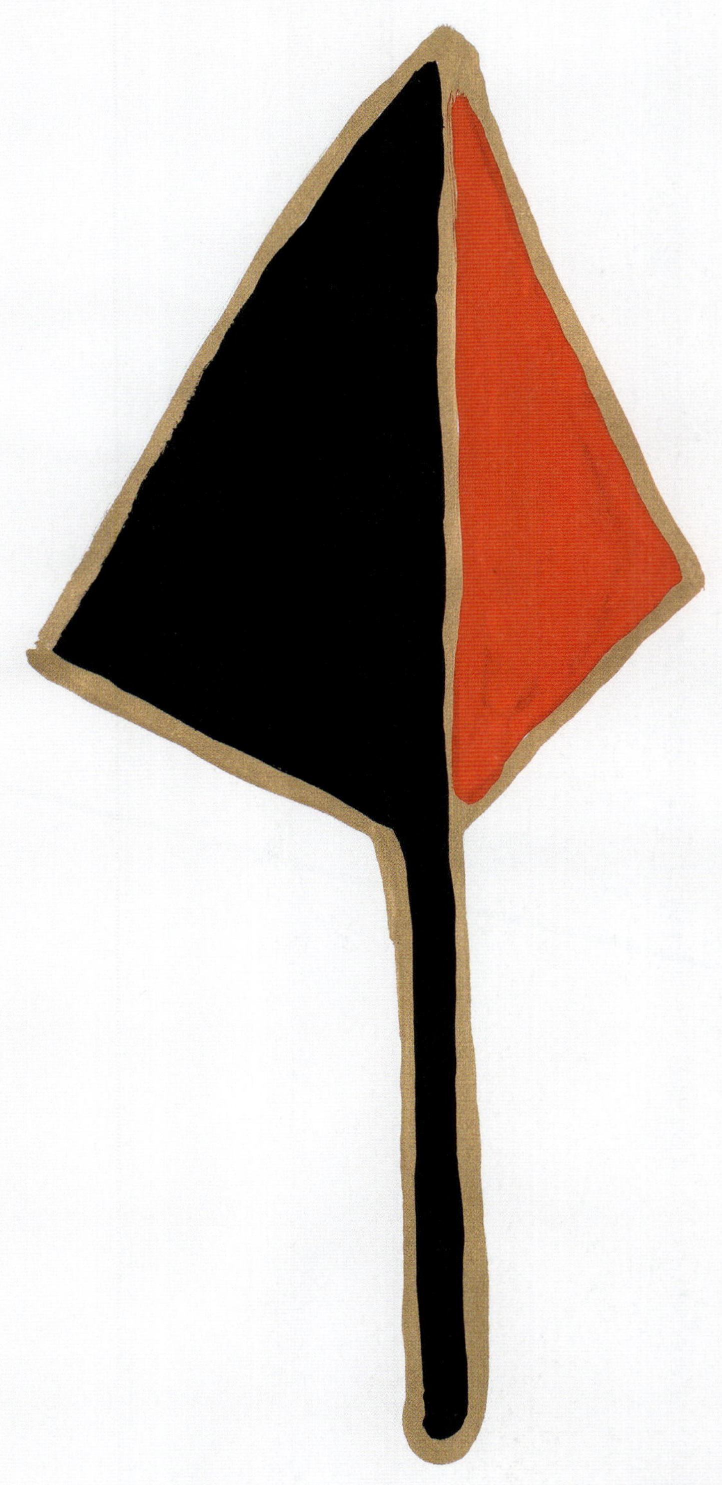

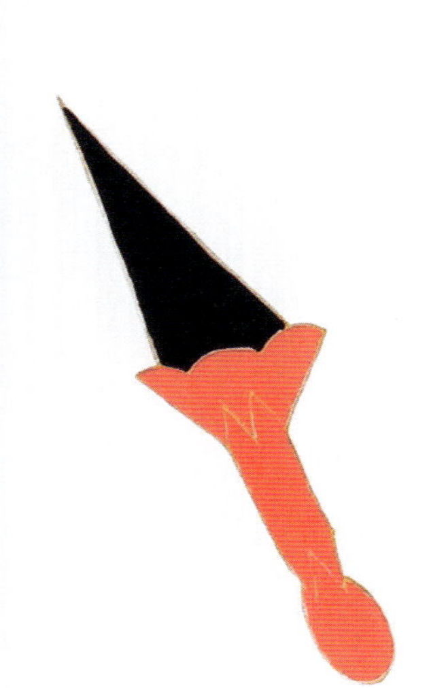

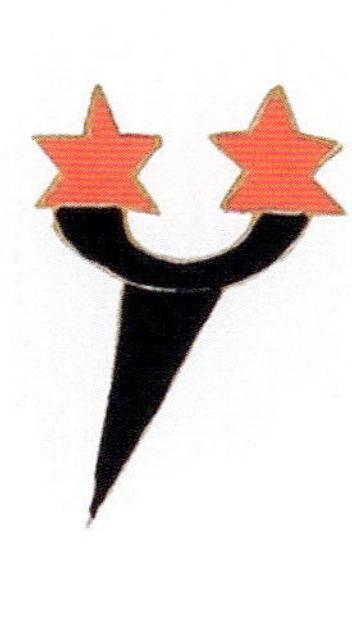

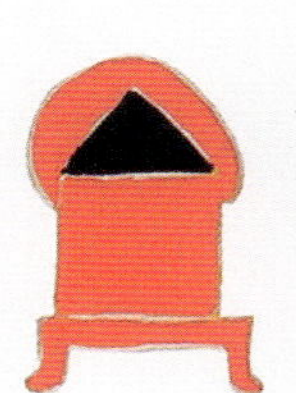

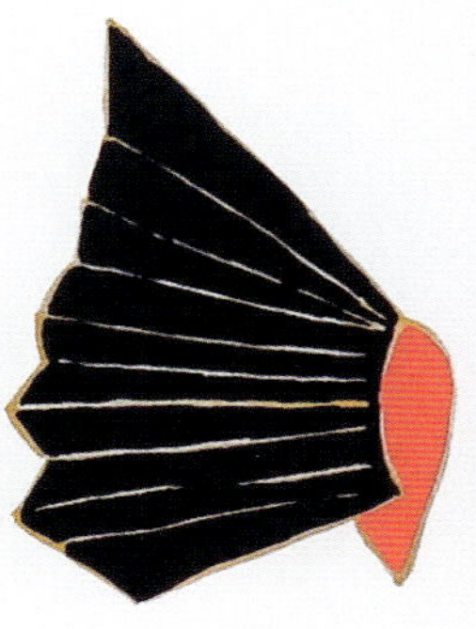

Untitled (I'm not afraid of who you are) (detail)
n.d.
mixed media on paper, c. 325cm x 37.5cm

The formal language of this work corresponds
with the series *Peterchens Mondfahrt*, 1992–94
and *The 5 rings of Musashi*, 1991.

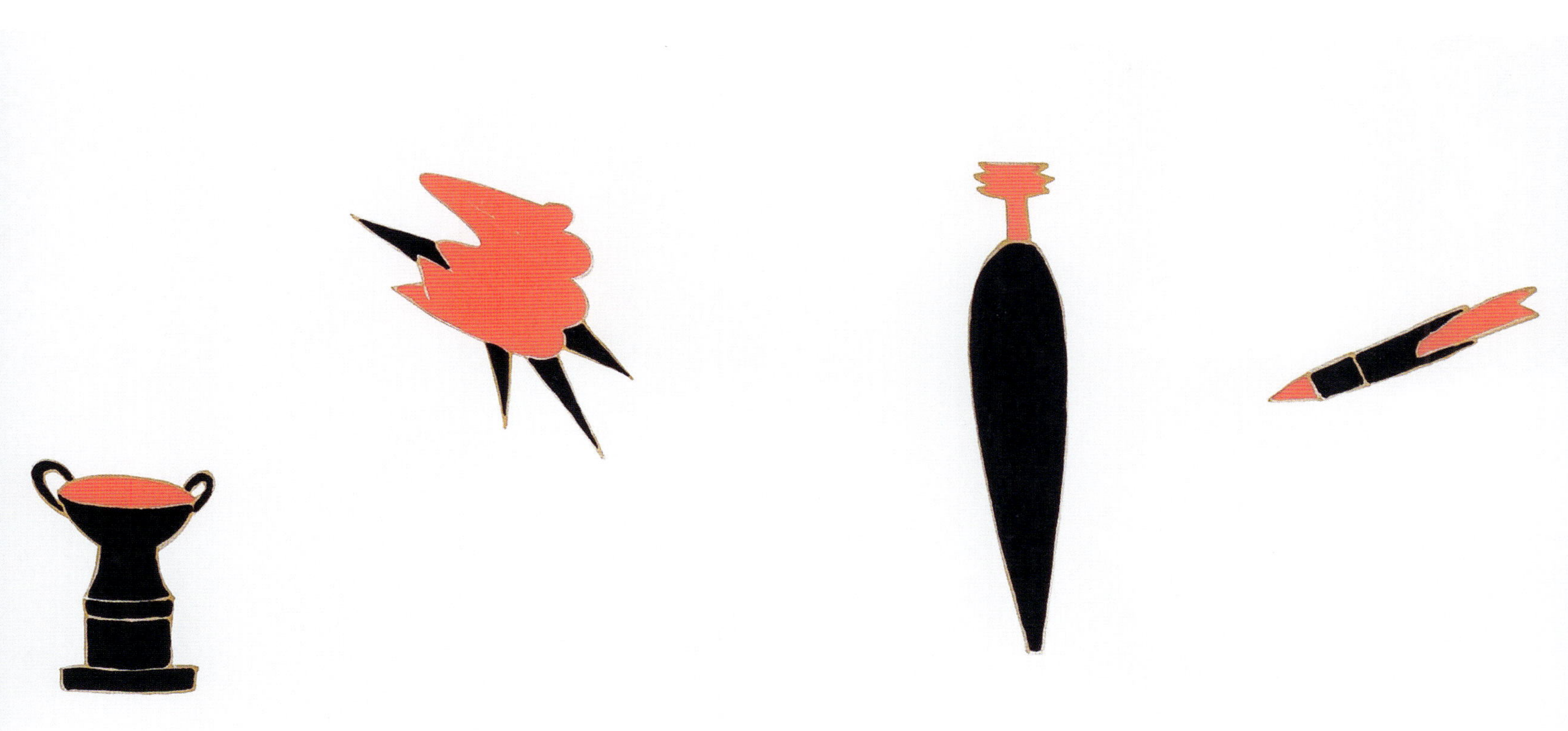

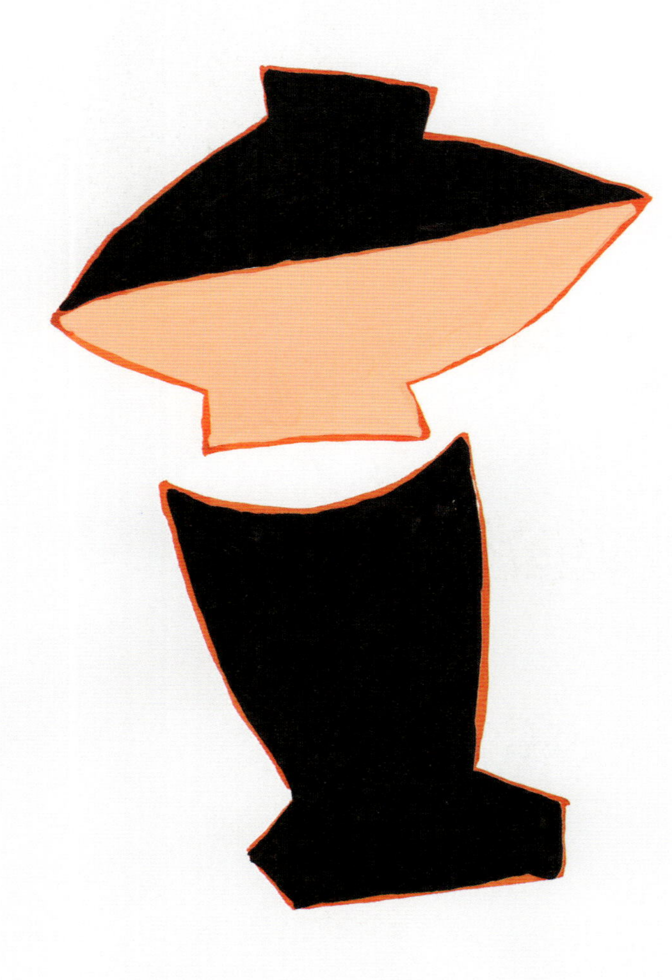

Two works from the series
The one, The other's, The other, 2012
aquarelle on paper, series of five, each 29.5 x 21cm

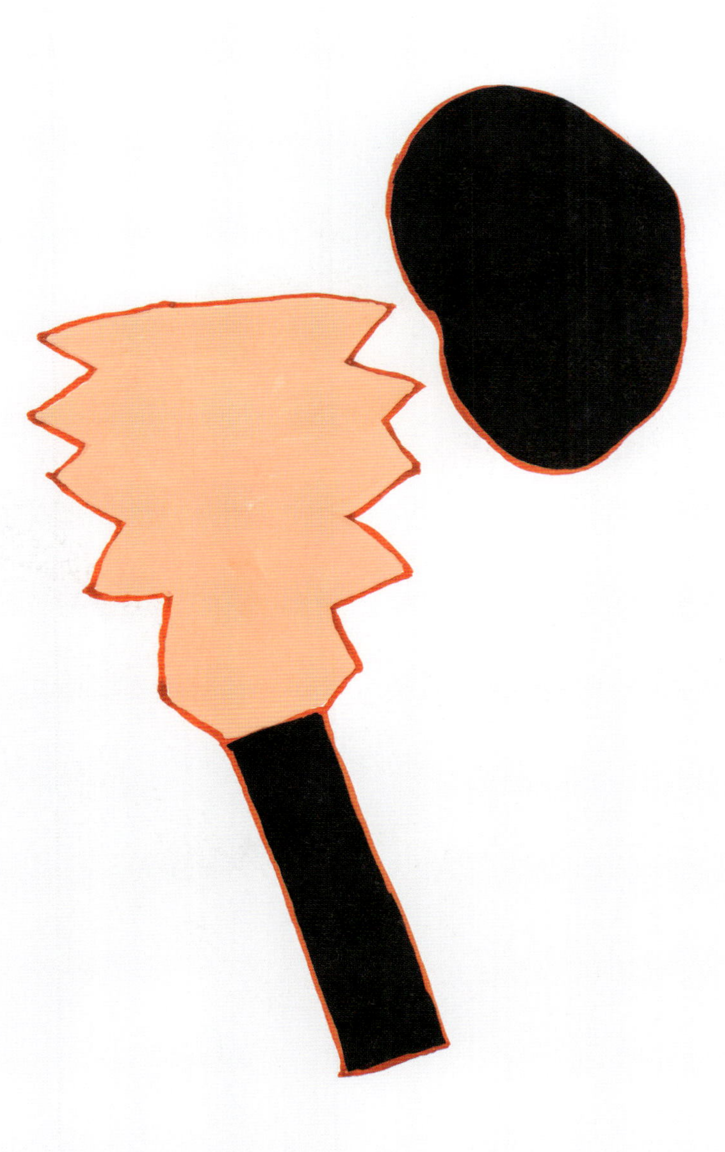

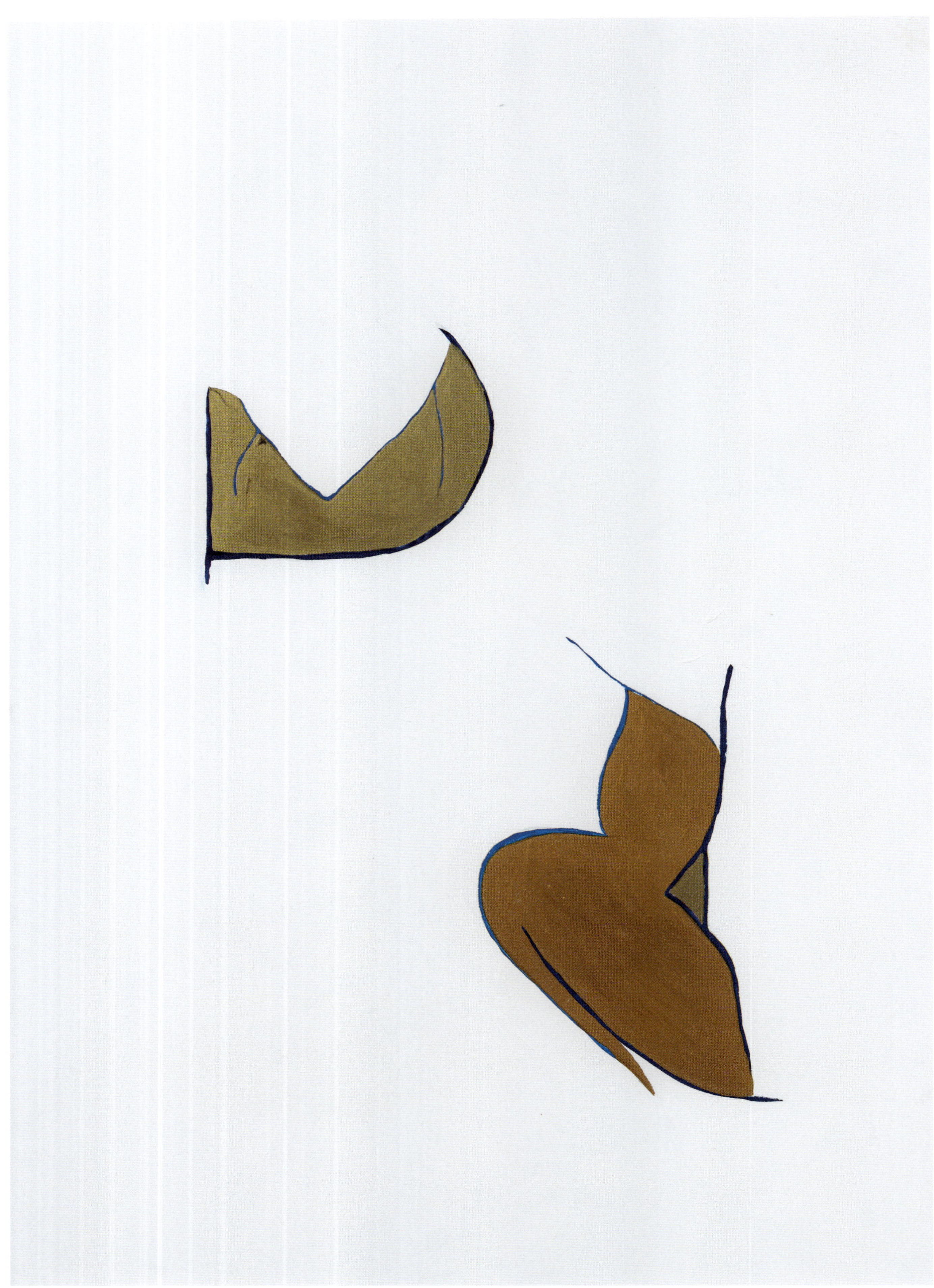

Untitled, n.d.
Probably from the series *The secret life of Milton Bozo*, 1989/90
acrylic and gold paint on canvas, 150.5 x 101cm

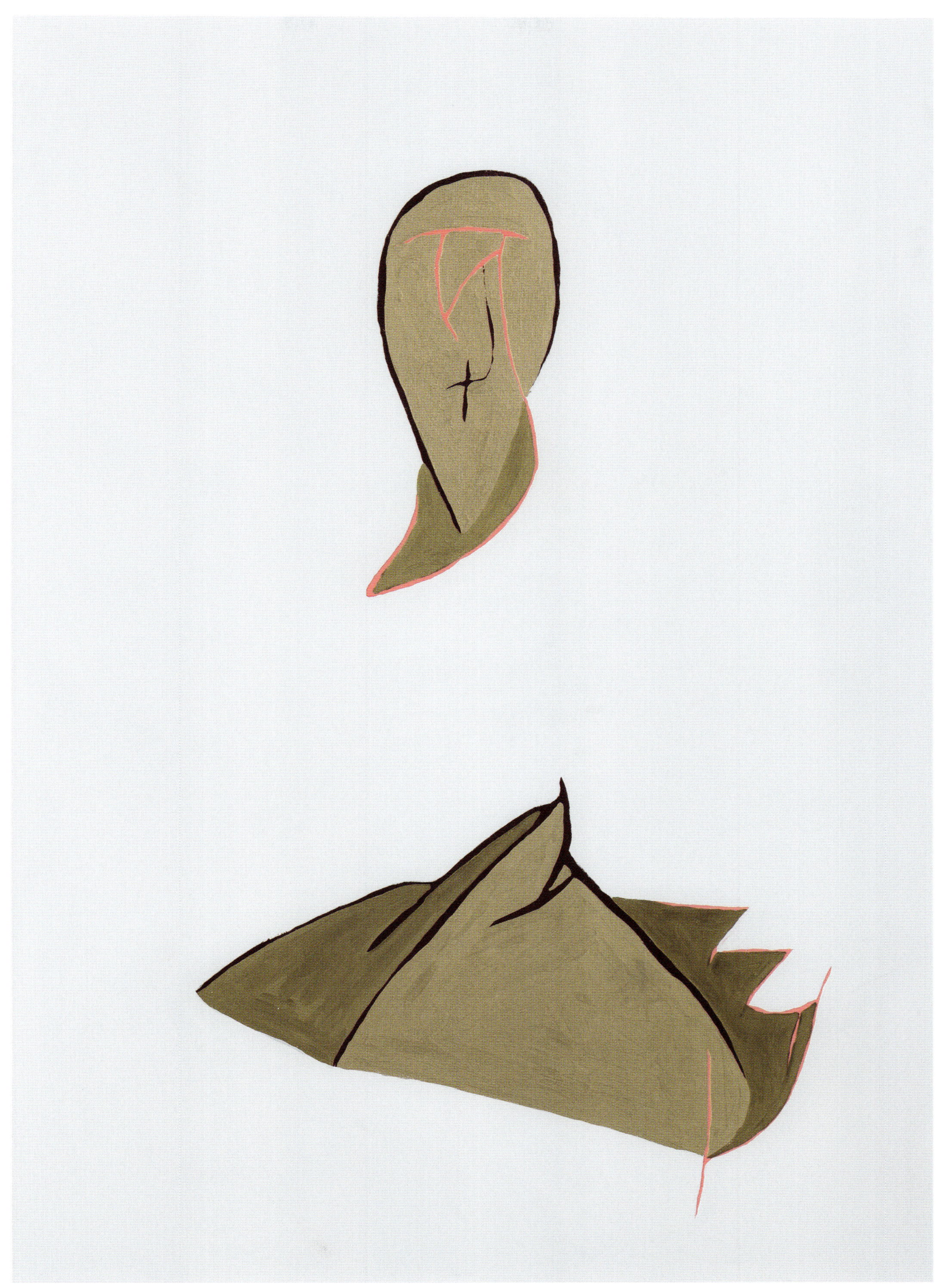

Untitled, n.d.
Probably from the series *The secret life of Milton Bozo*, 1989/90
acrylic and gold paint on canvas, 150.5 x 101cm

Walking on the Rope
The Lyrics of Marianne Eigenheer

By Claus Donau

Marianne Eigenheer once said in an interview, "I like to reflect, even in a playful sense, but I have to forget that all when I start painting."[1] Her artistic work is like a dance, for instance when she is painting directly on the wall, it's as if the image is drawn out of thin air. Influenced by literature, philosophy, voodoo rituals, fables, fairy tales and music, her figures, symbols, lines and signs enter, participate, then quietly disappear.

This applies equally to her texts. They start to reflect, but they don't aim to reach a certain result. Instead, they move freely in space, sometimes following a distinct thought, then taking a side path, finding the way back to the main route and continuing to search, as if dancing on a rope. She wrote, "For me, making pictures means doing something exciting. It's like walking across a rope where the other end is not visible."[2] With her writing, she is following the same desire to venture further and further into the unknown, weaving her own biography into the realms of her artistic œuvre.

After having said goodbye to her dream of becoming a composer, and after realising that studying psychology would be the wrong path, she turned to painting in order to be able to experiment without having to take others into consideration.

In her artistic work, text and image sometimes enter into a unity, like in a series of texts in watercolour on glass panes. Others become speeches, still others are printed in catalogue books. Her texts are characterised by the desire to move freely in thought, to research, to let poetry and literature, natural science and religion meet, with representatives of the most diverse genres as if they were her interlocutors. "How would you have put it, dear Italo?" she might have asked, and Calvino would have replied, "Marianne, all Cimmerian books are unfinished, for they continue into the beyond… in the other language, in the silent language to which all the words we believe we read refer." The endnotes presented here to accompany Marianne's texts go in search of clues.

[1] "*Marianne Eigenheer: Imaginäre Räume*", in: *Kunst machen? Gespräche und Essays*. Edited by Florian Rötzer and Sarah Rogenhofer. Berlin: Klaus Boer Verlag, 1990.

[2] Rötzer and Rogenhofer, *Kunst machen?* Berlin 1990.

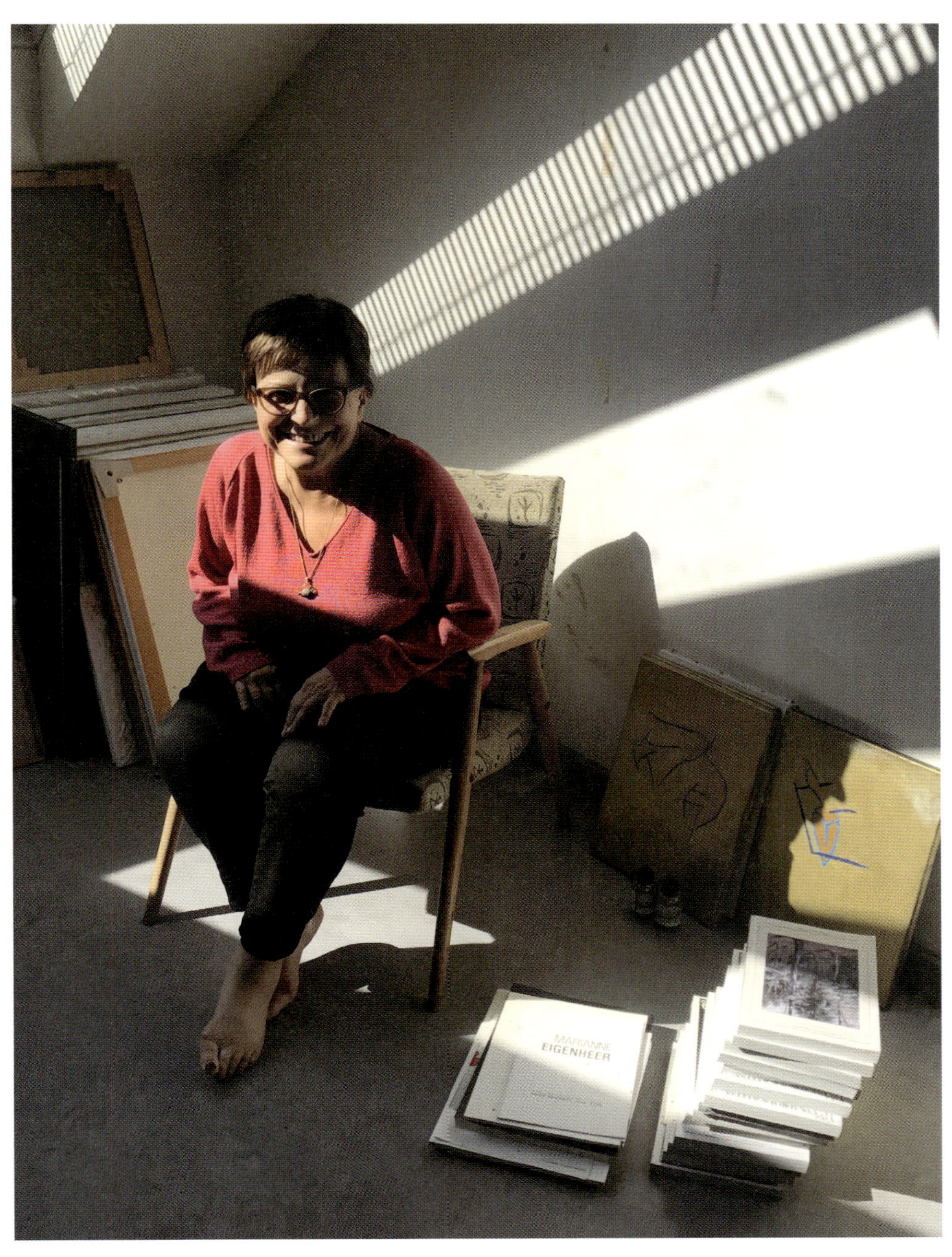

Marianne Eigenheer in her studio, September 2017
Photograph by Matylda Krzykowski

Endnotes

SPIDER WOMAN, HER BOUNDLESS PATIENCE AND ART'S NETWORK OF LINES: GOD IS A DJ

1   Marianne's speech was held on the occasion of an opening dinner at Galerie von Bartha, Basel, in 2017. "Spider Woman", also known as "Spider Grandmother", is an important figure in the mythology of many Native American cultures, especially in the Southwestern United States. "God is a DJ" is the title of a song by the band Faithless from their album *Sunday 8PM* released by Cheeky Records Ltd in 1998. Like many other music titles and citations from literature, "God is a DJ" pops up in Marianne's work several times, as well as in her Instagram posts (thank you, Karim Noureldin, for bringing this to my attention) and in her catalogues. As for her text works, she once answered a question of Hans Ulrich Obrist about unrealised works: "To mention just one of them, I have written some things, and I have, well, forbidden myself … Probably it would be a book of small texts. Not a novel, but words that fly around as if in the air." (From Hans Ulrich Obrist, "Flying animals, bodies and stars in the sky. Marianne Eigenheer, Hans Ulrich Obrist", *Lack/Lack*, Vol 3, sic! Raum für Kunst, Lucerne, January 2012.) She was an author as well as an editor, for instance together with Jean-Christophe Ammann for *Transformer. Aspekte der Travestie*, edited on the occasion of the exhibition of the same name at Kunstmuseum Luzern in 1974, publishing texts about Urs Lüthi, Luciano Castelli, Katharina Sieverding, Jürgen Klauke, Werner Alex Meyer, Luigi Ontani, Walter Pfeiffer, Marco, Pierre Molinier, Andrew Sherwood, The Cocettes, Andy Warhol, Brian Eno, Mick Jagger, New York Dolls and David Bowie.

2   The Hopis speak of a "Spider Grandmother" too. Conscientiously weaving her webs, she thought the world itself into existence. In the Navajo creation story, people travel up through four lower worlds, creating chaos and disorder until they are banished from each in turn. At one level, they are threatened by a devastating flood, but Spider Woman rescues them by weaving a web to create solid ground. There is another reference to the term "Spider Woman": Marianne admired Louise Bourgeois, the French-American artist, throughout her whole life. Bourgeois created countless works with the element of a spider – including her famous sculpture *Maman* from 1999 – and the international art scene often called her the "spider woman".

3   This frequently used quotation is shortened. The original is more sophisticated, which helps to understand why Marianne chose it: "Hence it comes that nothing is believed so firmly as that about which one knows the least, and that nobody pretends to be more sure than those who fabricate something for us – alchemists, for example, fortune-tellers, sworn astrologers, palm-readers, doctors and all the rest of the pack." From Michel de Montaigne, *Les Essais, Livre premier, XXXII: Qu'il faut sobrement se mesler de juger les ordonnances divines* [The essays, book 1, XXXII: That a man is soberly to judge of the divine ordinances], Simon Millanges, Bordeaux: 1580; Abel L'Angelier, Paris 1588; Abel L'Angelier, Paris 1595. For the German edition, see Michel de Montaigne, *Essais, Erstes Buch, Text 32: Göttliche Fügungen sollte man nüchtern beurteilen* in Michel de Montaigne, *Essais, Erste moderne Gesamtübersetzung von Hans Stilett*. Eichborn Verlag, Frankfurt a.M. 1998.

4   Carl Gustav Carus, *Briefe und Aufsätze über Landschaftsmalerei*. Verlag Gustav Kiepenheuer, Leipzig 1982.

5   Luke Howard, *Essay on the modifications of clouds, and on the principles of their production, suspension and destruction* ("modification" in today's English means "classification"). Essay read before the Askesian Society on 16 December, 1902 in London. First published in *The Philosophical Magazine XVI*, ed. by Alexander Tilloch, London, 1803. For the German edition, see Luke Howard, *Über die Modifikationen der Wolken*. Vortrag gehalten am 16.12.1802 im Plough-Court-Laboratorium vor der Askesian Society in London.

6   As far as we know, John Constable does not mention Luke Howard in his notes, nor does he mention Thomas Forster's *Researches into Atmospheric Phaenomena*, 1813. Cf. Gillen D'Arcy Wood, "Constable, Clouds, Climate Change", *The Wordsworth Circle*, Vol 38, Issue 1–2, ed. by Charles W. Mahoney, University of Chicago Press for the Boston University Arts & Sciences, Chicago 2007.

7   A work from Marianne's text-on-glass-series *Shingle Street*, 2004–2017 (watercolour on transparent glass, different formats; english texts).

8   Jean Genet, *Der Seiltänzer* [The tightrope walker], Merlin Verlag, Hamburg 1963. The poem "Le Funambule" was dedicated to the German-Algerian tightrope walker Abdallah Bentaga, whom Jean Genet met in 1956 and whom he supported. Genet's poem was first edited in 1957.

9   Lyrics from "Frankie Fell in Love" on Bruce Springsteen's album *High Hopes* released by Columbia Records in 2014.

10 Lewis Carroll, *Alice im Wunderland*, Philipp Reclam jun., Leipzig 1981. For the first German translation, see Antoine Zimmermann, *Alice's Abenteuer im Wunderland*, Macmillan & Co., London 1869.

11 François Jacob, "Reproduktion und Differenz" [Reproduction and difference], *Die innere Statue*, Kap. 4 "Reproduktion und Differenz", Ammann Verlag, Zürich 1988.

12 Probably a variation on a famous Louis Armstrong quote, "Man, if you have to ask what jazz is, you'll never know."

13 Junichiro Tanizaki, *In Praise of Shadows*. Leete's Island Books, New Haven/CT 1977.

14 When she was young, Marianne's mother wished her to become a pianist. As a child she received piano lessons and practised for several hours every day. After 13 years of practice, Marianne realised she did not want to follow the path her mother had chosen for her. Instead, she began to draw and paint, and studied art education at the Lucerne School of Art and Design.

15 Jonathan Cott, *Nahaufnahme. Telefongespräche mit Glenn Gould*, 4. Auflage, Alexander Verlag, Berlin 2007. For the English edition, see Jonathan Cott and Glenn Gould, *Conversations with Glenn Gould*, Little, Brown and Company, Boston/MA 1984.

16 This is the title of a series of works from 1976: "In fierce lines, written at a dramatic pace, pain and eros are sworn, as it were called out of life to the dead". In Annemarie Monteil, "Marianne Eigenheer: Man is the dream of the dolphin", *Basler Stadtbuch*, ed. by Christoph Merian Stiftung, Basel, 1996.

17 By citing quotes and song titles Marianne does not intend to boast about the depths of her experience as a reader but to express her constant reflection as an artist: "At the beginning of the 1970s, I found something like a home with Hubert Fichte, Antoine Artaud, Georges Bataille, and many others; at the same time, I discovered travel on various levels." Baron Samedi (also Baron Saturday, Baron Samdi, Bawon Samedi, etc.) is one of the Haitian "loa", which are spirits of Haitian voodoo. Samedi is the loa of the dead, along with Baron's numerous other incarnations like Baron Cimetière, Baron La Croix and Baron Kriminel. Le Guédés (The Ghede) are the family of loa that embody the powers of death and fertility. In the catalogue for the exhibition "Les Guédés dansent toujours", Marianne said: "In the mid-70s I studied, among other things, psychology of religion, the expansion of African-American religions (where the guédes of Haitian voodoo emerges) and their connection of death and sexuality […] The death of a person I had come to trust for the first time in my life triggered, like an eruption, huge drawings, in which for the first time, Baron Samedi and Mme Erzulie danced together, not like the dance of death but like the dance of life." See *Les guédés dansent toujours*, ed. by Das Esszimmer. Raum für Kunst, Bonn 2012. On the occasion of this exhibition, she created the series of works *Le mariage de Mme Erzulie et Baron Samedi*, 2012 (acrylic on canvas, 40.6 x 30.5cm / 16 x 12 in). Some years before, in 1977, she had already drawn a black-and-white charcoal sketch with a threatening figure of which you can see only a black face and a bright glasses frame (*Who is G.? oder Baron Samedi?*).

18 This quote, as well as the next one, relates to Georges Bataille's *Madame Edwarda* from 1941 (first published by Editions du Solitaire under the pseudonym "Pierre Angélique", fictitiously dated 1937; 2nd Edition: 1945; 3rd Edition: 1956. In 1956 it was published in Bataille's name by Jean-Jacques Pauvert, Paris). Dedicated to French poet Paul Eluard, the novel is part of George Bataille's *Das obzöne Werk* [The work of alterity] in which Madame Edwarda is a prostitute who calls herself the "Divinus Deus" (divine god). Access to divinity is gained through erotic transgression. In his preface, Bataille invites us to confront everything scary, especially sexuality, to dive into all that is dark, hidden. The "horse" quote relates to several scenes in *Madame Edwarda* where the act of love is compared to riding a horse, and the "Madame Thérèse" quote relates his citations of the statement of Saint Theresa of Avila: "I live without living in me, and I expect a life so high, that I die because I do not die."

19 Robert Walser, *Schneewittchen. Komödie in Versen* [Snow White – comedy in verse], Die Insel, Vol 12. Heft, Insel-Verlag, Leipzig 1901. At the age of 23, the Swiss writer Robert Walser published two plays inspired by the famous fairy tales "Snow White" and "Cinderella".

20 "Bilder zur Lage" is the name of a poem, a series of paintings and woodcuts, and an exhibition with catalogue. See Marianne Eigenheer, *Bilder zur Lage*, with a text by Max Wechsler, ed. by Grita Insam/Modern Art Gallery Vienna and Severina Teucher Gallery Zurich, 1982. See also the exhibition catalogue *Marianne Eigenheer: Bilder zur Lage*, Le Nouveau Musée, Villeurbanne, Lyon 1983, as well as the catalogue and exhibition at Museum Quality, Brooklyn/NY, 2015. One year later, in 2016, the exhibition "Neue und alte Bilder zur Lage" was opened at Galerie Bugdahn und Kaimer, Düsseldorf.

21 A painting from 1982 (acrylic on panel, 147 x 280 x 2.5cm / 58 x 110 x 1 in).

22 From the song "The Dream Before" by Laurie Anderson on the album *Strange Angels*, released by Warner Bros. records in 1989. Anderson dedicated it to Walter Benjamin: "Hansel and Gretel are alive and well, and they're living in Berlin. She is a cocktail waitress, he had a part in a Fassbinder film, and they sit around at night now drinking schnapps and gin […] He says: I've wasted my life on our stupid legend when my one and only love was the wicked witch. She said: What is history? And he said: History is an angel being blown backwards into the future. History is a pile of debris and the angel wants to go

back and fix things to repair the things that have been broken …" (followed by the original quote of Walter Benjamin, see endnote no. 28). One copy of Marianne's mural series *Hansel and Gretel*, 1991 is signed as "Hommage an Walter Benjamin" (Homage to Walter Benjamin). She often weaved fairy tales into her texts, too, especially those of the Brothers Grimm. In her reflection on the fairy tale *"Das eigensinnige Kind"* [The wilful child], for instance, she describes wilfulness as a positive quality that inspires you to question your own creative output.

23 *Misere des Herzens* (Misery of the heart) is a series of works from 1984 (ca. 225 x 160.5cm / 88.6 x 63 in, dispersion paint on cotton). Klaus Honnef said: "At first sight, animals. But only at first sight. . . Their curious shape, suggesting something bodiless and shadowy, as if they had no solid support from within, no inner core … Whatever resistance there is [to break out of the picture, the frame] takes the form of gentle opposition seeking to adapt rather than to rebell. All the same, the accommodation is an act of coercion and the paintings betray a docile melancholy". See Klaus Honnef, *Marianne Eigenheer*, trans. by Catherine Schelbert, in a catalogue published on the occasion of an exhibition at Kunstverein Schaffhausen/Museum zu Allerheiligen, 1985.

24 *What Is Behind That Curtain* is a series of abstract paintings from 1984 (acrylic on paper, different sizes). The title is presumably referring to *Behind That Curtain*, 1928, which is the third novel in the Charlie Chan series of mystery novels by Earl Derr Biggers.

25 Title of an exhibition at Galerie Bugdahn & Szeimies, Düsseldorf (1986) where Marianne's series of works titled *Il sorriso di Don Giovanni* (tempera and gold pigment on paper, ca. 170 x 74cm / 67 x 29 in) was exhibited. The quote refers to Mozart's opera *"Don Giovanni"*. For details please see endnote no. 1 for the text "Don Giovanni's Smile, or Why I Also Prefer Not to Be the Japanese Emperor's Nightingale".

26 This is the title of a song by the band Enigma from the album *The Cross of Changes* released by Virgin Records in 1993. One day in 1996, Marianne told Swiss critic and writer Annemarie Monteil that she liked that song and that a line of the lyrics had "stuck in my head". She used it for a group of blue line gradients to create the endpapers of Basel's chronicle *Basler Stadtbuch*. The motif was printed as a limited graphic edition, too. See Annemarie Monteil, "Marianne Eigenheer: Man is the dream of the dolphin", Basler Stadtbuch, ed. by Christoph Merian Stiftung, Basel, 1996.

27 This is the title of an exhibition held at Galerie Marianne Grob, Luzern in 1992 and Galerie Bernhard Schindler,

Bern, in 1994. The wall painting at the Galerie Schindler (340 x 1100cm / 134 x 433 in) was later painted over, like many other wall paintings. In 1994, Bologna Studio erAArte organised the exhibition "Little Peter's Moonride. The Journey continues…" The exhibition and work titles refer to Gerdt von Bassewitz's children's fairy tale *Peterchens Mondfahrt* (Ernst Rowohlt/Druck der Spamerschen Buchdruckerei, Leipzig 1912). The English title is *Peter and Anneli's Journey to the Moon*.

28 Title of an exhibition and accompanying catalogue held at Kunstverein Freiburg i.Br. in 1992, showing a large wall painting (200 x 1600cm / 80 x 630 in) and also title of a 1993 exhibition at Galerie Bugdahn & Kaimer, Düsseldorf. It refers to Walter Benjamin who in 1921 owned Paul Klee's painting *Angelus Novus* (New angel) which is a small (31.8 x 24.2cm / 12.5 x 9.5 in) monoprint from 1920 using the oil transfer method Klee invented. When Benjamin fled from Paris to escape the Nazi terror he hid the picture. Later it came into the possession of the German philosopher Theodor Adorno who passed it over to the Israeli philosopher and historian Gershom Scholem. Today it is in the collection of the Israel Museum, Jerusalem. About Angelus Novus, Benjamin wrote, "There is a painting by Klee called *Angelus Novus*. It shows an angel who seems about to move away from something he stares at. His eyes are wide, his mouth is open, his wings are spread. This is how the Angel of History must look. His face is turned toward the past. Where a chain of events appears before us, he sees one single catastrophe, which keeps piling wreckage upon wreckage and hurls it at his feet. The angel would like to stay, awaken the dead, and make whole what has been smashed. But a storm is blowing from Paradise and has got caught in his wings; it is so strong that the angel can no longer close them. This storm drives him irresistibly into the future to which his back is turned, while the pile of debris before him grows toward the sky. What we call progress is this storm." (Walter Benjamin, *On the Concept of History*, IX, trans. by Harry Zohn, 1940.)

29 Reference to "Tears of the Dolphin", a song title by the band The Surf Kings on their album *Up From the Depths* released by Innertube Music in 1999.

30 *The Book of Five Rings* is a text on kenjutsu and the martial arts in general, written by the Japanese swordsman Rōnin Miyamoto Musashi around 1645. Marianne used it as inspiration for *Das Buch der 5 Ringe von Musashi* (The book of 5 rings by Musashi), a series of paintings in red and black on white concrete walls. It was created in 1991 at the central bus station in Kiel, Germany – a poetic and precise discourse on female forms of articulation combining simplicity and enigma (each 200 x 800cm

/ 78.5 x 315 in). The murals were dedicated to famous women whose names were applied like signatures: *Elizabeth Murray meets Musashi, Laurie Anderson meets Musashi, Nancy Spero meets Musashi, Louise Bourgeois meets Musashi* and *Alice Aycock meets Musashi*. There is also a small painting *From the book of the five rings* by Musashi (tempera and gold pigment on paper, 106 x 100cm / 42 x 39.5 in).

31 In October 1987 Marianne went to Japan for a three-month residency. She might have been in contact with the Goethe-Institut, which is named after German poet and statesman Johann Wolfgang von Goethe, who now becomes "Johnny" in her speech.

32 *Lotte in Weimar*, written by Thomas Mann between 1936 and 1938, was first published in 1939 by Bermann-Fischer Verlag in Stockholm. The text is a vivid dual portrait and a complex study of Goethe and Lotte, the still-vivacious woman who in her youth was the model for Charlotte in Goethe's widely-read *The Sorrows of Young Werther*, 1774.

33 "Please Forgive Me" is a song by Brian Adams from the album *So Far So Good* released by A&M Records in 1993.

34 David Deutsch, *The Fabric of Reality*, Viking Adult, New York City/NY 1997.

MAYBE A LOVE LETTER TOO …

1 Peter S. Beagle, *Das letzte Einhorn*, Hobbit-Presse im Klett-Cotta Verlag, Stuttgart 1975. For the original English, see Peter S. Beagle, *The last unicorn*, McIntosh & Otis, New York 1961.

2 Giorgio Cesarano, *Der erotische Aufstand* [The erotic insurrection], 2. Teil, Text 53, Edition Tiamat, Berlin [West] 1984. For the original passage in Italian, which reads "L'angoscia è il memento vivere della corporeità", see Giorgio Cesarano, *L'insurrezione erotica*, capitulo secondo, testo 53, Dedalo, Bari 1974.

3 Giorgio Cesarano, *Der erotische Aufstand*, 2. Teil, Text 39, Edition Tiamat, Berlin [West] 1984. The original Italian reads "L'angoscia è il memento vivere della corporeità", and can be found in Giorgio Cesarano, *L'insurrezione erotica*, capitulo secondo, testo 39, Dedalo, Bari 1974.

4 Italo Calvino, *Wenn ein Reisender in einer Winternacht* [If on a winter's night a traveller…], trans. by Burkhart Kroeber, Hanser, München 1983. For the original Italian, see Italo Calvino, *Se una notte d'inverno un viaggiatore*, Einaudi, Turin 1979.

DON GIOVANNI'S SMILE, OR WHY I ALSO PREFER NOT TO BE THE JAPANESE EMPEROR'S NIGHTINGALE

1 On the one hand, the title "Don Giovanni's Smile" refers to Mozart. In his opera *Don Giovanni*, the character of Giovanni *is* desire embodied, he does not simply *have* desire. There is

nothing behind the force of this desire; it is only a game of masks, deceptions and disguises, and no one else pretends as much as he does. Don Giovanni does not exist, only what others call "Don Giovanni" exists. On the other hand, "Don Giovanni's Smile" ("Il sorriso di Don Giovanni") was the title of an exhibition with accompanying catalogue at Bugdahn & Szeimies Gallery, Düsseldorf, in 1986 and the title of a series of works on paper. "The Japanese Emperor's Nightingale" refers to the fairy tale by Hans Christian Andersen (cf. endnote 3).

2 Saint Luke painting the Virgin is a subject in art showing Luke the Evangelist painting the Virgin Mary with the Child Jesus. Marianne's statement: "I am like the Cretan princess Ariadne, dancing. And I don't need any Evangelist or Saint to paint me." In her text "Another Labyrinth", she creates her own story of Ariadne, writing, "It would be conceivable that Ariadne would no longer count on a hero today. She would take the ball of wool of Daedalus in her own hands and unroll it until she found the Minotaur, her stepbrother, in the labyrinth … Her desire for her own liberation would be strongly alive, that she would overcome her fear of this monstrous incestuous encounter, the fear of the being that is the same and at the same time completely different. An acting Ariadne would transform this labyrinth." Excerpted from Program No. 26, edited on the occasion of the exhibition "Marianne Eigenheer" in 1981 at Galerie E+F Schneider, Le Landeron (Switzerland).

3 The quotations in Marianne's text are from the fairy tale "The Emperor's Nightingale" (also: "The Nightingale") by Hans Christian Andersen. H.C. Andersen, *Gesammelte Werke*, Bd. 1 und Bd. 2. Manesse Verlag/Conzett & Huber, Zürich o.D.

4 Andersen, "The Emperor's Nightingale".

5 On 12 October, at the beginning of a three-month residency at Meguro Art Museum in Tokyo, Marianne wrote: "I never before lived for such a long time in a country where I don't know the language and where the basis of the society isn't the Judeo-Christian tradition and mentality. The best thing is to forget all that you know and to 'see' with your feeling, your body, your intuition. If my work is changing under the Japanese influence, we will see…" See *Artistes suisses au Japon/Swiss Artists in Residence in Japan*, ed. by Meguro Museum of Art, Tokyo 1987.

Marianne Eigenheer | Biography

Marianne Eigenheer (1945–2018) was a renowned Swiss artist and academic whose work has been exhibited extensively around the world. As a child, Marianne's parents had aspirations for her to become a pianist; instead, after 13 years of daily piano practice, she turned to drawing and painting. She attended art college in Lucerne, Switzerland, and launched a prolific career as an artist and teacher.

Marianne's work was featured in Achille Bonito Oliva and Harald Szeemann's seminal Venice Biennale exhibition Aperto '80 in 1980, as well as in numerous solo and group exhibitions in Germany, at Bonner Kunstverein, Galerie Volker Diehl, Zeppelinmuseum and Ludwig Forum für Internationale Kunst; in the US, at Holly Solomon Gallery and the Swiss Institute in New York; and at the Manege Central Exhibition Hall in St Petersburg, Russia, the Perth Institute of Contemporary Arts in Australia, and the Meguro Museum of Art in Tokyo, Japan. Her work has also been exhibited in Switzerland, at sic! Raum für Kunst in Lucerne, von Bartha in Basel and at the Kunstmuseum Basel in 2017.

During her academic career, Marianne was a professor and director of the Institute for Curatorship and Education at Edinburgh College of Art, where she was granted an honorary professorship in 2009. Previously, Marianne worked at several universities and art colleges across Europe, the United States and Australia, including the University of Art and Design, Offenbach, and the State Academy of Fine Arts in Stuttgart.

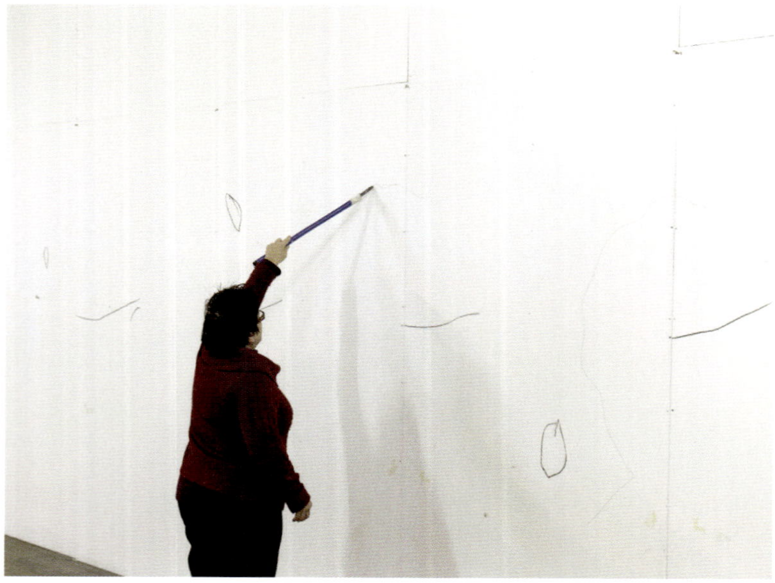

Marianne Eigenheer working on the wall drawing *Untitled* during "Marianne Eigenheer & Julius Heinemann in collaboration" at Performance Studio (V22), London, 2013
Photo: Julius Heinemann

Acknowledgements

Credits

This book is the result of a longstanding friendship and collaboration between the Estate of Marianne Eigenheer and von Bartha, Basel & Copenhagen. We would like to thank our contributors, writers and the many supporters of this project, especially Yasimin Kunz for her support and immense trust. Thank you to our authors, Max Dax and Jonathan Bragdon, Professor Klaus Honnef, Matylda Krzykowski and Nadine Wietlisbach for their wonderful contributions. Thank you also to Claus Donau for his extensive expertise, professional knowledge and insightful view of Marianne's texts.

Many thanks are also owed to Daniela Tauber from the von Bartha Team for her vision and skilful management of this project. We also extend our gratitude to Tom Marshall, translator, for handling Marianne's words with such care. Lastly, thank you to Black Dog Press, especially to Daphne Fordham-Smith for her profound project management (it was a pleasure working with you!); to Anton Jacques for designing this exceptionally beautiful book; and to Megan Jenkins Reagh, project editor, for sharing her excellent knowledge and sense of language.

Von Bartha & The Estate of Marianne Eigenheer would also like to thank all of Marianne's friends, companions, fellow artists, and the cultural workers who have played a critical role in keeping her work and legacy alive to this day. We are more than grateful for you and your perspectives as we continue to tell the story of the unique artist Marianne Eigenheer.

We would like to thank the collectors and owners of Marianne's works for their generous permission to publish the works of their collections:

p. 1 & 79: Courtesy Collection Muzeum Susch
p. 8, 66 & 71: Kunstsammlung Roche, Basel
p. 9, 108–113: Courtesy Kunstmuseum Basel
p. 14–17: Courtesy Private Collection Cologne Germany
p. 40–43: Courtesy Private Collection Switzerland
p. 67: Courtesy Private Collection Switzerland

We would like to thank our photographers:
Andreas Zimmermann: p. 2, p. 5, p. 8, p. 9, p. 10–13, p. 19, p. 57–63, p. 73, p. 82–89, p. 108–116, p. 117 top, p. 119–143, p. 152
p. 14 – 15: Photo: Kayla Kaufmann
Ben Koechlin: p. 20–27, p. 34–55, p. 64–65, p. 67, p. 78, 80, p. 98–105
Hester Koper: p. 29, p. 76, p. 77

If not otherwise indicated, all images are courtesy of the Estate of Marianne Eigenheer & von Bartha.

This book, which is a tribute to the late artist and not a *catalogue raisonée*, contains in part a previously unpublished body of work by Marianne. The works were discovered between 2021 and 2022 while browsing the artist's estate and archive in the course of working on this book. These works have been attributed and dated to a particular period of Marianne's œuvre due to their visual qualities.

Contributors

Jonathan Bragdon

(b 1944) is an American visual artist working in a range of media including graphite, watercolour and ink. Born in Wilmington, Delaware, Bragdon moved to the Netherlands in 1979, where he still lives and works. His practice engages elements of playfulness, emotion and automata to create abstract landscapes and representations of metaphysical concepts. He has exhibited widely in Germany, the Netherlands and Switzerland, and his work is represented in numerous international collections including the Stedelijk Museum.

Max Dax

(b 1969) explores the field of tension between art, music and pop culture. As editor-in-chief, he has directed the magazines *Alert*, *Spex* and *Electronic Beats* by Telekom. As a curator he organised the exhibitions BLACK ALBUM / WHITE CUBE at Kunsthal Rotterdam in 2020 and HYPER! A Journey into Art and Music at Deichtorhallen Hamburg in 2019. As a photographer he published the books *Palermo: La città e la musica* in 2007 and *Napoli – La città e la musica* in 2005. He has authored several books, including *Was ich sah, war die freie Welt* (What I saw was the free world), *Dissonanz – ein austauschbares Jahr* (Dissonance: an interchangeable year) and *Dreißig Gespräche* (Thirty conversations). In Berlin he runs the Santa Lucia Gallery of Conversations together with Lucia Margarita Bauer. He is an active member of the art/music collective LAWBF and of the band Brandt Brauer Dax Frick, with whom he is currently working on a project titled *Multi Faith Prayer Room*, an interactive social sculpture dealing with the utopia of an empathic human future.

Claus Donau

(b 1955) is an independent editor, lecturer and producer based in Basel. From 1994 to 2020, he was publishing editor and production manager at Christoph Merian Verlag in Basel. Previously, he worked as a theatre director and teacher in Berlin, Zurich and Basel, having trained with Jack Garfein, Dominic de Fazio, Peter Brook and Ned Manderino. Claus has won numerous awards including the Basler Theaterwerkjahr for his theatre production *Délire d'interprétation*, an anti-biography about Camille Claudel, in 1990. Many books for which Claus acted as a production manager have also won international competition awards, including accolades from the Schönste Schweizer Bücher in 2019, 2002 and 1994; the Schönste Deutsche Bücher in 2017, 2014, 2013 and 2012; and the European Design Awards in 2009.

Professor Klaus Honnef

(b 1939) is a professor emeritus of the Theory of Photography at the Kunsthochschule Kassel, a visiting professor and lecturer at German universities and colleges and a freelance curator and author. From 1974 to 2000, Honnef was chief exhibition officer of the Rheinisches Landesmuseum Bonn. Before that, from 1970 to 1974, Honnef was the managing director of the Westfälischer Kunstverein, Münster and an editorial director at the *Aachener Nachrichten* from 1965 to 1970. He is responsible for several groundbreaking art exhibitions, as curator of the outdoor exhibition Umwelt-Akzente in Monschau in 1970, co-organiser of documenta 5 and 6 in 1972 and 1977 respectively in Kassel, and curator of the virtual exhibition "The Face of Freedom", in 2012. In 1988, Honnef was awarded the title of *Chevalier de l'ordre des arts et des lettres* (Knight of the order of arts and letters) of the French Republic, and in 2011 he received the DGPh Culture Prize.

Matylda Krzykowski

(b 1982) plans, designs, writes and talks about physical and digital space. Her transdisciplinary, geographically mobile practice resonates worldwide in the forms of exhibitions, installations, talks, performances and exhibits, among others. Recently she co-curated the exhibition "Total Space" at the Museum für Gestaltung Zürich and curated The Energy Show – Sun, Solar and Human Power at Het Nieuwe Instituut in Rotterdam. She is currently the artistic lead of CIVIC at the Academy of Art and Design in Basel.

Nadine Wietlisbach

(b 1982) develops exhibitions, publications and other mediating and discursive formats in the fields of photography and art. She has been director of the Fotomuseum Winterthur since January 2018. From 2015 to 2017 she directed the Photoforum Pasquart in Biel/Bienne, and before that she was the curator and deputy director of the Nidwaldner Museum in Stans. She has worked for various institutions in South Africa and the USA, most recently at the Museum of Contemporary Photography in Chicago in 2015, when she was also awarded the Swiss Art Award for her curatorial and critical work. She held a lectureship at the Bern University of the Arts from 2013 to 2017, and in 2007 founded the independent art space sic! Raum für Kunst in Lucerne. She has served as an expert on contest juries in Switzerland and abroad.

Cover
Untitled (detail), c. 1976
wax crayon on paper, c. 150 x 1050cm

Inside front cover
Misere des Herzens (left and right), 1984
acrylic on cotton, 225 x 160.5cm

Page 1
Untitled, 1984
acrylic on cotton , 225 x 160cm

Page 2
Untitled n.d. (probably 1970s–80s)
pencil, coloured pencil and crayon on paper, 80 x 60cm

Overleaf
Is now a place? Where is the past?
The past can be dangerous for the future history is an angel,
From the series *Shingle Street*, 2004–2017
watercolour on glass, different formats

Inside back cover
We are the ship We are the captain We are the water And the air
We are the seagulls And the dolphins Playing around the ship (right),
From the series *Shingle Street*, 2004–2017
watercolour on glass, different formats

From the children's world of three colours figures move
clearly into the pictures quietly off the Wall The Memories
Rise I Dance with Antonin Artaud (left),
From the series *Shingle Street*, 2004–2017
watercolour on glass, different formats

von Bartha, Basel & Copenhagen
www.vonbartha.com
info@vonbartha.com

VON BARTHA

THE ESTATE OF MARIANNE EIGENHEER

© 2023 SJH Group

Published by Black Dog Press Limited in conjunction with von Bartha and the Estate of Marianne Eigenheer. Black Dog Press Limited is a company registered in England and Wales with company number 11182259 and is an imprint within the SJH Group. Copyright is owned by the SJH Group. All rights reserved.

Black Dog Press Limited
The Maple Building
39–51 Highgate Road
London NW5 1RT
United Kingdom

+44 (0)20 8371 4047
office@blackdogonline.com
www.blackdogonline.com

Creative Direction and Design by Anton Jacques
Printed in Latvia by Amber Book Print

ISBN 978-1-912165-37-7

British Library in Cataloguing Data. A CIP record for this book is available from the British Library.

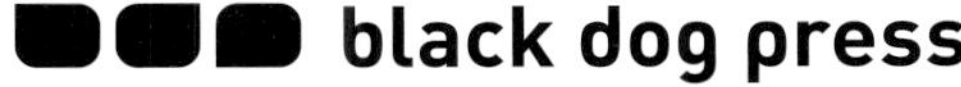 black dog press

IS
NOW
A PLACE ?

WHERE IS THE PAST ?
THE PAST CAN BE
DANGEROUS FOR THE FUTURE
HISTORY IS AN ANGEL